I0145845

Reflections in a ring of Light

BY

NANA DADZIE GHANSAH

DAkpabli

DAKPABLI & ASSOCIATES
ACCRA

REFLECTIONS IN A RING OF LIGHT

Copyright © Nana Dadzie Ghansah 2018

All Rights Reserved

No part of this book may be reproduced in any form by photocopying or by any electronic or mechanical means, including information storage in a retrieval system, without the written permission of both the copyright owner and the publisher of this book.

ISBN: 978-0-9981929-2-5

Cover Design by Nana Dadzie Ghansah and
Nene Buer Boyetey

Book layout by BIGGLESglobal Limited
P O Box NM 78, Nima, Accra, Ghana
Email: bigglesmultimedia@gmail.com
Tel: +233 302 333 502 | +233 244 634 204

Published by
DAkpabli & Associates
P O Box 7465, Accra North, Accra, Ghana
Email: info@dakpabli.com
Tel: +233 264 339 066 | +233 244 704 250
+233 247 896 375

"Can you remember who you were, before the world told you who you should be?"
- Charles Bukowski

Dedicated to:

...my late great-grandmother Adjoa Oduma aka Jooma, for introducing me to the art of storytelling.

... my late grandfather Kwame Dadzie Otoo aka Maapa, for encouraging me to reflect and write.

...my late dad, Kojo Bondam Ghansah, for recognizing my love of reading and fanning that flame.

...my mum Ama Oduma Ghansah, for being the first person to commission me to write a play for her class those many years ago and

... my wife Angela and kids, Alexis and Drew — you make it all worthwhile.

Table of Contents

Foreword
Prologue

On Life

Far from Home

Ghana on My Mind

The Art of Healing

Back To...Life

FOREWORD

Nana Dadzie Ghansah is a remarkable and multitalented individual whose personal charisma and authenticity often brings out the better qualities in people who interact with him. He is diligent, observant and very knowledgeable. He has been my close friend and a role model for close to four decades and I can comment on his work, based on a lot more than casual observation. He is a meticulous scientist and a self-taught professional photographer who has been able to single-handedly master archaic photography techniques such as platinum printing and wet plate collodion. He is also a prolific poet.

Life by its very design is not a linear experience and not all it throws at us can be explained using cold predictable logic. The arch of our existence here on earth, from birth till death is pockmarked with discreet events, observations and experiences, that often not only sear our memories and our consciousness but also influence our perspectives, our emotions and our judgment in confronting daily realities of our existence. In this regard, humanity's expression of emotions is universal. People are the same everywhere. We express almost identical emotions: love, joy, anger, anxiety, aspiration, insecurity, hope, sadness and envy irrespective of creed, race, gender, geography (location) or ethnicity.

This book brings to life, the reflections based on the Author's observation of personal and historical anecdotes and his experiences over five decades. He dives into some of the topical social issues of our time. The stories embody a rich tapestry of unique perspectives on everyday events experienced by many of us. He artfully simplifies multidimensional complex issues into easily digestible vivid but interesting descriptions. He does a remarkable job of infusing his narratives with relevance, combines humor and irony and maintaining emotional connectivity with readers. He concludes each story by sharing nuggets of wisdom, gathered over an eventful life odyssey from Besease, Ghana through Leipzig, Germany to Lexington, Kentucky.

The utility of this collection of stories is that they brilliantly lay out a mental drawbridge that leads directly either into the author's experience or an important observation. He is able to successfully pull the reader across a drawbridge and immerse him (her) emotionally into the experiences or anecdotes he describes. Interestingly, some of the stories are also quite effective in leading readers in the opposite direction across the same "drawbridge". I am talking about helping the reader to deal with some of humanity's common struggles: grief, joy, addiction, ageing and many more.

Sometimes, our inability to make sense of happenstance in our lives leads to avoidable anxiety and tension, loss of composure and the exposure of our lives to sub-optimal responses and decisions, which lead to even more anxiety and an almost perpetual state of disequilibrium. I boldly predict that readers will empathize with the emotions and motivations that the stories convey. The stories and the conclusions shared by the author build a drawbridge of wisdom that simultaneously illuminates our path out of some of our darkest fears and insecurities while providing a calming influence on our emotions.

I can describe him as one of the few truly wise people I have come across. I am most pleased to see him share his rich perspectives for the benefit of the many. A long-anticipated move finally comes to fruition!

J. Kweku Bedu-Addo
International Banker

PROLOGUE

"May it be a light to you in dark places,
when all other lights go out."
— J.R.R. Tolkien, from *The Fellowship of the Ring*

In A Ring of Light

I don't know where the memories came from, but they flooded my mind as I headed to my study to write a piece I had been thinking of doing. It was to be on existential nihilism, which posits that life has no intrinsic meaning or value. That all existence — our actions, thoughts, suffering, joy — mean nothing. I think the Greek skeptic Empedocles put it best when he wrote, "the life of mortals is so mean a thing as to be virtually un-life."

I do not know if it was me sitting at my desk that did it or my immersion in nihilistic philosophy over the past few days that set it off. Whatever it was, suddenly I was back in my grandfather's house where I spent the first eight years of my life.

I heard the rooster crow, signaling the start of a new day. I got out of bed, brushed my teeth, and headed out with my pail. I had to get water from the well each morning. The sun was just rising up over the horizon and the village was coming to life. I joined a group of kids, all about my age, heading to the well. The rising rays of the sun always made the drops of dew on the leaves glisten with colored light. They made those mornings beautiful. It took me about 30 minutes to get back with a full pail of water, which I would pour into a big, black drum that stood in a corner in the courtyard.

Then I swept that courtyard. That was my morning chore. I had to sweep it well because Maapa, my granddad, inspected it like a jeweler inspected a diamond. You see, my grandad demanded excellence in everything his kids and grandkids did — even sweeping the courtyard.

After a bath and breakfast, I would go off to school. I would think of how much I missed Mum on those mornings. When she headed the school in the village, we walked to school together. Now she was off to the city (Tema) and Dad was in England, so I had to walk to school alone.

My little brother was not of school age yet. It got better after I realized I could talk to the plants, the colorful birds, the restless insects, and the lizards that lined the path to school. They always listened. I told them all the stories I made up as I walked.

During recess at school, the other kids would sit around me in a circle to listen to my stories. The end of recess was never welcome. They always wanted to hear more.

I took the sheep and goats out after school. That was fun. Sheep are really, really simple. Goats are the epitome of obstinacy. There is a certain feeling of responsibility that grows as one does that. One learns what care is, even if it's for animals.

After dinner, I showered and then came study time with Grandpa. We did arithmetic and reading. I cannot remember the book and even though I struggled with the words, I read anyway. Study time ended with the highlight of my day — I got to write a letter to Mum. She still has them — that woman.

I always rested on a mat on the floor. Maapa could never get me to sit for that. In the ring of light cast by the flame of a lantern, I would reflect on the day and think of what to write to Mum. There were so many things to tell her.

I wrote about how much my little brother and I missed her and Dad. I would tell her how much we looked forward to her visiting soon. I listed the things I wanted her to get us on her next visit.

Sometimes I tried to write out one of my stories, but they were always too long and I would settle for a simpler narrative. I would write that in the ring of light, after which I went to bed. Grandad would mail the letter the next day.

Sitting in my dark study, I sighed, drained by the vivid memories of a time so long ago when I was a little boy in a village in Ghana — far from Lexington, Kentucky. I touched the LED lamp on my desk, which cast a ring of light over it. As I started typing, the similarities hit me.

I might be 5,000 miles away from Besease, I might be 43 or 44 years older, my grandad might be dead and gone, but I am still writing. In a ring of light cast by an LED lamp and not by a kerosene lantern, I sit down, reflect, and write. I am still writing in a ring of light cast by a lamp. Maybe not letters to Mum, because I can talk to her daily if I want to, but I'm writing about my thoughts, dreams, vision, hopes, aspirations, and stories. Yes, every time I sit down to write, I am nothing more than that little boy. The little boy who, in the ring of light cast by a kerosene lantern, wrote down his reflections of the day for a mother who was far away.

Suddenly, I remembered why I was in my study in the first place. I aimed to write a piece on existential nihilism. That life is meaningless. With all the memories still vivid in my mind, how could I buy into such a destructive philosophy?

It was almost as if life itself was reminding me that I could give everything that happened all those years ago meaning. The loneliness, the stories I made up to keep me company, my conversations with the plants and colorful birds and lizards, the trips to the well, my time with the goats and sheep, and writing in that ring of light every night.

However, is it a question of me giving those events meaning or do they have an inherent meaning in themselves? Did they make me who I am now, or am I giving them significance by what I do presently?

If I never rediscovered the joy I have in writing, maybe those experiences would have no significance. However, by immersing myself each evening into reflection and writing, I have given meaning to something that happened many years ago. In other words, we give our lives meaning. By actively living, we give this mean existence of ours a purpose. We make "the life of mortals less mean as to be virtually life."[1]

As I started typing in that ring of light cast by the lamp on my desk, I listened out for my grand-dad. He was always humming, and I strained my ears hoping I would hear him again. In the quiet of my study, the only noise was the clicking of the keyboard as I typed and the memories of a time when I would have started this reflection with the salutation, "Dear Mum."

[1] *Culled from a quote by the Greek philosopher Empeocles (ca. 495–435 BCE) — "The life of mortals is so mean a thing as to be virtually un-life." Pratt, A. Nihilism. Internet Encyclopedia of Philosophy. www.iep.utm.edu/nihilism/.*

On Life

"I would like to be a scholar in whatever I do, a scholar is
never finished, he is always seeking,
and I am always seeking."
— *Ahmad Jamal*

Being Thankful!

Once I stood safe on the island,
Watching as the ocean burned.
Up above on the highland,
Their pleas were not discerned.
As the bullets whizzed by,
And the buildings exploded,
Great and sweet was the pie,
That my hunger eroded.
They wail from hunger and thirst,
My overfilled cup runneth over.
Theirs is injustice at its worst,
From evil he doth me deliver.
I'm thankful but I hear their cries,
I'm grateful but I see their eyes.

That Rainy Friday

I don't know how I got there but when my eyes finally adjusted to the darkness, I was in a dark, fluid-filled cave. I was attached to the wall of the cave by a rope of some sort. It seemed to keep me afloat. For some reason, I wasn't gasping for air and felt totally calm. I do not know how long I stayed in there, for it was impossible to count the days or nights. It was pitch black.

Then came the quakes — out of the blue. They were scary. Each time the cave shook, I was propelled forward. I saw an opening forming ahead of me, at the opposite end of where the rope attached to the cave. I was filled with apprehension. I tried to hold on to the rope but with each quake, my hands slipped off. It was quake after quake, shaking the cave to its very core. It felt like forever.

After a particularly strong one, I felt forcefully propelled into the opening and for a while, my head was caught in it. Then I felt something grip my head and gently but forcefully pull.
I popped out of the cave in a rush of fluid, and what hit me first was the light. I tried to cover my eyes, but everything was so slippery. It was also so very cold. In the haze, I could hear a thousand voices and I struggled to figure out where I was. I seemed to have landed on a plank of some sort. Who pulled me out? Where was I?

Suddenly, something flipped me around and that is when I felt the slap across my backside. It was so hard it knocked the air out of me.

I took a deep breath and yelled, "What the heck was that for?"

I started kicking with my legs and arms; I was so mad. I was still kicking and yelling when someone covered me with a warm towel. Aaaah! That felt so good. It shut me up instantly.

My eyes were slowly starting to adjust to the light. I could see several women and soon I was lying in the arms of one of them. She held me close. Her breaths came out in short, sharp bursts and her heart was pounding.

Out of nowhere, I finally heard a gruff voice say, "Kofi, welcome. We'll call you Kofi Dadzie. Me Nana, Kofi Dadzie. Nana Dadzie!"

Where was I? Where were these people calling me names?

Then another voice, this time quite sweet, said, "June 10, 1966. About 8 pm"

Then I heard someone say, "Ama, well done!"

The young woman asked, "Is it still raining?"

Someone answered, "Yes!"

Who were these people?

The young woman looked at me and said, "Kofi! Nana'dzie"!

She sounded excited and hugged me really close.

While I was wondering about all this, the strangest thing happened. With an amazing sleight of hand, the young woman shoved something soft and warm in my mouth. I instinctively sucked on it and suddenly this liquid just poured into my mouth. I kept sucking not realizing how hungry I was. It was filling. I was still sucking when I fell asleep, still wondering where I was.

I came to as the sunlight streamed through the curtain, remembered the dream and chuckled. I stretched out my hand for my iPad careful not to make too much noise. I turned it on to read the headlines. The iPad came on showing the date — June 10, 2016.

I smiled, swamped with feelings of gratitude, wonder, and disbelief.

On the Unmarked Trail

Two years ago, I went hiking on one November morning in the Forest of the Abbey of Gethsemani near Bardstown in Kentucky. A friend had told me about the place earlier in the fall of that year and a month later, I paid my first visit. I fell in love with the place. Not only did I appreciate the solitude it offered, but I also discovered the beautiful forest across the Abbey and Thomas Merton. A few weeks later, I drove back for a hike in the forest.

On that cold but sunny day, I plodded on purposefully along the marked trails aiming to return to the Abbey where I had started. Somewhere along the walk, I came to a point with forks in the trail. There was one clearly marked, "To the Abbey." Then, there were two other trails that were unmarked and not even on the map. The first of the two was to my right and seemed to vanish into thick brush. The other looked like it went up a hill to my left. I made a decision to go up the hill.

I started up the fork that led to the hill and it kept going up. Tall trees lined the trail and the ground was covered by a thick carpet of leaves. The wind blew moderately through the trees, swaying them in a synchronized dance that rhymed with the song of the wind. It felt beautiful.

Soon, I could see into a valley and bounding down was a big deer. It was so graceful. I kept moving, thinking I had made the greatest decision as I totally enjoyed the views on the trail. It kept going up. Even higher, I saw another deer bound up and race towards a line of trees that seemed to crest the summit of another hill. The trees undulated gently, like they were opening up to accept the grace of the big animal. It vanished into them in a motion so fluid and graceful, it made me gasp. At this point, the trail had leveled out and I seemed to be at a summit. I was looking down into a beautiful valley. The trees and leaves reflected the midday sun into the most beautiful colors. I went around a bend, and suddenly the trail came to a dead end. Just like that. It didn't go any further. I looked all around to see if perchance there was a fork I had missed —nothing! There seemed to be no path through the thick brush and trees. The trail had ended.

I headed back and as I did, I thought about my decision to come up the trail. Somehow, I felt my little detour held a good life lesson.

There was a clearly marked path that led right back to the Abbey. However, I saw an unmarked side trail and decided to abandon the sure and dependent main trail and strike out onto the unknown of an unmarked trail. That trail was not even on the map.

As I got back on the main trail, it dawned on me that my striking off onto a dead-ending and unmarked side trail could be a metaphor for the paths we sometime take in life that end nowhere. I thought of when one abandons the sure and safe for the unknown and fails. I thought of the pain and sadness these decisions and the ensuing results bring. However, I also thought of the experience and consoled myself with the realization that even though I had taken the path that led to nowhere, I had absolutely enjoyed the experience. If I had to do it all over again, I would go up the trail without a second thought. That even though it had been a detour that led nowhere, it had been a most enriching and fun detour. Satisfied then with the result of my introspection, I finished the hike and went home.

Nevertheless, as the days turned into weeks and the weeks became months, the experience at the fork in the trail nagged at me. It was as if I was missing something. It came to me about three months ago. Now consider this:

What if when the trail ended, I had the tools at hand to cut through the brush or even down a tree or two to create another trail? Can you imagine how beautiful a trail it would have been? When we take the road less travelled in life, do we sometimes fail because we are not well-prepared for what we may face? Do we give up because we may have the comfort of the defined trail and thus refuse to take the extra step that could establish another path? Do we give up because we cannot summon the courage to march further into the unknown, but instead quickly retreat to the comfort of the defined trail? Does it mean if there was no defined trail to fall back on, one is forced to blaze one?

Still, how many of us are always ready to create a new trail even on a hike? Most do not carry machetes and axes when they go hiking. Sure, some terrains demand it but this one surely did not. Thus, I thought about it some more until it kind of hit me recently.

Dreams!

Unmarked trails that go off the defined track are the stuff that fuel dreams.

As we walk on our different paths in life, we all yearn for safety and security. So if the trail is marked and leads back to the warmth of the "Abbey," we are wont to not be distracted by unmarked side trails. However, life's beauty is not seen on those marked and secure trails. Not at all. The beauty of life is found on those unmarked trails that sometimes show up unexpectedly. When they do, only the curious venture to explore them. The incurious and those who yearn for security and predictability do not even hazard a glance at these side trails.

Even the curious and adventurous are not always ready to blaze a new path. Thus, there is often the need to turn around after the trail dead-ends. What happens then is the stuff that drives dreams. The beauty experienced on that side trail is often so profound that one never forgets it and seeks to return.

It is like seeing that beautiful woman or handsome man get on the train just when you are getting off. This might lead you to go past your station on subsequent times just for the opportunity to see this beautiful or handsome person again. It is this vivid memory that will often bring the curious back to those unmarked and dead-ending side trails in a bid to blaze new trails and change the paths people use and also change our world.

However, not only the curious go off onto these unmarked trails. They also attract those who seek to understand who they are and their place in this vast universe. They exert a pull on those who wish to find themselves and what their mission in this life is. Those unmarked side trails do just that.

So, be curious. March up that side trail that is not even on the map. It doesn't matter you are not prepared. It doesn't matter if you have to turn back. The beauty you experienced will feed your dreams, and those dreams will get you to return — and when you do, you will be ready. Ready to create a new trail up the hill with amazing views into a sun-drenched valley of amazing colors and beauty. And through all that, you might find yourself and your place in this experiment called life.

This Journey

This thing called life is a journey. Like with every journey, the travelers need to know the way and above all, a destination.

To get anywhere at all, one needs a sense of direction, a guide, a Global Positioning Concept (GPC).

To that end, some use Google Maps and others use Apple Maps or MapQuest. One guy uses only a compass.

Some know their destination from the beginning. Others discover it en route. Then are those who take each day as it comes, and even those who plod on aimlessly.

The way of some is smooth, while the path of others is riddled with obstacles. Some travel in style with glamour and glitz, where others do not even have shoes.

Some have to go through the valley of shadow of death, while others seem to have their paths through the meadows.

A few never make it, while others seem to live forever.

We get lost, but we find our way back to the path. Sometimes we even fall into deep, dark ditches — but we crawl out of them and keep travelling.

As the journey progresses, the travelers come to a realization — it is not what Global Positioning Concept one uses that ultimately matters; it's the interaction with the fellow travelers. Traveling alone is boring.

And in that, a most important fact soon became apparent:

WHEN EACH TRAVELER TREATED THE OTHER LIKE THEY WANTED TO BE TREATED, THERE WAS GREAT PEACE AND HARMONY ON ALL THE ROADS TRAVELLED.

Do all get to the destination? NO!

Do they all travel in style? NO!

Yet, it is the experience of traveling and how they are treated and treat others that matters when their journey ends.

Which brings me to some questions:

What matters more?

Spending each passing minute yelling out the superiority of one's GPC over everyone else's, even those who have no clue where they are going?

OR

Helping others on the trip by clearing the path, keeping

the lonely company, feeding the hungry, healing the sick, redirecting the lost, protecting the weak, and helping people find their destinations?

At the end of that journey, I doubt we are going to find an angry man with a white beard yelling,
"Even though you helped others on the trip by clearing the path, keeping the lonely company, feeding the hungry, healing the sick, redirecting the lost, protecting the weak, and helping people find their destination — because you used MapQuest instead of Google Maps, you are damned! All that matters is whether you used Google Maps or not!"

So, on this journey called life, do not be too concerned about what comes after. We are here for a purpose. Find yours, travel it, and if you can, lend another a helping hand.

Dignify Death

Especially around the holidays, I cannot help but think of my dad. There is this one particular Christmas he made so memorable. I was like eight or nine and decades later, I still think of it every holiday season. And when he does come to mind, the lessons he taught me and my siblings with his life and death follow.

These past few days, one lesson keeps coming back to me. It was an indirect lesson actually.

He taught us to find dignity in death. To dignify this rather morbid event.

Of all the lessons I got from Dad's life, this was the most powerful — not only because of how he made death look and seem so welcome but also because at the time, it made me rethink what I did for a living.

I am a cardiac anesthesiologist. When he died in 2008, I was also doing a fair bit of transplant anesthesia for all solid organs — hearts, lungs, livers, kidneys, and pancreas.

The patients I took care of (and still do) are some of the sickest patients out there and they are set to undergo challenging operations. I see surgeons doing all they can for lost causes. I see thousands of dollars being spent on patients in the form of surgical procedures who would be better off being left alone to die in peace. I see the fear of death and how tight we hold on to this life.

In the last few months before Dad died, I had become somewhat disillusioned about the importance of what we did. I had questioned the need for certain surgical procedures in certain patients. I had wondered if letting some really sick patients die without putting them through surgery was not the more humane thing to do. Instead of dying intubated and ventilated alone in the Intensive Care Unit, I wondered if it would not be more dignified to die at home surrounded by family.

Then Dad died exactly that way. He did die at the hospital, but he was surrounded by family. The doctors let him go as he wished. He prayed with the family, closed his eyes, and that was it.
Looking back, it's almost like Dad scheduled his death and I learned all this after the fact.

In a conversation with one of his friends about a month before he died, Dad said, "I'll be going on a trip soon and you'll miss me so much you'll cry like a baby."

At that, his friend just laughed. When Dad died, that friend of his literally broke down in tears and cried like a baby.

Dad died in March. The previous November, he was admitted on an emergency basis — the diagnosis was heart failure.

A few weeks before he died, he confided in Mum, "I was on my way out in November and your prayers and tears brought me back. Next time around, please let me go!" One of my younger brothers was home in March from London, where he lives.

In several conversations, Dad hinted at his passing and asked that we "stay united as a family and love one another."

Of course, my brother told him to quit that kind of talk.

A few days before Dad died, he was praying with his prayer group.

The member closest to Dad heard him say, "Take me home, dear God, take me home!"

The man felt Dad had finished what he was brought here for and needed to go. Period!

My dad soon got his wish and the look on his face the day I got home and got to see the body said it all. It was the most peaceful look I had ever seen on the face of a dead person! It was that look he had when we prayed as a family.

I left the morgue with a deep sense of calm.

Christmas is around the corner and for all Christians, it is a celebration of the birth of Christ. It is thus a celebration of the beginning. It is a joyous time and it is rightfully feted. Yet, inasmuch as we celebrate Christ's birth, we also celebrate his death at Easter. The Christian faith is based on the belief that he arose from the dead, a feat impossible for us mortals. We live and then we die.

So not being Christ, we need to realize that even as we celebrate life, we should accept the fact it comes with death as a package. This acceptance might soften the tightness with which we hold on to this life.

One may argue Dad's deep faith helped him deal with his death. That's true.

So, what is one to do who is not a Christian or lacks faith? Well, every religion has teachings about death. Every one of them does. Besides, one does not need faith to realize that there is nothing like eternal life. We must all die! Accept it!

Poll 1,000 people, and I bet the majority will be afraid of death. This fear makes us hold on to the life too dearly (like a bad relationship) and in the process lose all dignity when it comes to death.

Instead, let's face the end with all the courage and decorum we can muster. Tell those doctors to back off and allow us or our loved ones to die in peace and with dignity. Realize when our job here on Earth is done and be prepared to move on. Accept the fact that even as there is a beginning, the end must also happen. Let's do that, and we will die in peace and with dignity.

Dad apparently did just that.

Memento Mori!

Memento Mori is Latin for "remember you have to die."

The practice of remembering our mortality is an ancient one. Plato in the Phaedo writes, "Those who practice philosophy in the right way are in training for dying and they fear death least of all men."[2]

In ancient Rome, when victorious generals returned from battle, parades were held in their honor. Even as a general rode in these processions, at a time when most would feel a great sense of achievement and maybe even some hubris, the Romans had a way of keeping these generals grounded.[3]

In the chariot with a victorious general was a companion of much lower rank. His job was to continuously whisper the words "Respice post te! Hominem te memento!" into the general's ear. This Latin phrase means, "Look behind you. Remember you are a man." This reminded the general in spite of his recent victories, in spite of the adoring crowds, death was always just another battle away. It was reminder of their mortality and forced them to consider humility.

Rome fell centuries ago, but this concept of reminding

[2]Plato. Phaedo. The Internet Classics Archives. Translated by Benjamin Jowett.
[3]Tertullian's Apologeticum Found on The Tertulian Project by R. Pearse.
www.tertullian.org/works/apologeticum.htm.

ourselves of our mortality has lived throughout the years. For some, it is the skull and crossbones. For others, it may be a clock. For me, it is cemeteries.

I love cemeteries. They are my Memento Mori symbols. I go to cemeteries for the peace and serenity and to take great pictures. More importantly, they serve as a constant reminder of mortality. I am always reminded about how short life is. I can almost hear a clock tick.

The main purpose of my Memento Mori symbol is to remind me of the lack of time. Time. The years are passing by. Time. Every minute in this temporary life is precious and one has to seize each moment. Time.

As one wanders around and reads the epitaphs, pictures come to mind of lives lived, of dreams realized and shattered, of love, sorrow, pain, and joy. Overwhelmingly though, one realizes that irrespective of what these souls went through, it all ended one day. Their lives were finite. My life is finite. Yours too.

I always leave resolved to do more, worry less, and fill every hour — but alas, once the symbol of temporariness recedes, I slide back into the delusion that I have all the time in the world. Like a victorious Roman general, I need a voice in my ear whispering Memento Mori. I still have so much to do, places to go, people to see...

This Thing Called Wisdom

"The desire to reach for the stars is ambitious. The desire to reach hearts is wise." — Maya Angelou

Certain recent events in a land close to me yet ever so far away has made me think of the word "wisdom" all day. This thing called wisdom — what is it?

It is defined as: "the capacity of judging rightly in matters relating to life and conduct; soundness of judgment in the choice of means and ends; sometimes, less strictly, sound sense, especially in practical affairs."[4]

Throughout history, it is a virtue that has always been sought by many and yet few seemed to possess. The Greeks even had a Goddess for it — the beautiful Athena. The Christian Bible says one gets it by fearing God, even though I know some rather foolish people who say they fear God! The Quran says wisdom is given to whom Allah wills — Allah must be stingy! Psychologists try to measure it, and anyone who seems to have gobs of it becomes an oracle. So, what is this ephemeral quality called wisdom?

Well, wisdom seems to have to do with life, which is both biologic and interactional. Biologic in that a body has life and is alive. Interactional in that we live by interacting

---

[4]Mitchell, L. K., et al. "Wisdom across the ages and its modern-day relevance." International psychogeriatrics. U.S. National Library of Medicine, 29 Aug. 2017. www.ncbi.nlm.nih.gov/pubmed/28473003.

36

with others and our environment. A deep understanding and discernment of the environment is knowledge that enhances this interaction. In the same way, a deep understanding of the self and of other humans enhances life. I think this deep understanding of the self and of others constitutes wisdom.

Per my argument, wisdom is then a thorough understanding of the self and of others. It is a deep understanding of the human condition, the human psyche. A knowledge of one's strengths and weaknesses and appreciation of what makes humans tick. Our fears, hopes, egos, and desires. The wise person understands these human traits really well.

So, if a wise person exploits his/her strengths and always seeks to minimize the influence of inherent weaknesses, then inasmuch as they are aware of their strengths, the wise will be the first to point out their limitations and seek help for those things in which they are weak. In dealing with others, the wise person attempts to harness another's strengths even as he/she reduces exposure to their weaknesses. This is very much the opposite of what most unwise people do — exploit the weaknesses of others. The wise know ultimately that never ends well.

A wise person lives by the Golden Rule — treat others as one wishes to be treated. (Maybe that is why the Bible says in Proverbs 9:10: "The fear of the Lord is the beginning of wisdom...")

A good illustration of my theory is offered by the biblical

story of the Judgment of Solomon (I Kings 3:16-28). Solomon was king of Israel, probably from 970-931 BC, and reputed to be the wisest king that ever lived.[5] The story involves two women who lived together. They both had recently delivered. One slept on and suffocated her baby. On waking up and realizing her baby had died, she hid the body and then claimed the other woman's baby was hers. This led to a fight and the case was brought before King Solomon. He offered to cut the baby in two and hand each woman one half. At that, the real mother asked him not to while the other woman wanted him to go ahead and divide up the baby. He handed the baby to the real mother. A deep understanding of a mother's love helped the king make this amazing decision and illustrates his wisdom.

Thus, if wisdom is a deep understanding of the human condition, then understanding one's self as well as others can be learned. That is the good news. The bad news is the majority of people do not know who they are and are unwilling to so much as understand the next person. Is it any wonder wisdom is so scarce?

She is out there though. Wisdom is trying hard to draw our attention like in Proverbs 1:20-21; it is crying out loud in the streets, at the city gate, even in the public square — telling us to know ourselves and understand our fellow men and women. If only we would listen.

---

[5] Stefom, M. and Gordon C.H. Solomon, King of Israel. Encyclopaedia Britannica. 2017.

Dignity and Class

"Dignity consists not in possessing honors, but in the consciousness that we deserve them." — Aristotle

The Olympic Games ended tonight, and I enjoyed every minute of them. I know most Brazilians in the favelas that dot the Rio landscape were unwelcome guests at a party in their own city.[6] That is sad but a true fact of life in a world where many find themselves as unwelcome guests. In spite of all that, the games offered not only entertainment but several life lessons.

For me, one of the most compelling is the lesson taught by the dignity and poise of the U.S. track star Allyson Felix.[7]

In July, due to a nagging ankle injury she suffered in April, she lost in the 200-meter qualifying race. The athlete who beat her fell/dove across the finish line. Her dream to defend her Olympic gold medal from 2012 was dashed. She held her head high and consoled herself with the 400-meter, 4 x 400-meter, and 4 x 100-meter relays.

On Monday, August 15th, she lined up to run the finals

---

[6]Watts, Jonathan. "Forced evictions in Rio favela for 2016 Olympics trigger violent clashes." The Guardian, Guardian News and Media, 3 June 2015. www.theguardian.com/world/2015/jun/03/forced-evictions-vila-autodromo-rio-olympics-protests.
[7]Elliott, Helene. "Allyson Felix shifts into high gear to win the women's 400." Los Angeles Times. 3 July 2016. www.latimes.com/sports/sportsnow/la-sp-us-track-trials-20160703-snap-story.html.

of the Women's 400-meter. Running in Lane 4, she had the chance to cross the finish line and claim a gold medal when the Bahamian star, Shaunae Miller, fell/dove across the finish line to claim the gold. Allyson was beaten by 0.07 seconds. She was devastated but held her head high.

Three days later were the women's 4 x 100-meter heats. Allyson was in at the third spot. Just as she got ready to hand the baton over to English Gardner, she was bumped by the Brazilian runner in the next lane, causing her to lose her balance and miss the exchange. Even with that, she kept her composure and asked English to finish the race. She did, and the U.S. team appealed. They won the appeal and got the opportunity to rerun the race. They qualified and ended up winning the gold.

Dignity in the face of adversity is something few can muster. Those who do it always shine as bright as the morning sun, showing us all that it is possible.

Allyson injured her ankle in April and lost her dog in June and her grandfather in July. Still, she worked towards her goal. The 400-meter final loss would have discouraged many, yet she kept on. The 4 x 100-meter bump should have put the nail in her coffin, yet she had the presence of mind to tell English Gardner to finish the race.

She faced all these adversities with poise and class, always displaying a certain strength of character and dignity. That poise and dignity even translated to how she ran — graceful and effortlessly.

So, what is dignity and why does it matter?

Well, dignity keeps one above the fray of life and gives mental clarity to the daily chaos. It is defined as having self-respect and a sense of pride in oneself.

Life is hard and most of the time, people and experiences seek to strip away this sense of pride in one's self. It is up to the individual to constantly reinforce a sense of self-respect. It is worth reinforcing because it shows that even though one may not possess the honor, it is something that is deserved. So, since one behaves like being deserving of the honor, sooner or later, the honor comes along. If dignity is lost, it is like saying one does not have the honor and does not deserve it. How sad!

Thus, even though she lost by a hair in the trials, lost by 0.07 seconds in the 400-meter and was bumped in the 4 x 100-meter, she didn't despair. She knew that no matter what happened, she deserved the honor and it would come. And did it come!

After 16 days, the games are over, and life goes on.[8] The lessons learned this week will stay with me. Should I trip and fall, I hope I pick myself up with dignity and class. Just like Allyson Felix would.

---

[8] *"How Many Days Do the Olympic Games Last?" Olympic Games. www.olympics.mu/how-many-days-olympic-games-last.html.*

Olympiosis

I am suffering from a severe case of Olympiosis.

Symptoms are quite prevalent in the mornings, but are felt all day long — tiredness, yawning, red eyes, arthralgias, headache, deafness to alarm clocks, and gross irritability. It can be confused with a hangover. The difference is found by measuring the blood alcohol level in most patients.

The cause is thought to be the inability to extract the human mass away from a television set during the Olympic games. It was first described in the 1970s.

Most experts attribute the pathology to pure wonder at athletic prowess. Game and his team in a seminal paper postulate that the sheer determination exhibited by the athletes induces heightened admiration, leading to insomnia. Track et al. measured the level of light emitted from the medals the athletes receive and noticed a high correlation between the amount of gold won and the severity of Olympiosis and laryngitis.

Cases of Olympiosis spike during swim, track, and beach volleyball events. Men seem to be particularly afflicted during the beach volleyball events. This year, the CDC is reporting that doctors are seeing a spike around the women's gymnastics events too.

Four years ago, researchers in London isolated two viruses called the Phelps and the Bolt that might play roles in the severity of Olympiosis. This year, scientists in Rio de

Janeiro have isolated two more viruses — the Ledecky and the Biles. A group outside of Rio reported on a variant called the Manuel. A team at the National Institute of Health (NIH) is working on vaccines.

Olympiosis might be contagious, but the experts do not appear to agree on whether this is a fact.

The treatment is avoiding television sets. A good televisionicide will do the trick. Also, one should avoid contact with the internet in all forms. Symptoms usually subside after about three to five days of avoidance.

Failure to treat Olympiosis leads to a chronic, incurable state. The long-term prognosis is dire. It seems to lead to sundaynightfootballiosis, mondaynightfootballiosis, or even EPLiosis. Most chronic patients end up in rehabilitation centers, where they spend the rest of their lives watching TV and drinking beer or knitting.

A select group of patients seem not to progress to the chronic stage — I think I belong to that group — so for now, Olympiosis, bring it on!

All or Nothing

"It is better to take many small steps in the right direction than to make a great leap forward only to stumble backward." — Old Chinese Proverb

This was probably in 1988 or 1989, when Berlin was still divided into East and West. One of the places someone could cross over from East Berlin into the western part of the city was at Friedrichstrasse. The train station there was divided into East and West. The checkpoint to cross over was stuck somewhere between the two.

That day, I got to Friedrichstrasse around noon and made my way across the checkpoint manned by the DDR Grenztruppen into West Berlin. I descended a staircase that led to the subway. At the foot of the stairs stood a disheveled middle-aged man. He looked like one of the many drunks who hung around the Western part of the train station.

For a little background information, the East Germans had several shops on both sides of the train station where they sold knock-off Western products, especially booze. Hard liquor and beer cost about 25-50% less than in West Berlin, so any self-respecting drunk made his way to Friedrichstrasse to get the cheap booze.

Getting back to the story, I sat down on a bench to wait for the train, looked around, and noticed the disheveled man at the foot of the stairs again. He appeared as if he was looking up, expecting something. Then, all of a sudden, he took off towards the stairs. He made it up about a third of the way (there were about 20 steps), lost his balance, and came right back down, upright but backwards. That got my attention.

Still no train.

The man came to a stop, caught his breath, composed himself, and resumed staring at the stairs again. Then he darted up once more. This time, he made it only about halfway and then it was back down.

I was smiling now. I heard the train in the distance.

The disheveled man had me and everyone else on the platform riveted. I wondered how many times he had tried. He was staring intently at the stairs again. He looked like a bull ready to charge those crazy runners in Pamplona. He was Ahab, staring at Moby Dick. It was crunch time. I wondered if he would let me walk him up. I thought better of it when I considered it might injure his pride. Besides, the train was almost in and I needed to catch it.

He charged up the stairs again.

The train was pulling in.

Up and up and up — and for a second, he hung at the very top. Time stood still as he tottered. Just as he was about to start his backward descent, a stranger at the top of the stairs gave him a shove in the back. Geschafft! He made it!

I ran into the train just as the doors closed.

Another guy who had been on the platform but missed the finale asked me, "Hat er es geschafft?" (Did he make it?)

I nodded. That was all I could do, I was laughing so hard.

I recently remembered this, and it made me smile. It was funny, but like a lot of things in life it taught a lesson too.

When we are beset with problems and issues, the easiest tasks seem like climbing Everest. The disheveled man could have taken the stairs one step at a time, but he didn't. In his altered state of mind, it was all or nothing. The majority of us may not be drunk, but I bet sometimes we want to go up the stairs — not one step at a time, but all the way at once or not at all. Unfortunately, not all of us get a shove in the back when it looks like we are going to fall. Most of the time, all we find are people like me, standing on the platform laughing.

The Story of the Praisers

Once upon a time, there lived a great, wise, and wealthy Man who travelled the land helping the needy, feeding the hungry, and spreading wisdom and knowledge.

One day, he came upon a city that was in dire straits.

Its leaders were unwise, and the people were foolish, poor, and hungry. Overall, there was great suffering.

As soon as he got to know who the leaders were, he got them to assemble all the people together in the great square.

Over the next few weeks, he taught them all they needed to save themselves and their city and turn it into a place of opportunity for all. Using his many resources, he imported food into the starving city. For the first time in many months, the people of the city knew no hunger. There was great joy all around.

Happy he had given the people of the city what it took to be successful and grow their city, the Great Man resolved to leave the city. Before he did, he handed each resident a bag. He asked them to open the bags the day after he left. The people agreed.

On the day he left, everyone came to see him off. It was a day of great sorrow. They wished the Great Man would live with them forever, but he couldn't. There were other cities, towns, and villages all over the land that needed his wisdom and guidance.

The next day, each person opened their bag to find a thousand pieces of gold plus a message to go out and make their lives better with the gift.

Overall, the city was in great joy. The people came out into the streets, dancing and singing with happiness. The celebrations went on all night and continued for a few days.

Soon, the people got back to their normal lives again.

With the great windfall, some of the people started new businesses. Others built new homes. Others travelled the land.

The great scribes in the city started writing down all they could remember from the Great Man's teaching. They put it together into a Great Book.

For some, remembering and forever praising the Great Man became their raison d'être. Using the wisdom and knowledge he taught them to improve themselves and the city became of secondary importance. Using the gold, he left them, they built monuments to commemorate the memory of this Great Man. They built huge buildings, in which they went to sing his praises and talk about what he taught them about life. Soon, they convinced more and more people to give them their gold to build even more monuments to the Great Man and buildings where people could praise him.

They called themselves the Praisers.

These Praisers soon became a very powerful group in the city. A movement in fact. The elected a leader — the Chief Praiser. There were Junior Praisers, Deputy Praisers, Associate Praisers, and Senior Praisers. The majority were just common Praisers. They had come to believe the best way to grow as a person and help grow the city was to praise the Great Man day and night. The Praisers grew in power and wealth.

It wasn't long before the city started on another decline toward poverty, famine, and suffering. Most people had either used up their gold in unwise ventures or given it to the Praisers. The minority, whom had used their gold like the Great Man taught them, was not enough to carry the rest of the city.

The people cried out loud for the return of the Great Man. The Praisers praised him even more, singing his praises until they collapsed in exhaustion — but that didn't fill their hungry bellies.

So, the leaders in the town sent out a group to go find the Great Man and ask him to come back and save their city again.

The group found the Great Man as he wandered the land, but alas he couldn't make it over to the city himself. He promised to send his Son to help them.

The group returned to the city with the news. Great was

the jubilation. Great was the praise.

However, the Great Praiser was unhappy. He knew if the Son of the Great Man appeared, he would recognize the Praisers for what they were. He and the other leading Praisers feared they would lose their power.

They connived to destroy the Son should he appear.

Time passed as the people waited for the Son of the Great Man to arrive in pomp and style.

Time passed, but he didn't.

There was great despair in all the land.

Then one day, a traveler entered the city. He was as innocuous as they come. Over the next few weeks, he fed the hungry, helped the sick, consoled the dying, and reminded people of the message of the Great Man.

The people took notice and everywhere he went, there was a crowd following him.

The older ones thought, "He sounds like the Great Man!"

They wondered if he was the Son.

One day, the traveler went into the building where the Chief Praiser was leading praise. He saw how the people shouted and cried for direction, believing that only through praising would they grow as individuals and improve their lot in life.

The traveler stood up to speak, shocking everyone in the building.

He told them he was the Son of the Great Man and how their ways weren't going to lead to the life of which they dreamed; only by following the directions of his Father, could they be saved.

He reminded them of the books written by the great scribes long ago that contained all the wisdom of his Father. He told them he knew some of those books were hard to find but assured them if they listened and did as he directed, they would find the life of which they dreamed. He demanded the Chief Praiser give the people some of the movement's gold, just as his Father did, so they could make their lives better.

The people in the building were overjoyed.

"Gold! Gold! Gold!" they all chanted.

The Chief Praiser stood up and said he had no more gold than was needed to run the movement.

The Son, however, didn't believe him. Seeing a door behind the podium where the Chief Praiser stood, he asked what was behind it.

The Chief Praiser looked incredulous. The Son marched over and opened the door to reveal bags and bags of gold. The people were stunned even as the Chief Praiser fled.

The Son gave each person 1,000 pieces of gold and asked them to go out and feed the hungry, help the sick, and console the dying.

Leaving the rest of the gold in the building, he went forth to help the people.

There was great joy and anticipation as the news spread that the Son was finally in the city.

However, not all were happy. The Chief Praiser and his acolytes were livid. This stranger who called himself the Son of the Great Man threatened everything they had built.

After the Son left the Building of Praise where the gold was, the Chief Praiser sent two Deputy Praisers to get the rest of the gold. They did, and the Chief Praiser hid the bags.

He then went to the leaders of the city and lodged a complaint of theft against the Son of the Great Man. He also accused him of debasing the name of the revered Great Man and inciting the people to riot.

The Son was swiftly arrested and brought before the leaders. Witnesses appeared who saw him incite the people. Others appeared who saw him steal the gold, distribute some, and take the rest away. Then there were witnesses who claimed they heard him say praising the Great Man was foolish. A great gasp went from the crowd.

No one was called to show he had helped the sick, fed the hungry, or consoled the dying. No one stood up to say what he preached about — that they were to remember what the Great Man taught.

The leaders asked him if he was indeed the Son of the Great Man. He said he was.
They asked for proof. He said that the proof was in him trying to remind them of his Father's way and wake them up to the folly of their ways.

A soldier walked in to report they had found gold in the small abode of the Son. The Chief Praiser smiled.

The leaders had heard enough. They found the Son guilty of theft, blasphemy against the Great One, and treason. He was sentenced to death by hanging.

On the day the Son was hung, a wealthy man, whose child had been healed of a deadly disease by the Son, stood in the crowd.

He asked for and received the body from the leaders and buried it in his family's graveyard.

The Chief Praiser was proud he had removed what could have been a great obstacle indeed. They went back to praising.

Out in the city, among the poor and the needy, the sick and the dying, and the cold and the hungry, there was great sadness. A man who cared for them had been taken from them. Soon, they found out where he was buried, and it became a pilgrimage to visit his grave. With time, the belief developed there was only way to find success in life — by first undertaking a pilgrimage to the Son's grave for his blessing. And so, another movement was born — the Pilgrims.

Feeling Contemplative...

He heard of this hill where one could leave their burdens. He made his way there to unload his burden. He labored up slowly, weighed down by uncertainty.

Alas, he got to the summit. In the distance, he saw others unloading their burdens before a shining light. He hurried up towards the light that got brighter. As he got closer, he realized that the light came from a tree and that the people were unloading their burdens at the base of this mighty tree. Then it struck him — compared to the burdens most of those there had, his burden was a joke. His burden was almost minuscule. A deep shame came over him. He wanted to run.

Then he heard a voice ask, "Can you help me get this down?"

He turned. The man facing him had the biggest burden he had ever seen. He helped him get it off his back and to the base of the tree. For the next hour, he helped several men and women get their burdens off. He felt exhausted but light.

Then he thought of his burden. He reached back. It was gone! He looked around him. He couldn't see it anywhere, but then again, wouldn't it be dwarfed by the others?

Then it hit him — in being immersed at helping others unload their burdens, he had lost his. He had unloaded his burden by helping others unload theirs.

He looked up at the tree. He could swear the Light smiled at him. He smiled back. As he made his way down the hill, he vowed to come up often to help others unload their burdens. He felt so whole when the Light smiled at him — he sure did.

The Sign of the Roses

He came out of the house and turned south on Greifswalder. He had to go to Kreuzberg. He liked walking all the way to Arnswalder Platz to catch the tram to Warschauer, where he took the U-Bahn to Kreuzberg.

It was early, and there was a freshness in the air and a spring in his step. He loved doing the 15-minute walk each morning. It cleared his mind. He turned left on to Danziger. Soon he came to the bakery. As he walked by, he could smell the fresh bread, always very pleasant.

It was as he neared the flower stand that he heard the Voice. It was quite clear.

"Buy a bouquet of roses," it said.

He stopped, looked around him, shook his head, and continued.

As he got to the stand, the florist called out, "Guten Morgen!"

"Guten Morgen!" he responded.

Then he heard that Voice again, "Buy a bouquet of roses."

He kept going past the flower stand.

Then a third time the Voice called out, still but clear, "Buy a bouquet of roses."

He turned and walked back to the florist and got a bouquet of red roses. He felt silly, stupid, and somewhat crazy — but that Voice was pretty insistent.

Then he heard it again, "Give the roses to the most beautiful woman you see."

At that, his face broke into a smile. Now that would be easy. Maybe this was his own Genie, sent to help him pick up women. Now that he could live with — crazy or not.

A minute later, he saw this really stunning blond coming towards him and thought, "Bingo!'

"Not her," the Voice said.

"What?" he thought.

And not the redhead, the tall black girl, another blond, or the brunette. He realized he had walked past Arnswalder and decided to catch the tram at the next stop. As he continued on, in spite of all the stunningly beautiful women he saw all the way to the tram stop and on the tram ride to Warschauer, the Voice kept saying, "Not her!"

He got off the tram at Warschauer and hurried towards the U-Bahn entrance. Coming towards him was a rather pregnant lady who was walking slowly.

"She is the one," the Voice said.

"What?" he thought.

"She is the most beautiful woman you'll see this morning. Give the bouquet to her," the Voice commanded.

So, filled with apprehension at how the pregnant woman was going to receive him, he walked towards her.

As close as he could get, he called out a greeting to her, "Guten Morgen!"

"Guten Morgen," she responded, a surprised look on her face.

"You are the most beautiful woman I've seen all morning, and I want to give you these roses and wish you a very nice day," he said as he handed the roses to the woman.

Her face broke into the most beautiful smile as she said, "Danke Schoen" and took the roses.
All of a sudden, she looked transformed. It was as if she was straighter and stronger. Her eyes gleamed. She wished him a good day, turned, and walked off.

As she walked off, she seemed to walk faster.

He stared after her for an instant and then spun around and made for the U-Bahn entrance.

"Well done. That wasn't so hard," the Voice said.

Then there was silence.

"Why did I have to do this?" he muttered to himself,

hoping for a response.

Silence.

"Why did I have to do this?" he repeated, hoping for an answer from whoever had been instructing him.

But the silence persisted.

The rest of the day, he kept telling himself the woman was probably having a bad day and needed to be cheered up. However, he wondered why he had to be the messenger. And he couldn't get over the feeling there was more to the morning's event. So, he listened and listened and listened — and all he heard was...silence.

An Audience with the Father

After several months of pleading, I was granted an audience. I don't even know how I got there, but all of sudden I found myself before this large, rather ornate gate. As I looked around, the gate opened as if by remote control. The mansion that was revealed was breathtaking. It arose from the carefully manicured grounds like a symphony from an orchestra.

I walked along the only pathway visible. It was marble! As I walked, I marveled at the landscaping. How expensive it must be to keep that, I thought. The pathway brought me to a massive wooden door. Just as I was about to open it, it swung open. Standing in the doorway was an old man with flowing white hair and a white beard. He beckoned me in. He introduced himself as Peter and asked me to follow him.

Words cannot describe the beauty of the decorations, paintings, and statues that graced the mansion. Soon we came to another door, and this one opened by itself too. It revealed a large hall. At one end sat a throne.

Peter turned to me and said, "He will be out soon. Sit in that chair and wait. Once he appears, you have 30 minutes. Good luck."

He turned and walked off, even as the door swung shut behind him.

Then I heard a voice say, "Nanadadzie, my son, how can I

help you?"

I spun around to see an imposing figure sitting in the throne.

Around him was a certain glow. His face was lit by a broad smile that illuminated the lines of wisdom that gave his face such depth of character. His eyes were deep and seemed to hold a lot of something. I couldn't put my finger on it.

"Nanadadzie, you have 30 minutes. Use that time well," he continued.

"Are you God?" I asked.

"The One and Only."

"Where is Allah? I wanted to meet both of you."

"I am One and the Same."

"Should I call you just God or Dear God?"

"Call me Father."

"Father, do you know the mess going on down there on Earth in your name?"

"I know, Nana, I know. It's OK to call you Nana, right? Most people call you that."

"Of course, you can, Father. So, you know there's a lot of bad things being done in your name and you are fine with that?" I asked incredulously.

"Nana, they use my name in vain to do these bad things."

"So why do you allow that?"

"You humans have free will, you know that, right?"

"Father, free will to use your name for the Crusades? The numerous European religious wars? Slavery? Apartheid? Al-Qaeda? ISIS?"

"Nana, each human ultimately has to discover the Truth."

"But, but the carnage is great. Did you see Brussels? And Paris? Have you seen what Boko Haram is doing in Nigeria? The attacks in Mali, Bukina, and Cote d'Ivoire? The beheadings in Syria? Iraq? 9-11? What truth do you find from such carnage? That religion leads to violence?" I asked, my voice rising.

"Nana, my son, I could with a stroke of my finger wipe all that out. But what lesson would that teach mankind?"

"That you cannot mess with God. You did that back in the day!"

"I might have, but did it teach mankind anything?" he asked, looking at me sternly.

"So, we have to go through all this pain to learn? To learn what?"

"To learn to live together as one."

"Father, call me cynical but that isn't happening. The Church you left down there is in shambles.
You heard of all those priests and the kids, right? That was a disaster. Islam has been hijacked. The races hate each other. There are wars everywhere. Large swaths of the population are starving or dying from diseases. And we are supposed to live together as one? I'm sorry, but I have no faith that will ever happen."

"Nana, do you believe in me?"

"Father, to be honest, there are lots of times when I have my doubts."

"Nana, you are bound by time and space. I see eternity. Good always overcomes evil. The right shall dominate the wrong."

"You sound like my late Dad. By the way, is he around?"

"Yes, he is, but he is not the reason you are here. There is always a dark side to light. A bitter side to the sweet. Those who use my name for evil are the dark side of light. Ultimately, the light shines so bright, the darkness is unseen and unheard. Believe and be strong."

Suddenly, I heard a sound behind me.

I turned to see Peter in the doorway.

"It is time," he said.

I swung around to ask God a last question, but the throne was empty.

I sighed and walked out of the hall behind Peter. With each step, I heard a ringing sound. As we neared the main door, it got louder. The minute he opened the main door, the piercing scream of my alarm broke through, waking me up to another morning of life on this Earth with its violence, pain, and hopelessness. Or is all that leading to a time of peace, love, and hope?

That is when it hit me. What I had seen in his eyes. His eyes were full of certainty. Certainty that all will be well. That good will overcome evil. That right will dominate wrong. Certainty.

I sat at the edge of my bed and realized I wasn't so certain that good will overcome evil, that right will dominate wrong. I wasn't at all, but wished I had faith. I wished I believed, but I didn't.

I sighed.

As We Walked...

Then we entered the banquet hall — a huge cavernous place. It was the strangest place ever.

At one end sat guests who were gorging themselves on large plates of food. Their full bellies glistened in the harsh light as crumbs and drops fell from their full mouths to the ground.

In another section were several guests sharing a plate of food. Their faces were glum, for you could tell they did not have enough.

And then was the last section, where the guests looked like they were not even at the banquet. They were doubled over, faces contorted in apparent pangs of hunger. A few were even motionless on the floor.

I stopped, surprise etched on my face.

"Isn't there enough food for all the guests?" I asked.

He looked me like you would look at a clueless son and replied, "You'd think, right?"

And then He took me to the top of the mountain and said, "Visualize a world with no strife!"

So, I closed my eyes, and that is when I saw the chasm — a great chasm it was indeed — on one side was much prosperity and abundance and on the other much need, hunger, and suffering.

I opened my eyes and asked Him, "I see a great chasm. How can I visualize no strife with such a great chasm?"

He looked at me, smiled, and said, "Fill the chasm!"

"With what?"

"With empathy."

A Mother's Love

The woman pushed through the crowd of people with a strength she didn't know she had in her frail body. Soon she could see him, standing alone against the wall, blood pouring from a gash in his head. She hesitated only for an instant, and then ran towards him through the hail of stones. She ran. It felt like forever. A stone hit her in her back and another on her right shoulder, but she kept on. As she drew closer, she saw him look up towards her. She saw recognition in his eyes. He opened his arms and scooped her up when she got to him at the wall, protecting her from the stones.

The tears started immediately as sobs racked both bodies huddled together in the hail of stones.

And then the hail ceased. The woman peered out cautiously from beneath the young man.

She pushed him away, stood up, and turned to face the mob. A silence had fallen on the crowd.

"I did all I could, but my son became a thief," she said. "A common thief. Still, he is my son and I am his mother. Any mother among you knows how that feels. You will die for your son, wouldn't you? You'll protect him from all ill, wouldn't you? So, to you he is a common thief who needs to be stoned. To me, he is my son and I'll die protecting him."

With that she spread out her arms, straightened her back,

and assumed a position in front of the young man.

A murmur went through the crowd.

"Stone her too!" someone shouted.

A single stone hit her in the head. She fell. A moan went up from the mob. Her son, the young man, rushed to her and placed his body on top of her to protect her.

He couldn't stop crying.

After a while, a realization hit him. There were no more stones. He looked up. The mob was gone. He gasped.

"Mum, they are gone. There are no more stones!"

The woman on the ground moaned. There was a gash on the side of her head where a stone had hit it. The son took off his torn and bloody shirt and cleaned off the blood. He picked her up, even as she still moaned.

He heard a noise behind him and turned around. Standing there was Katu, the village beggar.

"Your mother loves you very much. Only a mother can love you that way. Come, I'll help you take her home," Katu said.

The last rays of the sun dipped beyond the horizon, illuminating the bond between a mother and her son as they headed home.

The Day Bertha Went on a Ride:
A Piece of History

I am intrigued by what I call the Frisome Women (Friggin' Awesome Women). I was raised by one who was raised by one, married to one, have a sibling who is one, and may be raising one. Smart, focused, pragmatic, creative, and tough, they have a certain sixth sense for what works! They don't mince words, don't suffer fools, and want to get things done. I am intrigued by what makes them tick. You all know one or may even be one.

Bertha Ringer[9] was a Frisome. She was born into a wealthy family in Pforzheim, Germany on May 3, 1849 (167 years ago on the day of this writing).

Her dad wanted a son and wrote in the family Bible, "Unfortunately, only a girl again!"

Bertha, however, was an intelligent girl who at an early age was very interested in technical things like the locomotive. When she was allowed to attend school at the age of nine, her interest was in the natural sciences. However, in that era, women were not allowed into institutions of higher education. It was the scientific belief that the lighter brain of women was logically unable to absorb and process as much information. Moreover, too much thinking was thought to be harmful to their reproductive abilities!

---

[9] "Bertha Benz. A Woman Moves the World". Mercedes Benz. Classics. www.mercedes-benz.com/en/mercedes-benz/classic/bertha-benz/.

The beliefs of the day irked her greatly. It didn't help when she read what her dad wrote in the family Bible. These factors might have lit up her subsequent determination to show her dad and the world that women could be great too.

On June 27, 1869, while on a trip with her mother, a poor young engineer joined them in their coach. They soon started talking and he told her about his dream of building a driverless carriage. She was hooked. By the next year, they were engaged. The man's name was Karl Benz.

In 1870, Karl owned an iron construction company. His business partner was irresponsible, and the company was failing. Karl was also a terrible businessman. As a single woman at that time, Bertha was allowed by law to invest in a company and she rescued Karl's business using funds from her substantial dowry.

They got married in 1872 and Bertha Ringer became Bertha Benz. They moved to Mannheim where she helped her husband start the Benz Gasmotoren-Fabrik — a company that manufactured internal combustion engines. Problems with the banks led to the closure of that business after a year.

In 1883, Bertha helped Karl Benz start another company — Benz & Cie. They made industrial parts. That business venture thrived. This allowed Karl to turn his attention to his lifelong dream — the invention of a driverless carriage powered by an internal combustion engine. In other words, an automobile. That era had several engineers who built versions of a driverless carriage but had not successfully marketed their work.

After several failed attempts, Karl finally finished work on his first horseless carriage in December 1885 and received a patent for it in 1886. It was powered by a four-stroke, single-cylinder, 0.67 horsepower engine and had three wheels — one in the front and two in the back. It was the Patent-Motorwagen No.1. For fuel it used the solvent ligroin that you bought from a pharmacy. It had no gear system and had brakes and wheels made out of wood!

By 1888, he had built two more — the No. 2 and No. 3. The No. 3 was much improved with a two-horsepower engine and a maximum speed of 10 mph (16 km/h).

He showed the Model 3 at the Paris Expo in 1887. In the late summer of 1888, it went on sale as the Benz Patent Motorwagen.

Well, Karl, like most great inventors, was also terrible at marketing and couldn't find any buyers or get anyone interested in his invention. Bertha had seen him build his Motorwagen and believed in the product. She thought it was ready for prime time and needed publicity. She had invested a lot of money in the venture and she needed to see some returns. Moreover, not too far away was a gentleman called Gottlieb Daimler and his partner Wilhelm Maybach who were also trying to build a driverless carriage.

So, one early morning in August 1888, she left her

husband a note, packed her two sons, 13-year-old Richard and 15-year-old Eugen into the Patent Motorwagen No. 3 and drove off to visit her mum in her hometown of Pforzheim — which was 66 miles (106 km) away!

Let that go through your heads for a minute! Sixty-six miles in a contraption that had never been tested before over more than a few miles in town! In 1888! On roads meant for horses and carriages! By a 39-year-old woman with two teenage boys! Now isn't that just friggin' awesome?

Now, the big idea wasn't really to visit her mum. It was to prove to her husband that his invention was great and ready for prime time and to give the car publicity.

The journey took her just over 11 hours. She stopped at several pharmacies to buy ligroin as fuel. The Motorwagen used a surface carburetor that doubled as a reservoir for 1.5 liters of fuel. (Subsequent models had a fuel tank and also, her experience probably birthed the concept of the gas station.) At one point, she had to repair the car's ignition and she improvised with her garter. When the fuel line became clogged, Bertha cleared it using her hairpin! When the wooden brakes began to fail, she got a shoemaker to make leather pads for them, thus coming up with the idea of brake pads. At one point, she had to get two young boys to help her sons push the car up a hill (that bore the idea for a gear system).

They arrived in Pforzheim tired and dirty, but safe. Once in Pforzheim, she sent her husband a telegram to let him know they had arrived safely. Can you imagine him freaking out?

She stayed for three days with her mum and then made the return trip to Mannheim using a different route. This way, she was able to introduce the car to even more people. The reception ranged from wonder to frank fear of the "Smoking Monster."

Beside getting a lot of publicity for the Motorwagen, she had also undertaken the first test drive of a car!

Her 120-mile trip was the catalyst Benz & Cie needed. Karl Benz became credited with inventing the predecessor of the modern car. By 1899, Benz & Cie was the world's largest automobile company with a staff that had grown from 50 to 430. That year, they sold 572 vehicles!

Karl and Bertha, along with sons Eugen and Richard, also formed a new family-owned car company, Benz & Sons, in 1906. The cars they made became popular in London as taxis because of their quality and reliability. It closed its doors in 1924.

Benz & Cie, on the other hand, stayed in business until 1926 when it merged with its main competitor, Daimler Motoren Gesellschaft (DMG) to form Daimler-Benz AG. The rest, as they say, is history!

Karl Benz went on to build the first truck and also to invent the flat or boxer engine that is still used in Porsches and other racing cars. Among some of his honors was a doctorate from his alma mater, the Technical University of Karlsruhe. He died in 1929.

On her 95th birthday on May 3, 1944, Bertha was honored by the Technical University of Karlsruhe, her husband's alma mater, with the title of Honorary Senator. Two days later, she died.

Among her many honors is also the Bertha Benz Memorial route. The route traces her path during the world's first long-distance journey by automobile in 1888 from Mannheim to Pforzheim and back.

What a woman! A mother, investor, test driver, mechanic, and inventor! Now tell me Bertha Benz was not a Frisome!

Can you imagine what she might have achieved if she had been allowed to study at a university? Can you imagine what Karl Benz would have done without her?

So, as you speed off in your AMGs, G-wagons, and SLs, spare a minute to wish her "Herzlichen Geburtstag" on the other side.

What is the saying again? Behind every successful man is a friggin' awesome woman!

Frau Bertha Benz, you were friggin' awesome!

Do it Well

"Gentlemen, we will chase perfection, and we will chase it relentlessly, knowing all the while we can never attain it. But along the way, we shall catch excellence." — Vince Lombardi Jr.

My friend, the Rev. Albert Ocran, has a radio show on Joy 99.7 FM in Accra on Sundays called "Springboard." He usually discusses motivational and educational themes. Sometime last year, he did a series titled "10 Critical Success Factors." Over a period of like eight weeks, he talked to a string of thought leaders and entrepreneurs about what they saw as their 10 critical success factors.

One Sunday while listening, I thought of my own journey to figure out this puzzle called life. It started actively back in 1995, during a period of broken dreams. In the process I realized that unlike getting a formal education, life lessons are not taught formally as we grow from childhood into young adulthood. They are imparted loosely by parents and other family members. Sometimes by teachers, friends, or at church. In a period marked by working hard to attain a professional degree or learn a trade, life lessons take the back bench. That is until life rears its ugly head.

I wondered if I could tease out 10 lessons from all that I had learned since I started my journey of figuring things out. Over the next few days, memories came rushing back; in that torrent, I was able to tease out 10 lessons — my critical factors.

Recent events have reminded me of one of these lessons. It is the one lesson that guides me most in my professional life. I am not always successful at letting it guide me, but I try.

It is a lesson gleaned from a story my mum told me as a boy. The story stuck with me and as I got older, it always seems to prove itself.

The lesson is: DO IT WELL!

It is the notion that whatever you do in life, do it well. Do it like you were doing it for yourself. Aim for excellence. Do that procedure well. Nurse that patient well. Defend that case well. Run that business well. Sell those goods well. Treat your wife or husband well. Raise your kids well. Preach that sermon well. Teach those kids well.

Now, let me see if I can tell the story Mum told me well.

In a city far away lived a very wealthy man. He loved new mansions. Every so often he had his favorite builder build him a mansion. He would live there a few months or maybe a year, and then get the builder to build him another. He had mansions dotting the city.

Then a major recession hit the city. For a long time, the builder did not hear from his wealthy client. Things were hard for the builder, but he managed. Then the economy recovered, and business started to pick up again. The builder was busy again. After almost two years, the wealthy man contacted the builder. He wanted another mansion. This time, the wealthy man wanted the builder to use the most expensive marble, wood, and stones. It was to be a masterpiece. The builder, however, was bitter. He felt the wealthy man should have reached out during the recession. He also felt the wealthy man never paid him enough for all the good work he did. He agreed to build the mansion but instead of using the best materials, he fudged. He used the cheapest marble and stones. The foundation wasn't well-laid, and the walls were weak. The roof shook when the wind blew, and the windows clattered. It was his worst work.

The day arrived when the builder invited the wealthy man to take ownership of the mansion. The wealthy man met him in front of the mansion all smiles. The builder handed him the keys.

Then the wealthy man said, "All these years, you have built me one great mansion after the next. I have been unwell these last few years and had to travel for treatment. I couldn't help you during the recession. Now I am back and want to say thank you. This mansion is my gift to you for always doing things so well. You are the epitome of excellence."

With that, he handed the shocked builder the keys to the mansion.

Even as the builder took the keys, all he could think was, "I should have built this well!"

He should have.

Do it well!

Those Darn Updates!

My son always walks his nanny/tutor to her car when she's leaving. The other day, I was opening the windows in the kitchen when they walked out together. It looked nice out.

Shortly thereafter, I heard the nanny drive off and then my son playing with the ball in the driveway. I went into my study to write.

It wasn't much longer after, that he came running into the study, quite wet. I looked at him, then pulled the curtain aside to look outside. It was pouring.

"When did it start raining? It was dry a few minutes go!" I asked incredulously.

My son looked me like I had just flunked kindergarten math, placed his right hand on my shoulder, and said, "Daddy, life updated. Since the last time you looked outside, life updated."

Initially, I laughed — but the more I thought about it, the more I liked it.

Life updated.

To a little boy born in the era of iPads, iOS, and apps, life doesn't move on — it updates.

Life 2.0...Life 5.1.1...Life 2017.03...

Unlike that company in Cupertino, California, those updates from life come often unannounced. Still, one has to download and install them. Life doesn't care if one doesn't have Wi-Fi or if one's device cannot handle the new updates. It doesn't even care if you didn't realize it had updated. Too bad, life just updates. You need to keep up, or it just leaves you behind to grapple with things using an old and outdated OS.

Sure, just like in life, we can neglect that update and carry on. However, sooner or later, there will be those apps we cannot use or those games we cannot play.

We can change devices, but sooner or later that new one is going to need updates too and there will be no getting out of it. You see, all those devices run on an OS and every OS needs updates sooner or later.

So be ready for those updates from life. Get yourself a good Wi-Fi connection. Download those updates, install them, and get going. If that device you have cannot handle the new updates, upgrade. Whatever you do, keep up with life. Sure, it can be a pain sometimes, but ultimately it is a gift. A really short gift. So, keep up with the updates! Make the most of it!

Now, if I could follow my own advice...

The Curse of Cassandra

"Yet, mad with zeal, and blinded with our fate,
We haul along the horse in solemn state;
Then place the dire portent within the tow'r.
Cassandra cried, and curs'd th' unhappy hour;
Foretold our fate; but, by the god's decree,
All heard, and none believ'd the prophecy."

~ From Virgil's The Aeneid (2.323).

In Greek mythology, Cassandra[10] was the daughter of King Priam and Queen Hecuba of Troy. Her brother was Paris, the man whose abduction of Helen, the wife of Menelaus of Sparta, started the Trojan War. Cassandra's other brother was the brave Hector, a hero of said war.

She was described as beautiful, elegant, intelligent, charming, insane, and cursed.

Legend has it that Apollo, the Greek God of Healing, Light, and Truth fell in love with the young Cassandra. She promised to be his lover, so he blessed her with the gift of prophecy. Well, when the time came for her to keep her promise, she spurned Apollo. Well, hell hath no fury than a Greek God spurned. Apollo cursed her — even though she would prophesy, no one would ever believe her.

So, no one believed her when she warned that Paris' abduction of Helen would lead to war and the destruction

---

[10] *"Cassandra." Encyclopaedia Britannica. 2018.*

of Troy. Nor did they believe her when she warned the Trojans not to drag the horse they found outside the city walls into the city.

After Troy fell, she was assaulted by Ajax, one of the Greek heroes, and then given to King Agamemnon as a concubine. He took her back with him to Mycenae. Even though she prophesied that they would be killed on their return to Mycenae, Agamemnon did not believe her. Well, upon their arrival in Mycenae, both of them were murdered by Agamemnon's queen, Clytemnestra, and her lover.

With her constantly prophesying and no one believing her, it is any wonder she was seen as being insane?

Cassandra has come to stand for those whose words of warning are never heeded. Those who see foresee the misfortunes that await but are laughed off as "Chicken Littles."

It could also stand for those who are blessed with gifts they cannot harness or can harness but just seem unable to make any personal, societal, or financial impact with those gifts.

How frustrating it is to be blessed with a gift that seems to go to waste! These feelings of helplessness, uselessness, and futility are enough to drive one mad. They are powerful enough to make one wish to end it all. One wonders if the Gods have conspired to play a cruel joke on these poor souls. It is as if the Gods have colluded to destroy these gifted ones by driving them mad. It almost confirms the saying, "Those whom the gods wish to destroy, they first make mad."

This all begs the question of, "Why?"

Why are some gifted ones never heeded? Why are some talented ones cursed into utter oblivion and non-fulfillment?

Could it be that like Cassandra, they reneged on a promise to the Gods? That these gifted men and women spurned the Gods? Could it be that their condition is just a price they are paying for betrayal?

In promising to be with Apollo and then later spurning him, Cassandra exhibited a lack of trustworthiness, a lack of character. This is what brought the curse on her.

Could it be that these gifted but unheeded, these talented but unfulfilled people are in this position because of the lack of character? That it may not be a curse at all, but a case of deficient moral rectitude that breeds distrust in them? Maybe the curse of Cassandra is not a curse at all, but a lesson in how important character is in life. That irrespective of gifts or talents, character may be the most important of all traits, gifts, and talents. Maybe Heraclitus was right after all when he wrote that a man's character is his fate.

Or maybe I am full of hot air — and really, only the Gods know!

Those Talents — Reflections on My Birthday

It is an innate human desire to live in comfort — a roof over one's head, three square meals, clothing, being able to provide for one's family and dependents — these are some of the hallmarks of a comfortable life. To achieve this, most people chase a career that pays enough to ensure these amenities.

However, this comfort does not necessarily equate to happiness. One may be comfortable, yet unhappy — a bad marriage, a chronically sick child, a terrible boss — all these can put a dent in one's joy. Another major source of unhappiness is a sense of not knowing who one is and one's purpose in life.

I seek with this write-up to contend that, even though a great career or wealth can give one all the comforts of life, true happiness is found when one finds or creates a purpose for one's life. There are many who never find themselves or their purpose in life.

How sad indeed!

When that purpose emanates from one's career, that is a huge bonus. However, this is not always the case. Most times, the desire for comfort is the paramount driver behind our career choices, not one's purpose in life. We then seek to create a purpose around that career, even though that might not feel like who we really are.

However, a rather good guide to finding or even creating

one's purpose in life is those innate talents one is blessed with. The prerequisite for finding these talents is self-knowledge and awareness. Knowing oneself, one's talents, and developing them makes it easier to craft a purpose for one's life. This is the ideal scenario.

In reality, many are those who never find themselves, recognize their talents, or even are able to use them to discover or craft a purpose for their lives.

Yet, as early as in childhood, the talents of each of us is evident. The one thing a child does repeatedly, in spite of all odds, is often a good indicator of this child's talent. Unfortunately, parents may overlook these important signs in their quest to raise a well-educated child. If one is unable to find that talent in childhood, all hope is not lost. Through prayer, introspection, meditation, self-reflection, imagination, and conversations with friends and family, one can still hone in on one's genius even as an adult. So, do not give up hope if you are still searching.

I'm always reminded of the biblical story of the Parable of the Talents when this issue comes up (Matthew 25:14-30). The parable as told by Jesus is of three servants who got talents from their master before he left on a trip. A talent from that time is estimated to be worth about $1,000 - $30,000 today.[11] The first servant got five talents, the second got two, and the last got one. The first two servants doubled their gifts. The last one did nothing with his. On

---

[11]Talent (measurement). Wikipedia. en.wikipedia.org/wiki/Talent_(measurement).

his return, the master was of course impressed with what the first two servants did with their talents. Jesus wasn't too happy with the last one.

In Matthew 25:28-29, Jesus said, "So take the talent from him and give it to him who has the ten talents. For to everyone who has will more be given, and he will have an abundance. But from the one who has not, even what he has will be taken away."

Now no one is going to come hound you for not finding or exploring your talent or talents. But like the parable shows, there is something to be gained from using it and a lot to be lost from not harnessing it.

Which means once these talents are found, it is important to do something with them.

Like already mentioned, the ideal scenario is building a career and creating a life purpose based on one's talents. One is then able to monetize and multiply these talents, just like the first two servants did. Unfortunately, that cannot always happen.

The next option is to make a hobby out of these talents. In reality, that is what is most common. Even though a hobby out of one's talents may not bring any money, it can serve as a balm to one's soul, the essence of one's spirit. It brings periods of true and intense happiness that reminds one of what life is truly about.

The third option is to harness these talents to improve the

lives of others, put a smile on others' faces, or change the world one lives in for the better. This path may be unrewarding materially, but it can bring great happiness and a sense of accomplishment. Besides, what is greater than helping make the world a better place or putting a smile on another's face?

The last option is to do nothing with these talents, a choice that is unfortunately quite common but sad.

Thus, we realize that even if we are unable to build a career out of our talents, there are other ways they can be explored and exploited. Therefore, there is really no excuse to leave talents untouched.

Each of us is blessed with a talent or talents. Find yours and harness it. It will bring you happiness like you never realized; it might make you rich, but above all, it helps make this world more beautiful.

Then, like the author Henry Van Dyke once wrote: "Use what talents you possess; the woods would be very silent if no birds sang there except those that sang best."

A Simpler World

I am no Mr. Fix-It-All, but I used to open the hood of a car and recognize the parts. Things like the cylinder block, the carburetor, alternator, radiator, battery, oil dipstick, and brake fluid reservoir were all quite easy to make out. Now, it takes a degree in advanced automotive engineering to find where something is in most cars and a PC running some arcane program to figure out what chip has locked up your steering wheel!

I miss the simple! I yearn for the uncomplicated. As an example, take my dream car — the 1970 Mercedes 280 SE coupe. The engine was simple. But if you ever have the chance to open the hood of one of Mercedes' AMG models, the story is totally different. All you can recognize is the signature of the mechanic who put the engine together on the engine block!

This yearning for the simple is not for just cars, and I seem not to be the only one who has it.

There seems to be a worldwide lust after the elemental, as the world has gotten rather complex.

I mentioned cars earlier, but an even more poignant example of this complexity is the phone. It has gotten so complex, it is now called "smart." We went from a device with a dial that one spun to a veritable handheld computer that, by the way, is also a phone, a camera, a voice recorder, a clock, a timer, a TV, a projector...whew! Talk about complex!

Yet as humans, we like the simple. We yearn for the unsophisticated. So, as life gets more complex, humans are turning to the simple and turning away from what is complex. We are turning to simple solutions and arguments for issues that are, well, complex.

In this gradual turn, science is seen as the biggest culprit. As scientific knowledge has increased, all the fields science encompasses have grown in a marked degree of inexplicability to the lay person. Try explaining cancer biology or quantum theory to a lay person and watch the smoke puff out of their ears. Thus, it is no surprise many see science as the driver of this complexity. This has spawned an anti-science wave that is evident all around the world.

There arises also a distinct anti-intellectualism. The intellectual always seeks to tackle the issues of the day through all-encompassing thought processes that take all factors into consideration. Well, that is often heady stuff most lay people have no inclination for. Are there no simpler solutions devoid of theories and maxims?

We also turn to those leaders who demonstrate a rather basic grasp of our rather complex problems and propose ordinary solutions. These leaders often have a populist bend and embody the very simplicity the people yearn for. They see things as black and white, good or bad, us versus them. Their choices are binary and simple. There is no middle ground to allow ambiguity and complexity. They enumerate the problems and have for each a distinct culprit, making it easy to fix — by getting rid of that culprit. Besides having a populist tendency to them, these leaders also lean towards the autocratic. It's as if people want to be led and not have to make decisions for themselves.

A fourth sign of this turn towards simplicity is the wish for the known and familiar and an aversion to what is new, foreign, and unfamiliar. Tribalistic tendencies increase as people seek the safety of the known. This breeds a certain xenophobia, which is not necessarily due to hate but more out of fear. A fear of the unknown that is seen as complex and unfathomable.

Lastly in this wish for the simple, people turn to a known and omnipotent Deity. To a great Being who knows it all and can keep one safe in this complex and evil world. Religiosity becomes more pronounced and a marked turn from the secular is seen.

In short, as the world gets more complex, do we become more anti-science, anti-intellectual, tribalistic, religious, and elect more populist and autocratic leaders?

It sure looks like it.

Is it our way of showing our yearning for what is simple?

Apparently!

Do these moves simplify the very complex problems that just won't go away?

Probably not!

You see, the wish for human comfort is a very strong need. We humans will do any and everything to attain happiness. If the complexity that has become paramount eats at this comfort, we will do all we can to change it. Once we think we have changed it, we will do all we can to keep the status quo. The enemy then becomes anyone who wants the complex. Above all, the enemy becomes anyone who attacks the leader who embodies the simplicity they yearn for. The support of that leader will only grow the more he seems to be attacked, for those traits that made him attractive. An attack on such a leader is seen as an attack against the very wish of those who want the simple. His supporters might do all in their power to prop up such a leader, as he embodies their most innate wish — for the simple.

The world faces an interesting yet disconcerting time. The sciences may lose the support they need. In a lot of scenarios, a simplistic offering for a complex issue may set us back or even endanger lives. The world may become smaller and more divided. Religious ideals may usurp the secular way of life.

Yet, nothing stays the same forever. Just as we yearn now for the simple, sooner or later, we are going to wish for more thoughtful responses to the questions, "Why?" and "How?"

Across the Room

That summer day in 2013 when my family and I visited the Musee de Louvre in Paris, we knew what the highlight of the visit was going to be — seeing Leonardo da Vinci's "Mona Lisa." We finally got to Room 6 — a.k.a Salle des Etats, a.k.a the Mona Lisa room.

I couldn't believe how many people were waiting to see it! The large room was packed, and the air was filled with phones and cameras trying to capture the painting. Even from the back of the room, I was struck by how relatively small the painting was.

As I strained my 67-inch frame to see over heads and shoulders, I felt one of my kids tugging at my arm. It was my daughter.

She said, "Daddy, look," and pointed behind me.

I turned. I gasped. I was looking at the largest painting I ever saw. Yet I had to see the "Mona Lisa," so I told her we'd look at it later.

About 10 minutes later, we were standing in front of the "Mona Lisa." To be honest, the hectic rush of the moment did not allow one to truly appreciate the nuances inherent in that great portrait. Pushed and shoved on each side by the throngs of visitors, there was no time to marvel at the fleeting smile, those eyes that followed you everywhere, or the delicate layers Leonardo painted over the 16 years he worked on his masterpiece.[12] [13] One has no time to appreciate his left-handed hatch marks or how he gently painted his outlines using the sfumato technique.

Trying to take that all in was impossible, so after a few minutes of basking in the presence of Lisa del Giocondo, we turned and walked back to the large painting across from the "Mona Lisa."

As we stood before it, I couldn't help but gasp again. My daughter's jaw hung open.

My son was simply saying "Wow," in a long-drawn-out cadence, and my wife said, "That's what I'm talking about!"

We were looking at Veronese's "The Wedding at Cana."

On June 6, 1562, the Benedictine monks of the Basilica of San Giorgio Maggiore in Venice, Italy commissioned Paolo Veronese to create a large painting for their new dining hall, which had been designed by the architect Andrea Palladio.[14]

The only stipulation of the monks was that the painting

---

[12]*Louvre.fr. (2017). Mona Lisa – Portrait of Lisa Gherardini, wife of Francesco del Giocondo | Louvre Museum | Paris. [online] www.louvre.fr/en/oeuvre-notices /mona-lisa-portrait-lisa-gherardini-wife-francesco-del-giocondo [Accessed 13 Nov. 2017].*

[13]*Isaacson, Walter. Leonardo Da Vinci. Simon & Schuster, 2017. Print*

[14]*"The Wedding at Cana." Wikipedia, 31 Jan. 2018, en.wikipedia.org/wiki/ The_Wedding_at_Cana.*

had to fill an entire wall of the dining room.

With the help of his brother, Benedetto Caliari, Veronese finished the painting in 15 months and presented it to the monks in September 1563. It was titled "The Wedding at Cana," measured about 22 feet x 32 feet (7 meters x 10 meters) and was oil on canvas. The painting was supposed to be viewed upwards, as it was 2.5 meters above the dining hall floor. This was meant to add to its air of expansiveness.

As a theme, Veronese chose the biblical story of the feast in Cana where Jesus turned water into wine (John 2:1-11). It is thought to be the first miracle Jesus performed.

Painting in the mannerist style typical for that era, also used by other masters like Michelangelo and da Vinci, Veronese combined the biblical narrative with 16th century Venetian decor. He merged the sacred with the profane, superimposing Venetian decadence on a spartan Galilean setting. There are about 130 characters in the painting (Veronese himself is in there too) — dogs, cats, and even birds. The composition is elegant, depicts the polished way Veronese reinterpreted the biblical story, and is masterfully done.

On September 11, 1797, French soldiers would steal the painting from the monastery, cut it into two, and transport it to France. After restoration in the 1990s, the painting now hangs in the Salle des Etats in the Musee de Louvre in Paris.

Sadly, of the almost 6 million people who stream into the Salle des Etats annually, less than 10% stop to admire this masterpiece.

The location of "The Wedding in Cana" has become its curse. It hangs across from da Vinci's "Mona Lisa." Thus, all who stream into this large room only have eyes for the portrait of one Lisa del Giocondo — aka Lisa Gherardini, aka Mona Lisa. The petite 30 inches x 21 inches painting distracts from the largest canvas in the entire Louvre!

This phenomenon stimulates some reflection:

How many times in life do we see great people or events dwarfed by perceived (rightfully or wrongfully) greater people or events? I think of all those basketball greats who could never win a championship because of Michael Jordan's success, how the movie "Forrest Gump" stole the thunder of "The Shawshank Redemption" in 1995, or how Princess Diana's death eclipsed Mother Teresa's in 1997. It almost seems like the world's stage can only hold one star at a time — which begs the question, "Is it always occupied by the greatest?"

Sometimes it is. Other times, due to hype and human subjectivity, it is not. It is in those instances that objectivity is sorely needed. Yet due to intellectual laziness, we as humans would rather go with the flow than try to see beyond the obvious facade.

It takes the innocence and curiosity of a child to draw our attention to what we may be missing.

Also, we all go through life with preconceived notions of what we want or where we want to go. Sometimes we become so enamored with our obsessions that we fail to see a grander picture of how things could be or where else a door might have opened.

A visit to the Louvre was a delightful experience and provided an overwhelming immersion in human creativity and ingenuity. It was also a great lesson in not getting hung up on society's hype and our own preconceived notions and looking beyond the obvious and at all the possibilities. There could easily be a Veronese across the room that dwarfs that Mona Lisa you have craved all your life, so turn around!

Park by the Interstate

It is some 90 miles from the Brent-Spence Bridge, which spans the Ohio River between Covington and Cincinnati, to Lexington. We crossed it around 8:30 pm earlier this evening, heading towards Lexington.

About two miles from the bridge, the thunderstorm started. It would pour for the next 60 miles like there was no tomorrow. It made driving quite tricky. Anyone who has driven through a thunderstorm can attest to that.

There were instances where the wipers could hardly keep up, and visibility was reduced to a few feet ahead. I noticed several cars had pulled over beside the interstate, waiting for the rain to subside. Most of them were smaller sedans. In such weather, traveling in a big SUV helped greatly — so we kept carefully driving. The whole wet spectacle was regularly set aglow by flashes of lightning, which just added to the foreboding aspect of it.

During this cautious crawl of driving in a thunderstorm, I thought of life.

Life, though good, has its share of suffering. It comes with it. When the trials and tribulations hit, it is like driving through a never-ending thunderstorm. Sure, like a weather forecast, paying attention to warning signs in life might spare one the misery of those tribulations. However, just like that same weather forecast, can one with any certainty pinpoint the time when those trials and tribulations may hit? Not really. So, one has to live this life and hope for the best.

In times of strife, is being well prepared like driving in an SUV during a thunderstorm? Is being unprepared like driving in a small sedan?

Maybe! Maybe not!

Driving that small sedan might make you ill-prepared for the thunderstorms of life, but you have the power to wait it out. Even though the conditions may make it impossible to continue in a small sedan and the only option might be to park and wait out the storm, it could turn out to be the wiser decision. Sure, time may be lost as one waits; but what is more important — life or time?

Then, what shows the big SUV is really that safe? That it can weather the storm? No matter how careful one might be, there is always other people's driving habits to consider. What says the storm might not actually get worse, even for the SUV?

Even though the SUV gives one an edge, ultimately, it is what one does or does not do that makes the difference. One might not have the big SUV to plow through the rain, but one can wait out the storm — and that might be the wiser decision.

When those trials and tribulations hit, being able to go on is great. However, if you are unable to, take a deep breath, park by the interstate, and wait. Even this thunderstorm shall pass. Besides, it might be the wiser move after all.

That Old, Deaf Dude

What should have clued me in was when his daughter said her dad had one hearing aid for the left ear and it was programmed so he could hear the music. I didn't think much about it. I asked her to take it out for safekeeping before he went back for his procedure. She said he would hear us in the operating room if we yelled in his right ear. I acknowledged the tip and went off to see another patient.

So, when one of the Post-Anesthesia Care Unit (PACU) nurses called about 90 minutes later and asked me to come and see the old musician who had just had X procedure done by Dr. Y, I drew a blank. Of all Dr. Y's patients that day, there was none of them that I remembered was a musician. I briefly thought of the old guy with the hearing aid, and quickly ruled him out.

As if the nurse sensed my dilemma, she gave me a name. It was the old man with the hearing aid! What the daughter said came back to me.

"Mr. EB? A musician? How?" I asked.

"Yeah, that's him," the nurse answered.

"I'll be right over," I said.

I headed for the PACU. Mr. EB was resting in a recliner. In spite of iffy vital signs, he wanted to go home. The look in his eyes signaled there was nothing I was going to say or do that was going to get him to stay a minute longer. In spite of his numbers, he looked great, but I wanted him to stay a wee bit longer.

"Sir, the nurse said you are a musician. How do you manage with your hearing?" I asked.

His daughter, who was still with him, proceeded to tell me a story that blew me away.

Besides the guitar, her dad played a lot of other instruments and sang too. His favorite genres were gospel and bluegrass music. He had lost his hearing and some of his eyesight, but he could still play with the help of his hearing aid and — check this out — having one other musician stand on the side where he wore his hearing aid, so he could feed off the beat and rhythm!

He still wrote music and performed at bluegrass concerts like at Renfro Valley here in Kentucky, and also gave free performances at nursing homes. Mr. EB's daughter showed me a short video of one of his shows with his band.

As I sat there with my jaw hanging close to the floor, the old guy grinned at me and started regaling me with stories. He is one of the oldest living artists to have played at the Grand Ole Opry, had been honored at the Smithsonian, and honored right here in Kentucky too. His catalog of written songs exceeded 200.

Mr. EB told me of life during the Great Depression and how he had taught himself to play the guitar, much to the surprise of his dad. (I would later Google him and confirm everything he told me and learn even more.)

As I had walked into the PACU, I had planned to tell Mr. EB I wanted him to wait another half an hour before being discharged. But aside from a few pesky interruptions, we talked for almost 30 minutes. I got to observe him for 30 minutes and was happy to discharge him home. However, in those 30 minutes, he re-taught me an invaluable lesson. He reminded me where there is a will, there is always a way.

At his advanced age, with his eyesight, hearing, and health failing, he could have packed it in. Not him. He had figured out a way to beat Father Time at his game and was living life and making the most of it. Life is truly what you make it.

We as doctors and nurses pride ourselves in helping others gain good health or maintain it. We see ourselves as givers. However, we are also takers. Amid all the pain, we also hear and see patients' stories of strength, resilience, and hope. These stories are priceless in that they remind one of the strength of the human spirit and what will, and determination can achieve. In that, the patients help us as much as we help them. Thus, I am really grateful I met the "old, deaf dude."

The Man Under the Bridge

He sat under the bridge.

From the car, he looked like one of the many panhandlers who seemed to be everywhere these days — but he wasn't asking for any money. He just sat on the low wall under the bridge. Beside him lay a rather dirty looking backpack. He looked disheveled, emaciated, and had a long, haggard face.

What caught my attention was what he seemed to be doing. He had what looked like a board in front of him and he was drawing or sketching. I kept wondering what he was drawing that made him so oblivious to his surroundings.

As I sat in the car at the red light, I wished I had my camera with me to capture the scene. A lonely man sitting in the shadows of a bridge, oblivious to life around him, drawing. It just held so much meaning I wished I could immortalize it.

As the light turned green, I thought of the countless times I wished I had my camera with me to capture a moment (and I do not mean my iPhone camera!). However, even when I've had my camera, there were scenes I could not capture just because of where they were. I think of the many times I've thought of stopping on a narrow road to capture the fog in a valley or the shadows the setting sun cast. For safety reasons, I've had to forego the capture of those unforgettable moments.

Yet such instances are indelible and inspire people to express them in different art forms.

As I drove on, I thought of how else the moment under the bridge could be captured and immortalized.

A photographer would of course capture it in pixels or on film, seeking to get the highlights and shadows right and maybe even the expression on the guy's face, framing it against the starkness of his surroundings.

The artist might sketch or paint the scene, paying attention to the hues and tones to impart the tenor of the moment.

A musician might write a piece about the lonely man under the bridge.

A rapper might bust some funky lyrics about "chilling under the bridge."

Even a sculptor may capture the moment in stone or metal.

Besides not having my camera, I cannot draw, sing, rap, play an instrument, or sculpt.

So, I kept driving and thinking about those few minutes under the bridge.

Who was he? Was he a man down-and-out on his luck? Was he a tired panhandler? Or was he an artist seeking inspiration at the most unlikely place?

What was he drawing? Was he drawing the face of a loved one from the past? A daughter he missed? A life left behind? Mistakes made with dire consequences? Dreams unfulfilled and hopes dashed? Was he drawing his future, or sketching the pangs of hunger that wracked his frail body? The next masterpiece?

In that moment under the bridge, one saw an island of raw humanity in the hustle and bustle of life. I wondered how many drivers in their cars, in a hurry to reach their destinations, saw that lonely man. It was quite reminiscent of how the busyness of life prevents us from seeing life in all its starkness.

As these thoughts went through my head, I realized how I could memorialize that impactful moment. I could write about it. So, I picked up my pen and wrote:

"He sat under a bridge..."

Crawl Turtle, Crawl!

"You've got two problems. The first is to find a problem and the second is to solve it. Good day." — The physicist Clarence Zener to then-graduate student John Goodenough at the University of Chicago in 1946.[15]

John Goodenough is a creative late bloomer.[16] He invented the lithium-ion battery when he was 57. Now at the age of 94, he and Maria Helena Braga, a Portuguese physicist, may be on the cusp of another momentous discovery — a battery that uses an anode made of pure sodium or lithium and glass as the electrolyte. Such a battery would be cheap, lightweight, and not susceptible to fires. It could store more energy and allow the powering of electric cars at much lower costs, making them viable competitors to petroleum-filed cars.

Even though there are doubts about the invention, if anyone can pull this feat off, it would be John Goodenough.

Born in New Haven, Connecticut in 1922, he suffered from dyslexia as a child. He was enrolled in a boarding school at age 12 (by parents who were rather aloof). In spite of his learning disability, he somehow got into Yale

[15]Gregg. Helen. *"This Current Quest"* The University of Chicago Magazine, Summer 2016, mag.uchicago.edu/science-medicine/his-current-quest.
[16]LeVine, Steve. *"Not Good Enough for Goodenough."* Quartz, Quartz, 5 Feb. 2015, qz.com/338767/the-man-who-brought-us-the-lithium-ion-battery-at-57 -has-an-idea-for-a-new-one-at-92/.

at age 18. At that time, dyslexia were poorly understood and managed.

At Yale, he studied math. His studies were interrupted by World War II.

After the war, a scholarship for veterans allowed him to study physics at the University of Chicago under giants like Enrico Fermi.

Goodenough arrived at the University of Chicago in 1946 (he was 24). The registration officer in the physics department was John Simpson, then a new instructor fresh off the Manhattan Project and later a pioneer in the study of cosmic rays.

He took one look at Goodenough and said, "I don't understand you veterans. Don't you know that anyone who has ever done anything interesting in physics had already done it by the time he was your age; and you want to begin?"

That did not deter him. With the solid-state physicist Clarence Zener as his advisor, Goodenough would go on to finish his Ph.D. in 1952. It must be noted that back then, professors were not allowed to collaborate with students on their theses.

He would later work at MIT and at Oxford, where his work would lead to the invention of the lithium-ion battery. He is presently at the University of Texas.

John Goodenough epitomizes those who find their creative spark late in life. Unlike what Mark Zuckerberg once said, young people are not smarter and more creative than older people. Studies do show that creativity may actually blossom with age, a sweet spot being in the late 40s.

When asked about his creativity at such a late age, John Goodenough said, "Some of us are turtles; we crawl and struggle along, and we haven't maybe figured it out by the time we're 30. But the turtles have to keep on walking. This crawl through life can be advantageous, particularly if you meander around through different fields, picking up clues as you go along. You have to draw on a fair amount of experience in order to be able to put ideas together."[17]

I take great solace in the life and work of a man like John Goodenough. I discovered a knack for writing six months before my 50th birthday so I can relate to being a turtle, and I bet there are a lot of you out there like that. I can also relate to meandering around in different fields, collecting clues along the way.

Sure, there are days when the ticking clock sounds really loud. There are days when I wonder why I even bother. There are days when I want to toss my laptop through the window, but I don't.

---

[17]Kennedy, Pagan. "To Be a Genius, Think Like a 94-Year-Old." The New York Times, The New York Times, 7 Apr. 2017, www.nytimes.com/2017/04/07/opinion/sunday/to-be-a-genius-think-like-a-94-year-old.html.

I keep writing.

You see, like the Greeks used to say, "Man know thyself."[18]

That is the most important bit. That is the first problem. It matters not when that discovery is made because without that knowledge, one wanders aimlessly through life.

So, feel blessed you know who you are. Armed with that, you can find a way forward, irrespective of how old you are. What really matters is to keep at it.

Forget that the hairline is receding, the hair is grey, the six-pack is gone, hot flashes have set in, there are wrinkles everywhere, and everything sags.

Grab that spark, claim your turtle-ship, and keep crawling!

---

[18] *"Know Thyself." Wikipedia, Wikimedia Foundation, 4 Feb. 2018, en.wikipedia. org/wiki/Know_thyself.*

Finding the Why

"He who has a why to live can bear almost any how." — *Friedrich Nietzsche[19]*

By the early 1930s, Vienna in Austria was the capital of psychiatry, psychology, and psychotherapy. The work of two men — Sigmund Freud and Alfred Adler — had established the first and second Viennese schools of psychotherapy.

Whereas Freud taught that neuroses were a result of suppressed sexual tensions, Adler was of the opinion that the fight for power and control marked the genesis of neurotic issues.

Towards the end of the 1930s, a young Jewish doctor finishing his residency in psychiatry and neurology at the Steinhof Psychiatric Hospital in Vienna was working on a theory that was going to become the third Viennese School of Psychotherapy. His name was Viktor Frankl,[20] and his theory was based on finding meaning in one's life and born from existentialism. He would call it logotherapy.

Frankl believed as long as one could find meaning in any circumstance, it made life bearable.

---

[19]*Nietzsche, Friedrich Wilhelm. Twilight of the Idols or How to Philosophize with a Hammer. New York: Oxford University Press, 1998. Print.*
[20]*Frankl, Viktor E. The Unconscious God: Psychotherapy and Theology. New York: Simon and Schuster, 1975. Print.*

He surmised one should not ask what the meaning of his or her life is, but rather one must recognize the onus is on the individual to give meaning to his or her life. He theorized in any situation in life, if we are not able to change the conditions, then it is incumbent on us to change our perceptions. The best way to do this would be to find meaning in the situation or circumstance, regardless of how unlucky or terrible it might be. So, Frankl believed even in times of suffering, one could find meaning in the suffering. This discovery would make the suffering tolerable and modify one's reaction to it. Thus: "He who has a why to live can bear almost any how."

Frankl's work, however, was interrupted by the outbreak of World War II and the Nazis taking over. He would be sent to the Theresienghetto with this wife and then later to Auschwitz. His wife was sent to the concentration camp in Bergen-Belsen, where she died.

When he arrived in Auschwitz, he had the manuscript of the theory he was working on in his inner coat pocket. As was the practice, he had to take off all his clothes which were confiscated along with any other possessions he had, including his manuscript. He and the other new inmates received the old garb of prisoners who had already been gassed.

Devastated at his situation, he put on the old clothes he received. Sticking his hands in the pockets of the coat he had just gotten, he felt something. He pulled out a piece of paper. On it was the "Shema Yisrael," the most important Jewish prayer (Deuteronomy 6:4-9 and 11:13-21; Numbers

15:37-41).

As he would later write in his famous book, "Man's Search for Meaning":[21]

"How should I have interpreted such a 'coincidence' other than a challenge to live my thoughts instead of merely writing them on paper?"

Frankl went on to do just that — he found meaning for his suffering in Auschwitz and three other camps. He survived and after the war published his thoughts in several great books, finally establishing what came to be the Third Viennese School of Psychotherapy.

"O that on this and every other day, I may find my why so I can bear any how."

That should be everyone's daily prayer.

---

[21] Frankl, Viktor E. Man's Search for Meaning: An Introduction to Logotherapy. New York: Simon & Schuster, 1984. Print.

That Bitter Cup

"So arm in arms, with arms, we'll fight this little struggle,
'Cause that's the only way we can overcome our little trouble." — Bob
Marley in the song "Zimbabwe" 1979

A strong tenet of Christian faith is God sent His son Jesus
to this Earth to assume human form, be crucified, and
have the shed blood from his crucifixion wash away the
sins of mankind. This was to ensure salvation in the afterlife and prevent all who believed from burning eternally in
hell's fire.

Anyone who grew up in a Christian home had this
drummed into them from Sunday School into adulthood.

Does that mean that this life is unimportant? There are
those who definitely hold that view and live for a future in
the "City with Streets Lined with Gold." However, I for
one believe this life is valuable too. I hold that we are here
to give life meaning and Jesus' life was supposed to show
us how to live this life and give it purpose.

By his words and actions, he taught his disciples and the
throngs who followed him to be humble, kind, not judgmental, help the needy, heal the sick, love their enemies,
and give Caesar his due. He surrounded himself with
society's outcasts and stood for the common man. He
taught prayer in private and forgiveness. He harped on the
Golden Rule — to love your neighbor as yourself. One can
argue these are actions that ensure passage into heaven.
Well, I argue these are lessons indispensable to living in

this lifetime.

Furthermore, we could also actually call Jesus a revolutionary. I mean, chasing the merchants from the temple is as revolutionary as it gets. He definitely thought the practice of Judaism at that time needed some drastic changes. There are authors who claim he also had a political message of Jewish independence from the Romans. Whatever the case, he surely preached change and through that, incurred the wrath of not only powerful Jews but also of the Roman masters.

So, if God became Man and lived to exemplify how life should be led, were his actions going to have the same consequences as those of a normal man? In other words, if he was a revolutionary and — most revolutionaries throughout history have had violent ends or paid dearly for their beliefs — was he going to have a violent end or pay dearly for his beliefs too? (If you doubt revolutionaries have violent ends, look through history - Martin Luther King Jr., Meena Kamal of the Philippines, Spartacus, Joan of Arc, Malcolm X, Steve Biko, Abraham Lincoln...)

Being the Son of God and able to walk on water, raise the dead, turn water into wine, and heal lepers made him an extraordinary man. He may have assumed human form, but he was not your typical powerless person. So, one could argue he could easily have avoided whatever violent end most revolutionaries befall.

Yet as we all know, he did not avoid this violent end. He might have tried to pray it away as he said in Luke 22:42,

"Father, if you are willing, take this cup from me; yet not my will, but yours be done." But ultimately, he ended up dying violently...and that might have been his biggest lesson.

You see, we humans hate change. We are creatures of habit and we like things to stay the way they are...forever. Anyone or anything that threatens to change the status quo is not looked at favorably. When powerful people have a lot to lose from this change, they react vengefully, often with dire consequences for the change agent. Thus, change never comes easily. It is often led and incited by men and women brave enough to incur the wrath of the powerful or even the oppressors. These are the change agents, the revolutionaries. They may be militant like a Castro or peaceful like MLK. It doesn't matter — they incur a lot of wrath from the powerful anyway.

So, did Jesus with his life and death teach us to be change agents if we see change is needed? Did he teach we should fight for that change regardless of the consequences? Did he show us a violent end might just be what is waiting for the revolutionary, yet we should fight anyway? I think he did, and that might be the most important lesson he taught. To stand for what one believes in, as long as one has right on his or her side!

Well, like the mortal that I am, I have to ask, "Isn't it easier said than done?"

Connecting the Dots

"Think left and think right and think low and think high. Oh, the thinks you can think up if only you try" — Dr. Seuss[22]

Steve Jobs called it "the process of connecting things."[23] George Scialabba dubbed it "intelligence having fun."[24]

It is defined in The Oxford English Dictionary as: "the use of imagination or original ideas to create something new."

I am talking about creativity!

It is probably the most important of all human abilities. The trait that leads to inventions and innovations. It is through creativity the human race left the caves, understands nature better, has controlled diseases, and travelled into space. Creativity has endowed us with the poetry of Shakespeare, the paintings of Cezanne, and music of Mozart. On the flip side, it has enabled us to create terrible weapons that can kill millions at the touch of a button.

And yet, most educational systems around the world pay no heed to this really important trait.

Typical education systems aim to improve, measure, and

---

[22]Held, Jacob M. (ed.) Dr. Seuss And Philosophy: Oh, the Thinks You Can Think! Lanham: Rowman & Littlefield Publishers, 2011. Print.
[23]Wolf, Gary. "Steve Jobs: The Next Insanely Great Thing." Wired, Conde Nast, 4 June 2017, www.wired.com/1996/02/jobs-2/.
[24]Quote Investigator, quoteinvestigator.com/2017/03/02/fun/.

tease out those who possess a related ability. That of intelligence. The structure of most schools is such that intellectual ability is constantly measured through tests. Those who lack this ability find themselves at the end of the line struggling to make do in a world that has only one measuring parameter.

In a way, it is understandable that school would harp on intelligence — defined in The Oxford English Dictionary as: "the ability to acquire and apply knowledge and skills." These institutions are supposed to prepare one for life, and life needs those with knowledge and skills.

However, life also has problems that need to be solved and knowledge is often not enough.

What is needed is the ability to connect the dots — creativity.

So again, why has this quite important trait taken a backseat to intelligence?

For years, the thinking was there was one kind of intelligence that was measurable through tests like the Intelligence Quotient (IQ). General intelligence or, like some people call it, "g." This general intelligence determined the ability of any human to acquire knowledge, grab critical concepts, and learn skills.

In 1983, the Harvard psychologist Howard Gardner

published a book titled Frames of Mind.[25] The book explored a very interesting theory. He postulated each human being does not possess just one kind of intelligence — the kind measured by tests. Instead, he maintained there are seven different kinds of intelligence and each person uses a combination of these in daily life:

- Logical-Mathematical ("number/reasoning smart") scientific and mathematical thinking.
- Linguistic ("word smart") - writers, poets, speakers, lawyers.
- Musical ("music smart") - think Mozart, Michael Jackson.
- Visual-Spatial ("picture smart") - artists, painters.
- Bodily-Kinesthetic ("body smart") - athletes, dancers.
- Interpersonal ("people smart") - salespeople, religious and political leaders, counselors.
- Intrapersonal ("self smart") - having an effective working model of oneself.

He would later add "naturalistic" intelligence. [26]

Looking at the list of intelligences, one realizes most educational systems put all the onus on the "logical-mathematical" and "linguistic" — reading, writing, arithmetic. In societies like the U.S., there is also a lot of importance placed upon the "bodily-kinesthetic." Due to this concentration on the "logical-mathematical,"

---

[25]Gardner, Howard. Frames of Mind: The Theory of Multiple Intelligences. New York: BasicBooks, 1993. Print.

other intelligences are often neglected. To gain attention, one must be a genius in the other intelligences.

Further, by its very nature, an education rich in the "logical-mathematical" is the very antithesis of the creative mind. Such an education demands conformity and discipline, traits not often seen in the highly creative.

When one watches children, it is evident most humans are not only endowed with intelligence but also with creativity. Yet somehow, by the time most people are young adults, that creative bit of them has been suppressed greatly or even lost. When decisions about a future profession are made, the issue of creativity hardly plays a role. Rather, decisions are made logically and mathematically.

Gardner's theory of multiple intelligences has its detractors.[27] Their biggest problem with it is it cannot be measured like general intelligence. Interestingly, another trait that cannot be measured is creativity; this may contribute to the reason why it is so neglected. In a world where the "logical-mathematical" reigns supreme, whatever is not measurable is unimportant and can be neglected.

However, can any society afford to neglect creativity? Should all our students, irrespective of how creative they might be, be channeled into the "logical-mathematical"

---

[27] *Ascd. "Chapter 15. MI Theory and Its Critics." MI Theory and Its Critics, www.ascd.org/publications/books/118035/chapters/MI-Theory-and-Its-Critics. aspx.*

fields? Should there not be a push to help develop all intelligences since that might shift the onus from the "logical-mathematical" and open the door to including creativity in our education?

Creativity is quite different from intelligence. Intelligence is the ability to gather knowledge and use it effectively. Creativity goes a step beyond that. It is the ability to go beyond the "intelligence frame" to where those disparate dots are and connect them into something new.

Something innovative.

Like Steve Jobs said in a 1995 interview with WIRED magazine: "Creativity is just connecting things. When you ask creative people how they did something, they feel a little guilty because they didn't really do it, they just saw something. It seemed obvious to them after a while. That's because they were able to connect experiences they've had and synthesize new things. And the reason they were able to do that was that they've had more experiences, or they have thought more about their experiences than other people."[28]

Creativity is all about connecting the dots from experiences. Note Jobs didn't use the word "knowledge" but rather "experiences." Having more experiences and thinking more about these experiences seem to be a better engine for creativity than knowledge. Excessive knowledge

---

[28]*Wolf, Gary. "Steve Jobs: The Next Insanely Great Thing." Wired, Conde Nast, 4 June 2017, www.wired.com/1996/02/jobs-2/.*

might actually act as that inner critic against those novel ideas that often do not make sense to the rational mind, the logical-mathematical mind.

Creativity demands imagination. Letting the mind go to places it has not ventured before. It requires one forgets the rational and wander into the irrational. Like George Bernard Shaw once said, "Imagination is the beginning of creation."

Thus, we see an interesting juxtaposition. Imagination is irrational. Logical-mathematical intelligence is rational. Any wonder creativity is stifled in our schools?

So, what about an educational system that right from the get-go seeks to figure out the strength of each child? Which intelligence or intelligences they are endowed with? How creative they are? Then instead of railroading all children through a "logical-mathematical" educational setup, lessons are tailored to the strengths of each child or groups of children? What if this is not done only in special schools, but it's the norm in all schools?

Just maybe we can create a world where no one is useless or dumb or not smart, and instead have societies where the strength of each person is harnessed, and creativity becomes the true driver of our lives.

This Thing

All over the world, wherever the English introduced their language to the Indigenes, an adulteration of the English language ensued. It got mixed up, slanged, patoied, pidginized, and even drawled out.

It was no different in Ghana where we not only made English our official language, but also created our own pidgin version of it. Not satisfied with that, we borrowed a few words to add to our everyday discourse. In the process, we have at times so altered the meanings of the original word or phrases that not even Chaucer could make them out.

Sometimes, we translate directly from the vernacular into English, using that literal translation as an expression. A good example is the expression "skin pain," a term that means "jealousy." In the Akan language, jealousy is "ahoa" (skin) "yaw" (pain) — and just like that, we have a term. One old and popular phrase that is probably older that most living Ghanaians can remember is the term "distin." The term was birthed from the phrase "this thing."

The term was used to describe anything or any event whose name the speaker could not remember or did not know. Often these were people whose command of the English language was fragmented. However, with time, it got into popular usage. Here is a good example of its use:

Remember back when cellphones first appeared on the market? If I tried to describe one to a friend and I couldn't remember the name, I could have said, "I saw "distin" you can use to make calls that is wireless."

Boom! I didn't miss a beat!

Thus, "distin" grew and with time became the Swiss Army knife of everyday Ghanaian conversation, morphing into other branches of our discourse.

So now, one can hear the term, "It was a sad distin" — meaning "It was a sad day" or "It was a sad event."

The term has also crept into our bedrooms where all things conjugal fall under the broad umbrella of "distin." Here one even hears variations like "to distinate" or "the distinate."

I'll leave the meanings to your imagination.

Matter of fact, all parts and participants of that male-female interaction can be described with "distin."

"His 'distin' doesn't work anymore, but that is not catastrophic since we live in the age of Vitamin V," Ama confided to Abena.

One can only marvel at the versatility of the word!

I cannot end distin without my favorite "distin" story.

This past July, I was in Accra with the family and took the kids to Coco Lounge at Stanbic Heights for brunch.

Street-level parking was full, so we used the underground lot and thus had to take the elevator up. The minute my son saw the elevators, as he is wont to do, he ran over to the door and started pushing repeatedly on the call button.

Suddenly, an attendant appeared — like out of the blue. He was an older guy.

He pushed my son's hand away from the call button and yelled, "Why you pressing, pressing, pressing? Don't you know you'll break the distin?"

At that moment, all I could imagine was my son breaking a distin.

I still laugh when I remember that funny distin.

The Age-Old Query

Let do a simple imagination experiment.

It's late 2006. Out there in the universe is a planet inhabited by aliens as curious as the human race. They have been exploring the wide blue yonder and chanced upon the planet Earth. Let's call this alien planet "Ahom" and the aliens that live on it "Ahomfians."

Now, these Ahomfians are different than us. You see, they cannot see us humans. They, however, see structures. They see our houses, churches, skyscrapers, and mobile homes. They are fascinated by them.

One of the Ahomfian explorers recommended studying our planet. Their ruling council agreed.

The explorer designed a study to look the strange structures on our planet. He picked a random street somewhere in the suburbs of Middle America with beautiful single-family homes.

A team of Ahomfians was sent down, and these aliens fitted all the homes on this random street with a multitude of sensors. When they returned to their planet, they were able to monitor parameters like the temperature of the homes, heat emissions, sounds, and vibrations.

The study started in 2007, a year before the crash of the real estate market.

The 30 homes on that street were all new constructions, and but five of them were occupied. The Ahomfians, unable to see the humans in those homes, noticed a difference in heat emissions and other parameters between those homes and the other 25. The 25 homes felt "alive." The others seemed "dead."

Then 2008 came around, and the economy crashed. All of a sudden, more of the homes seemed to "die." By the end of 2008, only 10 of the homes were "alive"

The aliens wondered what had happened.

Then after about a year, things seemed to change. More of the homes started to come "alive." The heat emissions went up. The homes emitted more vibrations and sounds. By the end of 2009, all the homes were emitting heat and sounds and seemed "alive."

After five years, the team wrote a report. Their conclusion was on the new planet they had "discovered," there were immobile structures that seemed to go through several life cycles — the timing of which was quite unpredictable. They recommended more studies.

Now if these aliens could see us humans, they would have realized these homes come "alive" when they are occupied and feel "dead" when they are not.

Makes one think of life, doesn't it? Doubt me? I'll show you.

When one has life, the body is alive. Death ensues when life ends.

Aren't our bodies just receptacles for whatever makes us alive, just like those homes the aliens studied? Thus, when a body is occupied by this life agent, that human is alive but dies when that agent leaves? The spiritually inclined will call this agent the soul and make it responsible for the gift of life.

Or is it?

Let's go back to the homes analogy and think of what makes a home worth living in. It has to be structurally sound, affordable for and attractive to the buyer, and in a fitting neighborhood. If any of those things change, homeowners tend to sell and move on. Thus, homes that suit this bill tend to attract buyers and thus become "alive."

If we go back to the body, can we also apply this analogy?

One may say that there are biological factors that are conducive to life and when they are absent, life escapes. Can it also mean that if one was to construct a body, say out of stem cells, such that it was receptive to life, it could come alive? Would this life agent find this body and occupy it?

Let's take this a step further. Is life created when a biological system becomes viable? So, if I were to use stem cells to create all the various human organs and string them together into my own Frankenstein so his heart beats and his neurons I grew in the lab seem to transmit messages, would he come alive? After all, he would be biologically viable.

I guess my question is the age-old query, "What is life?"

Is it a spiritual occupation of a human body, making it alive, or does life ensue as a result of viable biological processes?

If one believes in the former, then life and death are all-or-nothing processes. You are alive, then you die. Dead or alive! No protracted transitions. One can disagree with my premise and cite the myriad examples of people who had near-death experiences and their stories. That somehow, the life agent or soul has a change of heart and returns, restoring the viability of the body's biological systems; this further illustrates this school of thought's belief that a life agent is behind the viability of life.

However, if one believes in the latter, then life and death are not all or nothing. As long as we can prolong the viability of those biological processes, life hangs around to a degree. As long we can keep the CPR going, as long as we can cool the body to 18 degrees Celsius, as long as we can keep up with the blood loss, there may be a chance. Then life is a result of biology, not the effect of a life agent.

What is life?

I think I'll play an Ahomfian card and say, "More studies are needed."

Life as a Sisyphean Task

In Greek mythology, Sisyphus was punished for his sins and rolls a huge boulder up a hill in the Afterlife, only to have the boulder roll back down to the bottom of the hill once he gets to the summit.[29]

Sisyphus is believed to have been the founder and king of Corinth who was smart, cunning, and ruthless. He had no regard for Gods or men and ruled with an iron fist.

Of all the escapades of Sisyphus, the two that stand out the most and probably drew the most ire from the Gods was when he imprisoned Hades, the God of Death, and when he conned his way out of the Underworld.

He was so cunning that at his appointed time, Hades himself came for him. Well, Hades showed up with handcuffs and Sisyphus asked him to demonstrate them. You can imagine what happened. Hades handcuffed himself onto the wall and Sisyphus had the key! The God of Death in handcuffs! So, for a while, no one could die. Ares, the God of War, pissed off that wars were no fun anymore (no one died), went over to Casa de Sisyphus and freed Hades. After telling Sisyphus to report immediately to the Underworld, Hades promptly scurried away.

So, Sisyphus had no choice but die. Before he did that though, he asked his wife not to bury him but to throw his

---

[29] *"The Myth of Sisyphus." Greek Myths Greek Mythology, www.greekmyths-greekmythology.com/the-myth-of-sisyphus/.*

body into the Town Square. She was also not to put a coin under his tongue. One uses the coin to pay the ferryman on the River Styx, so he can get you to the other side. Nothing is free, you see. Not even when you are dead.

The dear wife did that, so when he showed up before Hades' wife, the Queen Persephone, in the Underworld, he was totally not ready. He claimed he wasn't buried properly and had no coin. So, he sweet-talked Persephone to let him go back to alleviate all the mistakes his wife made! The nerve! And Persephone obliged!

He returned to life, where he promptly forgot about death and partied like it was 1999! For years!

Finally, Zeus had it. Sisyphus had to go. Hades wasn't risking another trip to Casa de Sisyphus.

This time, Hermes, the God of Transitions, more cunning than Sisyphus himself, went to get him. Hermes hauled his behind down to Hades where he was sentenced to hard labor, rolling the boulder.

Which finally brings me to my point. Is there a moral to this story? Well, several. Don't piss off the Gods, would be one. Another might be all good things must come to an end.

I can imagine if the Gods punished a man, and a King at that, they would probably give him a punishment that not only sought to break his spirit but also was unlike anything he was used to. So hard labor for a King would be a good punishment. But then, how do you break the spirit of someone so cunning? Someone so full of spirit? Someone who apparently is goal-oriented and a visionary? Well, you take the purpose out of their lives. You put them in a situation where their very existence has no meaning. Like rolling a boulder up a hill for it to come crashing back down once you reached the summit. For you to do it endlessly — no end in sight, ever!

For us mere mortals, isn't that our very existence? Rolling boulders up the hill of life only to have then come down just when we hit the summit? Isn't life a series of these fruitless trips?

The little victories in life are when we get to a ledge somewhere along the hill and rest. We look back at the distance we have traveled and pat ourselves on the back. Unlike Sisyphus, we do not know yet the boulder is going to roll back down. We kid ourselves that once we get to the top, it'll stay. So, we labor to get this boulder up there. Sometimes we get to a summit and think we've made it. We look up and see another peak and keep rolling. That is our curse.

Maybe, the point of life should not be in where you get the boulder to. It should be in the experience. In the day-to-day activities. In the relationships and contacts, one creates. In finding some joy in this endless task. In knowing you can roll the boulder up.

Sisyphus has been doing it all these years. Something beside the curse must keep him going. Maybe the knowledge that even if the boulder rolls down, he still can get it up there. That no matter how many times he has to do it, he can summon the strength of spirit to move it. Maybe he has discovered that as he rolls this boulder up there, the experience is much more rewarding — the very process more fulfilling than the goal.

Very few are those who live life like Sisyphus the King. For most of us, it's the life of Sisyphus, the boulder-roller. Find your joy in your labor. If you do, let me know how you did it.

I can't.

Goodbye, Whitney!

Feb 22, 2012

If life is but a play, or to be post-modern, a movie, in which we all are nothing but actors and actresses, then Whitney Houston gave me the soundtrack to my movie. Like a maestro, she could match the highs and the lows with her amazing octaves and seemed to mirror the emotions I was going through. Whitney once said when she listened to Aretha Franklin, she could clearly feel her emotional delivery and she could feel it coming from deep within. She (Whitney) wanted to emulate that — and did she!

My love affair with Whitney started probably in 1985 or 1986. Like the rest of the world, I listened to her croon on her first album "Whitney Houston."

Even now I can hear her sultry voice, "So I'm saving all my love, yes, I'm saving all my love, yes, I'm saving all my love for you..."

I can also still hear Tom Scott on the sax.

It was a heady time. I was head over heels in love and knew what I was going to do with the rest of my life. Like Whitney, I felt the sky was the limit.

Then came 1987. In August of that year, I headed out to Germany to study —alone. I was 21. I left behind a girl I was crazy about, my parents, my siblings, and my friends.

In my suitcase were several cassettes. One was the newly released "Whitney" album.

As I heard her sing, "You're still my man," it matched the words I had heard during a last conversation.

I cannot recount how listening to those songs in my room in Radebeul, Germany reminded me of what I had left behind. Whitney always managed to draw out that emotion in song, in the timbre of her voice, in her lyrics.

The years went by. She dropped "I'm Your Baby Tonight." It brings memories of Moritzbastei in good old Leipzig, rain in October, the chill in the air, but so was love...or so I thought. It was a time of deep loss and regrets and what if's? And the soundtrack she provided was perfect.

As she got married, I also got involved in a relationship that would change the trajectory of my life. Even then, she always provided the soundtrack. Even as things spiraled down for me, I could always count on her. In times of deep thought, I'd pop in a Whitney CD, turn down the light, relax in the armchair, and just float on her voice. Her voice was that love I couldn't lose. It was always there. Be it on "The Bodyguard" or the "Waiting to Exhale" soundtracks, Whitney's voice was always reassuring, sultry, sorrowful, powerful, and emotional.

Slowly, the songs stopped coming. I missed them at first, but then I could always turn to her old tunes. Then were the stories and misadventures. I could feel the love for her slipping. Soon, I stopped caring and she became just another girl. However, I knew deep in there was something for her. Any time I heard anything positive about her life, I perked up.

Then she died.

I cannot describe the sorrow I felt. I never knew her, and she probably didn't even know I existed, but I was devastated. If our lives are just movies, then the music we love is the soundtrack to our lives. Whitney matched my movie in ways only she could. I felt like I had lost a part of me. I also felt sad because she couldn't deal with this ordeal called life. She provided a lot of joy to a lot of people but couldn't take care of herself. Life, like they say, is a bitch and she succumbed to it. I felt sad for the choices she may have made that destroyed her. I empathized, because this thing called life scares me too.

Last week was her funeral. The service was powerful. In life, she gave me hours of her beautiful voice. With her death, she helped me put my finger on why I don't have faith. True, I lack faith and have always wondered why. OK, let me explain.

As I watched the service, I was struck by the words of Pastor Marvin Winans. He preached about the importance of prioritizing things in our lives. Then he said not to worry because God says, "I got you!"

That got me thinking about my lack of faith. I know God watches out for me, but being human, my weaknesses, and the uncertainty of life sometimes make His power seem insufficient. No matter how great God is, I am human and can totally mess it up. It is this fear that prevents me from having faith. It is not lack of faith in God, but fear of my own foolishness. If anything illustrates my point, it was Whitney's life. By all accounts, she always spoke of her love of God. Despite all that, her demons got the better of her. No amount of God's grace could save her from herself.

So, she is gone. Gone with her voice, her grace, her beauty.

Like Shakespeare said, "The evil that men do lives after them. The good is oft interred with their bones."

For me, the joy she brought me is going to live forever — because that is what I want to remember. Everything else pales in comparison.

Miss Whitney, even now you may be singing "The Greatest Love of All" to adoring fans in another realm. Lucky them. Don't forget to rest in peace!

Write Your Novel

On April 25, 1884, Sir Walter Besant, an English historian and novelist, gave a lecture titled "Fiction as One of the Fine Arts" at the Royal Institution in London.[30]

In the lecture, he argued the novel was an artistic form like a poem or a painting, the writing of a novel was governed by laws a writer should master, a writer should have artistic talent, and moreover, a novel should aim to raise a reader's moral conscience. Back then, the novel was viewed as a non-serious literary form.

The lecture was published a month later in a newspaper with the title "The Art of Fiction," and led to a series of rejoinders by several writers of the day. Among them was British-American novelist Henry James.

James' response, which he published in September 1884, was also titled "The Art of Fiction." In it, although he agreed with Besant that the novel is a work of art, he took issue with the former's proposal that the writer of a novel be guided by laws. He maintained the most important job of the novelist was to make sure the story was interesting.

One other point he agreed with Besant on is characters in a novel should be clearly defined. In the seventh paragraph of the essay is this memorable quote:

---

[30]Campbell, Donna M. "The Art of Fiction" by Henry James, public.wsu.edu/~campbelld/amlit/artfiction.html

"What is character but the determination of incident? What is incident but the illustration of character?"

Think about this for a minute.

This is one of those quotes that easily escapes its area of origin and wafts into the everyday due to its connotation. It is not only a guideline for novelists, but also seems to carry lessons for life in general. This should not be a surprise, since a novelist tries to capture life and weave it seamlessly into a story.

So, back to the quote.

The novelist may see in these lines a call to create characters in a novel who mesh into the incidents that define them and to build incidents that clearly elucidate the characters they encompass.

If one creates a character with negative traits, he must be placed in incidents that define him.

However, the character's ability or inability to surmount or succumb to his dark side and rise or fall is what should make the story.

In real life, however, what does, say, the first part of the quote even mean?

"What is character but the determination of incident?" Does who we are draw us to certain situations in life? Does character predetermine what conditions we find ourselves in in this journey of life? To a point, I think. A drunk frequents bars and is more apt to get in a fight. An aggressive driver is more prone to get traffic tickets and see the confines of a courtroom. An empathic person is going to hear sad and heartbreaking stories from others more so than the self-centered one.

We all know of that friend who seems to always be in trouble, or the one who always suffers the worst misfortune, or even the one with the Midas touch.

I bet you look back and think of a trait that always seems to land them in these situations.

Also, the words and deeds that may emanate from a character can have effects far and wide. An uncaring leader who by his words incites hate in a society can awaken and embolden her darker elements.

Character determines incident.

The second part of the quote is actually easier to understand.

"What is incident but the illustration of character?"

Our character is our fate. Our character decides how we react to many of life's vicissitudes. Our character is evident when we fail to empathize with the unfortunate or are unable to draw the right parallels and equivalences in life. When we equate the actions of those who resist hate and oppression to those who seek to perpetrate and spread these cancers of society, we show dramatically who we stand with.

If we accept Shakespeare's assertion that all the world is a stage and we are all just two-bit players in a cosmic production, then the ability to rise above our base instincts and traits and aim for a higher point is what ultimately tells the story of our lives. It is what determines the plot of our performances.

Even though our characters might place us in incidents that are negative, it is ultimately our reaction to these incidents that matter. That is what defines us.

Like Viktor Frankl wrote in his book Man's Search for Meaning, "When we are no longer able to change a situation — we are challenged to change ourselves."

So, go ahead and write your life's novel. Fill it with joy and pain, laughter and sadness, love and hate. Make love. Sing. Dance. Who you are will determine the songs that play and even where the wind blows but dig deep and rise. Rise to let those dark incidents illustrate a strength and resolve to write the best novel ever.

The Art of the Nude

"Naked I came from my mother's womb, and naked I will depart." —
Job 1:21

For centuries, artists have painted it. Photographers captured it. Poets have written odes about it — the nude human body, unencumbered by the restriction of clothing.

Yet, nudes have always been controversial. Inasmuch as some see them as works of art, others perceive them as offensive. There is a certain societal stigma attached to models who pose for nudes or artists and photographers who create or capture nude images.

Just last week, I had to remove two artistic nude images I posted because they were reported to Facebook as being obscene.

Thus, drawings, paintings, and photographs of the naked human body walk a rather fine line between acceptance and abhorrence. Yet, from Gustave Courbet's "L'Origine du monde," through Ruben's depictions of voluptuous women to the works of Avedon, Newton, and Ritts, artists and photographers have always sought to depict the human body as it is.

Why the fascination?

Well, the human body — male and female — is really the most beautiful and intricate creation in all of Nature.

Whether one is marveling at the curves and endowments of a woman or the sinews of muscles that adorn a man's arms and chest, there is a certain aesthetic that cannot be denied

It is this beauty that draws artists. However, to really depict the body in all its beauty, well, it has to be nude.

Even as some aspire to use the nude as a depiction of beauty, others use it to titillate our senses and arouse desires. Unfortunately, society often puts all nudes into the latter category.

The ability of nudes to do both — depict beauty and arouse our desires — is another reason why they are such attractive subjects for artists.

You see, the human body in the nude depicts what is possible. If one sees it as a blank canvas, it becomes rather powerful. This power is from its inherent potential to tell whatever story the artists or photographer wants it to tell.

From the moment I saw the work of Herb Ritts many years ago in a bookstore in Berlin, I wanted to use nudes to tell a story too. A few years ago, after I put a studio together, I started shooting nudes. It would take a while for me to find my style.

To tell the story I wanted them to, I decided to use the human body as a treasure to be discovered, a dream to be fulfilled, and a journey to embark on before our strengths and dreams are covered by the clothing of our fears, weaknesses, and the script the world writes for us. It would become the symbol of untapped human potential that is enveloped in uncertainty, doubt, fear, and misgivings.

By shooting with mostly one light source and shrouding the nude body in shadows, I seek to show our potential as humans from birth is "...formless and empty, with darkness hovering over the surface of the deep..." (Genesis 1:2) — and something great can emanate out of all this. That if one looks closely, one can see the forms and lines of something wonderful in those shadows.

As difficult as it is to get society to buy into one's vision of artistic nudes, it's even harder to find models who are comfortable enough to pose for these images. To find one who is comfortable with his or her body and believes in seeing the nude body as a canvas is always inspiring and reminds one of what's possible.

Even as one searches for a model whose nude body can be used to depict how our naked potentials are shrouded in the darkness of uncertainty and the clothing of our fears, one is reminded that life is really a search for who we are.

So, maybe we need to start our search from the beginning — in the nude. My images just aim to remind you to look beyond the shadows for the form and the lines.

It is a Cold and Desolate Distin

"Distin" is a Ghanaian term used to represent a word or phrase when one doesn't readily come to mind...or when the word the writer really wants to use is not family-friendly.

My group also provides anesthesia services at a surgery center that is separated from St. Joseph's Hospital by a high rise with doctors' offices. The three buildings are connected by pedways. If we have to go there in the middle of the day, we use the pedways.

As one walks to the surgery center, part of the path takes one along a line of doctors' offices. The names of the respective group, doctor, or doctors is inscribed on a plaque that adorns the side of the doors to the offices.

Being that I know most of these physicians, I play a game of peek and compare.

All the doors to the offices have sidelights made of clear glass. Some of the doors also have clear glass components, so I can peek into these offices and compare how the reception area is decorated to the nature of the particular doctor or doctors. Spartan, flamboyant, colorful, drab, well-lit, or dark?

Most times, they do not match at all — an observation I attribute to the possibility that most of the doctors have absolutely no hand in how their offices are decorated.

I had to go to the surgery center this afternoon and as I walked along, I played my little game.

Suddenly, I came upon an office that was unlit. It felt deserted, cold, and looked empty. There was no artwork on the walls. On the carpet in the reception area was a small pile of unread mail. The difference really struck me then — all the offices exude a certain kind of warmth. I stopped to read the name on the plaque beside the door and suddenly, it made sense.

I was standing in front of the office of a physician who died about a month ago. That is why that particular office felt so deserted and cold.

I continued walking but couldn't stop thinking about how different that office looked and felt. It was as if Death had not only claimed the former occupant but had also touched the office itself with his cold and chilling fingers. That Death had stamped his alienating and depressing nature into the very being of the room, taking away what enlivened it, and leaving behind a dismal and gloomy space. It made me want to ask Death if he always had to be so cold and miserable. Unlike Midas who turned everything he touched into gold, whatever Death touches becomes cloaked in frosty joylessness.

Luckily, he didn't answer me but as I walked on, I grudgingly had to accept the sad truth — death is one cold and desolate distin.

The Hardest Thing

It always amazes me how a simple song can bring back long-lost or even repressed memories with such clarity. Music is really the soundtrack of our lives.

Whereas my son is totally into Afro-Caribbean music, my daughter seems to enjoy rock classics, indie, grunge, and Motown.

When we are in the car, she often loses the battle for which station to listen to by a ratio of 3:1; so, occasionally, I'll throw her a bone. I did so yesterday.

Scrolling through the Sirius-XM stations, I landed on one playing a Tom Petty song she likes — "Into the Great Wide Open."

Suddenly, I was back in Leipzig, Germany. It was 1992 or 1993, I think. Medical school. Time for the more serious clinical rotations. I wanted the community hospital experience. so, I picked a hospital outside Leipzig. It was about 19 miles away, and I had to be on the floor (ward) by 6 a.m. to prepare for rounds.

I would wake up each morning when the alarm went off at 5 a.m., wondering whether this was how life was going to be for the rest of my life. In a mad dash, I would get ready and set off in my trusted 1989 VW Golf, still wondering. On the occasions that my then-girlfriend spent the night, I rushed out with her still sleeping soundly without a care in the world. I was always so jealous of that.

For some reason, two songs stuck with me on those commutes. They would play often on the radio station I listened to. Both were by Tom Petty from the album "Into the Great Wide Open."

The first song was "Learning to Fly." The other was, well, "Into the Great Wide Open."

I remember one particular morning in the dead of winter when there was quite a bit of snow, so traffic had slowed to a crawl. I knew I was going to be late. The sky was grey, and I wished I was back in bed. In the space of 15 minutes, the DJ played both songs. That day, I was struck by the refrain of "Learning to Fly":

"I'm learning to fly, but I ain't got wings
Coming down is the hardest thing.

Then the refrain of "Into the Great Wide Open":

"Into the great wide open
Under them skies of blue
Out in the great wide open
A rebel without a clue"

To be honest, I found the songs quite unhelpful. One told me I had no wings, and the other said I was clueless. The songs somehow reminded me of how alone I was — far away from family, "into the great wide open," trying to grow my own wings so I could fly. Even back then I knew coming down was not the hardest thing. What was the hardest thing then?

As the song played on the radio yesterday and I was taken

all the way back, I felt those sharp pangs of nostalgia. The years have gone by since those days when I drove to Borna from Leipzig, but I must say those words have proven to be quite true.

I ventured "into the great wide open" all by myself and so far, I'm surviving. I have fallen often because of the immaturity of my wings. I still do, but I am not giving up.

And that "...without a clue" thing, how right was he! After all these years, I still wake up at 5 a.m., still steal out of the house careful not to wake my wife and kids, and still wish I was back in bed.

And then as the song finished playing, it hit me. Coming down is not the hardest thing. It's having the courage to take off again. Again, and again — even though the wings are not ready or immature. Knowing that you may come down much sooner than later but doing it anyway — over and over in spite of crashing repeatedly till one day, you stay up - and maybe even soar to the heights like an eagle.

The years teach you that. Finding it in myself to wake up each morning even when I didn't want to, taught me that. Overcoming fears, anxieties, bad habits, and procrastination and just doing it teaches that.

It took my daughter's taste in music to remind me of that.

One day when she and her brother get ready to step into the world, I may send them off with some Tom Petty. He was a good companion to me once upon a time. Maybe he will be a good one to them too...in the great wide open.

Riddle, Riddle!

I woke up that Saturday morning wrapped up in my usual existential dilemma — the great question of how to make time for all the other things that did not fall under work and family.

Studio time won out that morning, and I drove there hoping to do some encaustic work. Alas, I had no brushes, so I headed to Home Depot to get some natural bristle brushes.

A visit to Home Depot is always a welcome distraction. But on that day, being in the deliberative mood I was, I got the brushes, paid for them, and headed out.

I was almost at my car when I saw him on the ground near where the carts are parked. A woman and another man stood beside him. He looked unconscious. I walked quickly over. All of a sudden, I was the doctor. All thoughts of studio work forgotten. He was breathing, had a pulse, and no visible injuries. The woman told me his name and gave me a history. I called him. Slowly, he responded. I stayed until the paramedics showed up. I had a working diagnosis. It wasn't what the woman thought. I told them. As they took over, I drove off.

I hadn't driven even half a mile, when a voice in my head said:

"YOU ARE WHAT YOU DO!"

That got me thinking. Really?

On my way home, I had to go through Kroger to get a few groceries. I wheeled my shopping cart to the cash register with my favorite cashier. She is an elderly lady with beautiful, short grey hair that gave her a rather noble look. She worked a lot for her age, I thought. We exchanged greetings. Then I saw a tube carrying oxygen running into her nostrils.

"I didn't realize you are on oxygen," I remarked.

"I wear it when I get tired and at night," she answered.

She works all the time.

Like she was reading my mind, she said, "I have the grandkids, you know."

"COPD?" I asked.

"Yes," she answered.

I paid for my groceries, wished her well, and headed out. I hadn't even hit the door when the voice returned:

"LIFE GOES ON, WHETHER YOU LIKE IT OR NOT!"

You don't say, Mr. Voice!

These two occurrences occupied me as I cooked my special for dinner late that afternoon. As I cut the veggies and cleaned the meat, the voice came again:

"YOU CAN STEP AWAY OCCASIONALLY AS LONG AS PLAN TO RETURN. YOU WON'T LOSE ANYTHING!"

Hmmm!

It was a few days before I could sort of put it all together. It felt like deciphering riddles, like I had to figure out parables. I knew the occurrences and voice messages had to do with my existential dilemma. Then it kind of hit me:

One really is what one does most of the time, not what wants to do, plans to do, or wished he did. If you steal most of the time and preach some of the time, you are not a preacher. You are a thief. Since life goes on whether we like it or not, we have no choice but to accept who we are and keep at it. If what it takes is wearing oxygen, so be it.

Despite life being all-demanding and asking us to be what we do, it is all right to occasionally step away from the usual. To be someone else every now and then. To splurge on one's wishes and dreams. Just as long as we bear in mind that it is temporarily, we do no harm.

It is when we forget who we are and what life demands of us that we lose our way and end up in the valley of the shadow of despair.

I am grateful for the answers, but I keep wondering if Life cannot more simply present its answers to the worries that engulf us. I mean isn't it enough that one is trying to hold on? Does one need the pain of a riddle too? I guess if one is what one does, and life give its answers through riddles then life must itself be a riddle. Ha!

That Deadly Sin

This evening, we went to one of our favorite eateries in Cincy. The portions are always ginormous, and I have never been able to finish everything on my plate.

Today, I dared myself and finished off the serving.

As I sat there with my belly full, visions of my left descending and circumflex arteries closing off gradually were accompanied by whirrs of a sternal saw buzzing in my ears.

As those faded, the words of Pope Gregory I popped up from nowhere, "...and as long as the belly is distended, all of a man's virtues come to naught."[31]

Oh dear! The deadly sins! Gluttony!

You see, in the 4th century, the Greek monk, Evagrius Ponticus, drew up a list of eight human weaknesses that showed an obsession with the self. In order of increasing seriousness, they were: gluttony, lust, avarice, sadness, anger, acedia, vain, glory, and pride.[32] His student St. John Cassian would help spread it in Europe.

In the 6th century, Pope Gregory co-opted the list as part of Catholic Church doctrine and slimmed it down to the

---

[31] *Gregory the Great - Moralia in Job (Morals on the Book of Job) - Book XXX, www.lectionarycentral.com/gregorymoralia/Book30.html.*
[32] *"Guide to Evagrius Ponticus." Sitewide ATOM, evagriusponticus.net/life.htm.*

seven deadly sins.[33]   From the most serious to the least, they are: pride, envy, anger, sloth, avarice, gluttony, and lust.

Even though theologians like St. Thomas Aquinas[34] questioned the notion of ranking the seriousness of sin, the list has persisted. The sins were made even more popular by Chaucer's The Canterbury Tales from 1387.

There were those who even thought that each deadly sin had a special punishment in hell. Ernst and Johanna Lehner discuss that in their book Devils, Demons and Witchcraft.[35]   In Dante's Inferno, gluttony was punished in the 3rd Circle of Hell. In that circle, souls of gluttons are watched by the worm-monster Cerberus and punished by being forced to lie in a nasty slush that is produced by never-ending icy rain.

The Deadly Sins are no joke.

Yet if this evening was the night I finally bit the bullet, then I must say the meal that had probably sealed my fate was worth every bite. As I took a sip of wine, I tried to reconcile myself to my possible ignominious destiny. My

---

[33] *"Seven Vices and Seven Virtues (Wrath)." Faust, www.faust.com/legend/seven-deadly-sins/.*

[34] *St. Thomas Aquinas. "Question 84. The Cause of Sin, in Respect of One Sin Being the Cause of Another." SUMMA THEOLOGIAE: The Cause of Sin, in Respect of One Sin Being the Cause of Another (Prima Secundae Partis, Q. 84), www.newadvent.org/summa/2084.htm*

[35] *Lehner, Ernst and Johanna Lehner. Devils, Demons, and Witchcraft: 244 Illustrations for Artists and Craftspeople. Dover Publications, 1999. Print.*

gluttony was going to kill me and send my sinful soul to the 3rd Circle of Hell. My body with its distended belly, devoid of any virtue, would crawl around in the vile, icy slush. The sad bit is, I won't change anything!

I smiled and as I did in most times when I stuff my face, I thought of my favorite onscreen glutton — Mayor Shelbourne, Mayor of Swallow Falls from the movie, "Cloudy with a Chance of Meatballs I." In a scene, he finds Flint Lockwood and orders a special meal to be made by the Flint Lockwood Diatonic Super Mutating Dynamic Food Replicator (FLDSMDFR). He wanted a pizza stuffed inside a turkey, the whole thing deep-fried and dipped in chocolate.[36]

Now that is gluttony!

---

[36] *"Quotes." IMDb, IMDb.com, www.imdb.com/title/tt0844471/quotes.*

In the Praise of Eros

Seven men decide to talk about love after an evening of eating and drinking. That is the theme of Plato's Symposium,[37] a really amazing philosophical work on the topic of love. The work, dating back to 385-370 BC, is thought to be purely fictional, but the characters are not.

There is Phaedrus, an Athenian aristocrat and follower of Socrates; Agathon, a tragic poet and host of the banquet; Pausanias, Agathon's lover, also thought to be a lawyer; Eryximachus, a physician; Aristophanes, a successful comic playwright; and Socrates, the great philosopher and Plato's teacher.

Alcibiades, a prominent Athenian statesman and general, came in totally drunk towards the end, had nothing to add to the discourse on love, but instead gave a rousing tribute to Socrates.

A symposium in old Athens was an elaborate affair that excluded the wives and was usually held at a private home. The men would first dine and then retire to a part of the home with couches where they would drink, sing, make toasts to each other, be entertained by dancers, have a civil discussion, or make speeches about a philosophical topic. Even though wives were not present, there were escorts available for the discerning gentleman, of course.[38]

---

[37] *The Internet Classics Archive | Symposium by Plato, classics.mit.edu/Plato/symposium.html.*
[38] *Simpson, David. Plato's Symposium, condor.depaul.edu/dsimpson/tlove/symposium.html.*

In Plato's Symposium, the men agreed to stay sober. They even sent the entertainers away and picking up on a suggestion by Phaedrus, each man agreed to make a speech to honor Eros, the God of Love.

Phaedrus got to start, and he said love is the oldest of all the Gods and that it ennobles both the lover and beloved. He went on to say love induces bravery and sacrifice — like on the battlefield.

"Not birth, nor wealth, nor honors, nor aught else shall so inspire a man as Love."

Then it was Pausanias' turn. He drew a distinction between profane and sacred or noble love. He likened profane love to relationships driven by the search for only sexual gratification. To him, a sacred or noble lover was after a long-term relationship. Such relationships bred the qualities Phaedrus had mentioned earlier in both lovers.

"There is more than one love. Vulgar love is worthless, inconsistent and fleeting; but the love of the virtuous character abides throughout life."

Eryximachus, the physician, thought love governs everything in the universe — plants and animals, the human and the divine, medicine, music, astronomy, and good health.

"...a good practitioner knows how to treat the body and how to transform its desires."
The comic poet Aristophanes spoke after Eryximachus. He

narrated an interesting myth that has become the basis of androgyny. He claimed we were once all twice the people we are now, so we had four legs and arms and two heads. However, due to our threat to the Gods, Zeus cut us in half. Ever since, we have wandered the Earth looking for our other half to rejoin with it and become whole.

"Love is simply the name for the desire and pursuit of the whole."

Agathon was next. He posited that love is young, sensitive, dainty, wise, and tiptoes among blooming flowers. Thus, love shuns old age and seeks only beauty. He further stated love then imparts justice, moderation, courage, and wisdom.

Socrates, however, pointed out to Agathon that he had objectified love. His contention was Agathon made it seem love was only beautiful and good. Socrates thought love was neither beautiful or good. He explained how he had come to this conclusion by telling them of a story told him by a woman called Diotima.

She thought love was a not a God but a spirit that mediated between the Gods and man — neither beautiful nor ugly, neither wise nor ignorant. She thought true love was a desire for the good and beautiful. She listed the path to this ultimate step.

We are first aroused by beauty to desire someone we do not have. Yet, all beautiful bodies share something in common. When we realize that, we move beyond the physical. Now we desire more than just the physical. We see the beauty of the soul more than that of the body and we yearn to reproduce to immortalize this love and beauty, either physically or spiritually. Then, we start seeing beauty in wisdom and knowledge. Finally, at the very top, we understand the very form of absolute and divine beauty — The Form of the Beautiful: "an everlasting loveliness which neither comes nor goes, which neither flowers nor fades."

Diotima thus claimed true love transcends the physical and is platonic. The aim of love then is "the perpetual possession of what is good."[39]

A woman who was not even present schooled a bunch of men who are trying to figure out what love is. Go figure!

It is true that the Symposium is a work of fiction and yet, it was an event that was plausible in those times. Those men lived in times when such discourse was respected. Fast forward to today. Can anyone imagine seven men of any ethnicity meeting over food and drinks and talking about love with such class and insight?

First, hip-hop would be playing in the background, its lyrics dripping with misogyny. The conversation would be littered with the "B" and "H" words. There would be ample descriptions of how to hit "it." There would be whoops of laughter as the men regale each other with

[39] "Symposium (Plato)." Wikipedia, Wikimedia Foundation, 10 Feb. 2018, en.wikipedia.org/wiki/Symposium_(Plato).

stories of "B's" and "H's" they have hit — real or imagined. Any one of those men who dares to get all sensitive would be called the "P" word and be told to go find his "D" and "B."

Any wonder we have boys growing into men who think women are objects to be grabbed, groped, poked, molested, and assaulted?

Sure, the message of the Symposium is a bit more on the idealistic side. For most, love is that thing that burns between lovers and leads to great, mind-blowing sex. Yet if one looks close enough, everyday life has smatterings of this "Form of the Beautiful."

Look the miracle of birth and the love a mother feels for her child, the bravery that drives a soldier to sacrifice his life to save his fellow men, the love that drives living organ donors to donate organs to others, so they can also live healthy lives, the selflessness of that woman who toils in a refugee camp, the doctor who plunges into that war zone to care for children....

In all these actions, we see a yearning to perpetually possess what is good.

So, somehow, Diotima was right.

Now imagine we lived in a society where all men and women yearned to attain the highest level of love. We may never reach it, but in the process, we may move beyond a raw yearning for the physical that breeds pokers, gropers, molesters, and assaulters.

Those Renaissance Men

"A man can do all things if he but wills them." — Leon Battista Alberti

Once upon a time, they were called the Renaissance Men. Now, we call them polymaths. Those absolutely brilliant men and woman whose interests and expertise go from the visual arts into mathematics and music and even into engineering and inventions.

Perhaps the world saw the greatest collection of these men during the 3rd European Renaissance that started in Florence, Italy in the 14th century.

Besides the Black Death, another factor that played a big role in the birth this important cultural movement was the philosophy of Renaissance Humanism. Championed by men like Petrarch and Boccaccio, this philosophy found its origin in the classical work of ancient Greece that saw "man being a measure of all things" and the Roman concept of "Humanitas."[40]

The concept of "Humanitas" is best seen in the work of Cicero. He thought a man should be educated in the humanities — grammar, rhetoric, poetry, history, and moral philosophy — to make him a good man, orator, and public servant.

---

[40]Grudin, Robert. *"Humanism." Encyclopædia Britannica, Encyclopædia Britannica, Inc., 22 Nov. 2017, www.britannica.com/topic/humanism#ref127870.*

The humanists of the era saw mankind as being limitless in their capacity to improve and also as capable of all things. Therefore, they encouraged an education that covered as many fields as possible and encouraged wide learning.

It is no wonder the era bred men like Leon Alberti (an architect, painter, classicist, poet, scientist, mathematician, and skilled horseman) or Leonardo da Vinci, whose interests in invention, painting, sculpting, architecture, science, music, mathematics, engineering, literature, anatomy, geology, astronomy, botany, and cartography led him to do some amazing yet sadly unpublished work in all these fields. Of course, there was Michelangelo, a painter, sculptor, architect, and poet and Filippo Brunelleschi, an architect, engineer, and sculptor.

There have not been very many female polymaths. One of them from the 18th century was Maria Gaetana Agnesi. She was a university professor, a great linguist, a geometer, a theologian, a logician, an algebraist, a mathematician, and a philosopher.

Since then we have seen such well-rounded geniuses in every generation — men who excel not only in the humanities, but also show a knack for the sciences, are musically inclined, and even are great sportsmen.

Some modern Renaissance men are Bill Gates, Story Musgrave (a physician and an astronaut), Brian May (an English astrophysicist, record producer, guitarist, songwriter, and musician), and Viggo Mortensen (an actor, a poet, a musician, a photographer, and a painter).

The fact that these types of men and women are capable of so much just gives credence to the humanist view that "a man can do all things if he wills them."
Could it be the habit of dabbling in both the humanities and sciences leads to special individuals, or only special individuals can dabble in both?

I go with the former.

I believe the human being is capable of a lot, and most people do not tap into all their abilities.

Furthermore, I think the habit of tapping into these two disparate fields creates a special kind of human being. If one adds sports, the ante is totally upped.

While the sciences spawn fields like computer science, robotics, genetics, engineering, and astronomy, the humanities encompass things like poetry, painting, sculpture, prose, philosophy, history, music, and performing arts such as dancing.

The sciences make our lives better, but the humanities make us better people.

A car simplifies your life, helping you get from Point A to Point B faster, but a symphony by Mozart takes you to a beautiful place where the aesthetic of life is contemplated.

Moreover, the sciences may give us the doctors, engineers,

and inventors, but the humanities often breed the leaders and thinkers who move public opinion and policy. A bad leader can negate the work of the world's best scientists in a heartbeat. A hospital with the best doctors is nothing without a good CEO or even paradigm.

Thus, these Renaissance men not only knew how to make things that made our lives better, but they also knew how to make themselves and others better. That is special right there.

In a world where STEM (science, technology, engineering, math) seems like the place to be in the coming years, let's not forget the lesson the Renaissance men teach us. If we want a well-rounded society, we need some "Humanitas" too.

Like Cicero wrote in his Pro Archia Poeta:[41]

Haec studia adolescentiam alunt, senectutem oblectant, secundas res ornant, adversis perfugium ac solacium praebent, delectant domi, non impediunt foris, pernoctant nobiscum, peregrinantur, rusticantur.

(These studies sustain youth and entertain old age, they enhance prosperity, and offer a refuge and solace in adversity; they delight us when we are at home without hindering us in the wider world, and are with us at night, when we travel, and when we visit the countryside).

---

[41]*Marcus Tullius Cicero: The Speech for Aulus Licinius Archias, the Poet, www.forumromanum.org/ literature/ cicero/ arche.html.*

The Coming of the Light

There are no records of either his birth year or day. The Bible makes no mention of that. Historians think he was born between 2 BC and 7 BC. His birthday is not December 25 either. That date was picked by the first Christian Emperor of the Roman Empire, Flavius Valerius Aurelius Constantinus, aka Constantine the Great.[42][43]

Constantine may have converted to Christianity after a vision he had of the cross in 312 and subsequently released the Edict of Milan with Lucinius on June 5, 313. This proclamation granted for the first time toleration of the Christian faith and restored property that had been confiscated from Christians during the Great Persecution (303-311) ordered by the Emperor Diocletian.

In making December 25 the official birthday of Jesus, Constantine sought to blend Christian and pagan traditions. Back then, there were two rather important pagan festivals that were celebrated in December by the Romans to commemorate the winter solstice and the Gods.

The first, Saturnalia, started on December 17 and lasted seven days. This festival honored Saturn, the Roman God of Agriculture.

---

[42] *Sol Invictus and Christmas, penelope.uchicago.edu/~grout/encyclopaedia_roma na/calendar/invictus.html.*
[43] *Holloway, April. "Why Is Christmas Celebrated December 25th?" Ancient Origins. Ancient Origins, n.d. Web.*

The second, which started on December 25 and ended on January 1, commemorated the birth of Mithras, the Persian God of Light. This celebration was known as the Festival of Natalis Solis Invicti (Birth of the Unconquerable Sun).

Interestingly, the Scandinavians also celebrated the Yule festival from December 21 until January 1.

Constantine merged many of the traditions from these festivals with the Nativity story in the Bible — and Christmas was born.

Thus, the first recorded instance of Christmas being celebrated on December 25 is from the year AD 336. In 350, Pope Julius I declared that the birthday of Jesus was December 25.

Moreover, if one reads the biblical stories surrounding the birth of Jesus, there are clues that point to a birth in either the spring or fall. For one, the shepherds were out with their sheep. That would be highly unlikely in the cold of winter. Since it occurred around a Jewish holiday when Jews traveled back home in their numbers, that made a census by the Romans possible. Thus, historians think it was either around Passover (March or April) or Sukkot (Festival of the Tabernacles) that happened around September or October. It might explain why there was no room in the inn for Joseph and the pregnant Mary.

Another argument for the fall months is made by the British theologian Ian Paul, who starts his calculation from (Luke 1:26-27):

"In the sixth month of Elizabeth's pregnancy, God sent the angel Gabriel to Nazareth, a town in Galilee, to a virgin pledged to be married to a man named Joseph, a descendant of David. The virgin's name was Mary."

Whatever the case may be, this festival of Christmas (Christ's Mass) is now such an international phenomenon that is not always associated with Jesus Christ, that even non-Christians celebrate it.[44] It has become a time when friends and family meet to celebrate the good in their lives. A time when we seek to bring joy into the lives of other with gifts and our company.

To a larger degree, it has also become a commercial holiday during which the retail industry seeks to generate as much revenue as possible through a campaign of guilting us all into spending excessively on gifts for loved ones.

The genesis of the holiday and what it has become is enough to make any skeptic feel jaded and disillusioned about Christmas. However, I think there is reason to be hopeful. To do that, let's look at the festivals that Christmas supplanted back then in Europe. These were festivals that celebrated the winter solstice — a day when the darkness of winter ended, and the days got longer. They were festivals that celebrated rebirth and a new beginning. They

---

[44] *"How December 25 Became Christmas." Biblical Archaeology Society, 8 Dec. 2017, www.biblicalarchaeology.org/daily/biblical-topics/new-testament/how-december-25-became-christmas/.*

were celebrations driven by hope — hope for the warmth of the coming spring and the life it brought.

Around this same time, if one wandered south towards sub-Saharan Africa, one would experience the dry season and Harmattan. A time when the dry winds of the desert blew over the lands and most vegetation had died from the arid conditions. The Tamashek tribe in Mali would meet in those months to celebrate the year and look forward to the new one.

Is this the spirit of renewal Constantine sought to tap into when he declared December 25 the birthday of Jesus? Did he seek to remind all believers of the Christian faith to consider renewing their faith and strengthening their hope? Maybe those Saturnalia and Natalis Solis Invicti celebrations were rather raucous and had more to do with excesses than with deep reflection. Yet, the basis of that jubilation was darkness was ending and light was on the way.

So, no matter how skeptical you may be this time of the year, no matter how deep your doubts are about the whole Nativity story, you cannot deny this can be a time when we all look forward to the light that is imminent. A light that can warm our lives. For those in drier and warmer climates, it may be a time to look forward to the rain that brings life.

It is a time of hope for the better. A period when we show our joy and gratitude for being alive and having friends and family to share food and drinks with.

However, even as we celebrate the season, let's remember those whose lives are filled with pain, despair, and dread. Those for whom a winter solstice never comes. Those for whom the message of renewal is but a sad mirage. Like the raucous celebrants of the Saturnalis, let's carry our joy into their lives.

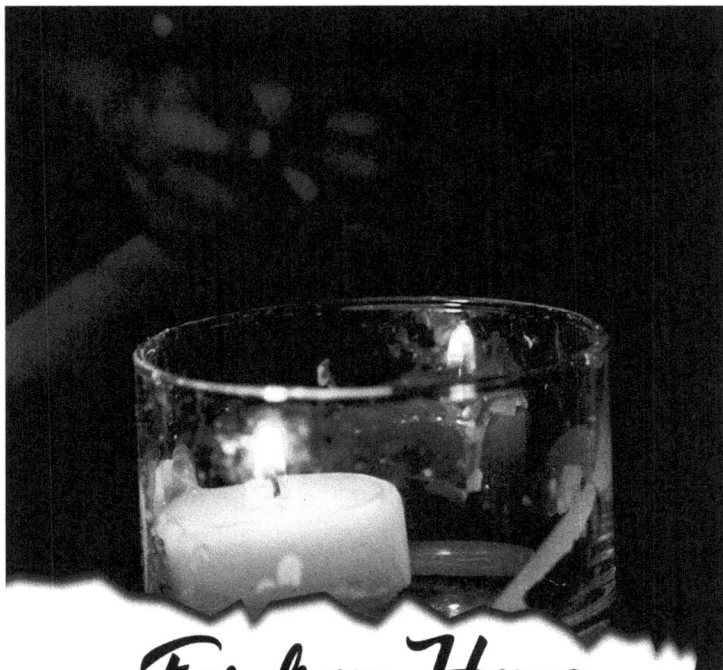

Far from Home

"A big part of the anti-immigration narrative is the perception that the majority of immigrants are poor, uneducated, and unskilled."
— *Fabrizio Moreira*

To Jazz

Jazz!
Smoke-filled rooms
Ripple with chords and beats
And long-drawn-out notes
Filled with bluesy tales of pain
That harken to days of sorrow
Far away from home
On ships
And cotton fields.

Jazz!
A confluence of the Afro
The Latin and the Classical
Brewed in sultry Orleans
With a touch of gumbo!
From the cradle of the blues
Crept Ragtime swinging,
Into bepopy, dixie Big Bands.
The Improvisation of the Cool!

Jazz!
Give me some Satchmo
Buzzing on his trumpet.
Can I have my Lady Day?
Strange fruits, anyone?
Hey! Duke is kinda Dizzy
Cos' Coltrane blows at Miles' place.
Ella baby! Nina dear!
Charlie, Monk, where art thou?

Jazz!
Smooth!
Cool!
Free!
Daring!
The sum of the parts
The result of the mix
What can be
If we let it flow!

My Sentiments Prior to Naturalization

March 12, 2010

In about a week, I will be sworn in as a U.S. citizen in the courthouse in downtown Lexington. This is the culmination of a 13-year-long journey.

I should be excited, because after all I get to be a citizen of a great nation with endless opportunities. Like an orphan, I should be happy I have wealthy parents who are going to adopt me.

Unlike the orphan though, I have been able to observe my prospective parents for many years and what I see troubles me.

It's not the economy; it's not even terrorism, race relations, or gender politics. It is the unwillingness of those in power to understand each other and try to see things the other person's way. There is almost a total aversion to finding the middle ground.

The political landscape is as contentious as it's ever been. Liberals can't stand conservatives. Republicans are at the throat of Democrats. Either you are with us or against us. Whatever the other person believes in is bad for the country. And on and on it goes.

The political process in this country has been turned into a zero-sum game. At one point or the other, the country is swung to extremes – right or left.

Like a couple on the verge of divorce, the other cannot do anything right.

I am reminded of an old movie from 1989 titled "War of the Roses" starring Michael Douglas and Kathleen Turner. In what was akin to a divorce death match, we watched the tragedy of two people in a marriage gone sour (Oliver and Barbara Rose) who refused to find a middle ground.[45]

Now, I look at the U.S. and can't help but think, "Oh God, I am being adopted by the Roses!"

Whatever happened to finding a compromise? Respecting the other point of view? Working together for the good of the country? Sometimes neither the conservative nor the liberal view is right. Sometimes, it's just common sense! However, because the political process is seen as a zero-sum game, party affiliations, ambition, power lust, and ideology are increasingly trumping common sense!

The malignancy is spreading to the news media, radio talk show hosts, and even the average American. For the last few months, I have been asking friends and co-workers which party I should vote for after my naturalization. If you ask a Democrat and a Republican this question simultaneously, stand back and watch them transform into Gladiators!

---

[45] *"The War of the Roses (1989)." IMDb, IMDb.com, www.imdb.com/title/tt0098621/.*

The sad part is, I have grown to love my adoptive parents-to-be. In the time I've known them, they have given me a lot of opportunities to make a lot of my life. I would love to give back to them, but I wonder if there will be any recipients.

In most biological systems, the normal is in the middle and the control mechanisms (under healthy conditions) always force the system back to the middle. Disease results when the system escapes the control mechanism and swings to one extreme or the other.[46]

Maybe we need to learn from nature. Maybe what is needed is a third middle-of-the-road party that can keep things in focus by forcing the Republicans and the Democrats to the middle. Maybe Congress shouldn't vote on major issues, but the people vote in referenda. Maybe Senators shouldn't stay in Washington so long. Whatever the case, I pray reason wins at the end of the day.

Come Friday, I'll don my suit and tie and drive to the courthouse to get sworn in. I just hope I don't get home to find my adoptive parents swinging from the chandelier!

---

[46] Vaidhyanathan, Vishnampet S. *Regulation and Control Mechanisms in Biological Systems. PTR Prentice Hall, 1993.*

The Angry Men

Once upon a time, the Earth was flat. People stayed where they were, afraid to go too far least they fall over the edge into an abyss.

Then science and technology changed all that. People realized that the Earth was round and dared to believe they could get to other side, one way or the other. A wave of exploration and globalization was ushered in. New lands and markets were found. That brought with it wealth for some, but pain and suffering for many. It ushered in a wave of terrorism.

Yes, terrorism!

Whole races were decimated and destroyed, people traded like cattle across seas. Curiously, all that pain and suffering was somehow justified by the religious beliefs of those days.

With time, the conquering race settled back to enjoy its spoils, content to leave the decimation it had wrought behind. After all, those other people were on the opposite side of the world — far, far away.

Then an interesting thing happened. Technology struck again and ushered in another wave of globalization. This time, it virtually flattened the earth and created a global village. Even as goods and services streamed one way, the forgotten people on the other side started streaming the other way. For some weird reason, terrorism always seems to follow globalization and this time around, it is no different. And it is again finding justification in religion.

Now there are angry men overall, standing up to defend what they have, who they are, and their ways of life. I wonder if there were such angry men hundreds of years ago among the people who were killed or traded. I guess their angry voices were drowned out by the din of gunfire and the screams of women and children.

This time though, at least for now, the din of gunfire and the screams of women and children are really far away, so the voices of the angry men are really loud and clear and can be heard all over the global village.

Hundreds of years ago, globalization changed the lives and cultures of many. Maybe the angry men are astute students of history, see this happening to their cultures, and are fighting to preserve what they have.

Who will prevail? The forces of technology and globalization or the angry men?

I wish I knew...I wish I knew...

What's in a Phrase

I moved from Philly to Atlanta in 1998 to start my residency. I immediately fell in love with the city — the vibe, the people, the culture, the weather.

What really struck me was how respectful Southerners are.

"Yes, sir" — "Yes, ma'am" — and "Yes, please" were commonplace.

One phrase I heard a lot was, "Bless your heart."

For a while, I couldn't make heads or tails of it.

One day at work, a nice, older Southern lady complimented me on how I spoke and asked me if I always understood the Georgia accent. I said I did, but I didn't understand a phrase. She asked me which one.

I replied, "Bless your heart."

With an impish smile on her face, she took my hand in hers and said, "You don't understand 'bless your heart?' Aww, bless your heart!"

In the meantime, the nurse I was with was bent over in laughter.

Over the years, I've come to understand the loaded phrase that is "Bless your heart."

It is one adept phrase, much like a Swiss Army knife!

Even Mark Twain uses it in his essay "Fenimore Cooper's Literary Offenses."

Possible Use Number One

Imagine a colleague telling you, "I was texting while driving and bumped a cop's car!"

Well, instead of saying, "You idiot!", you can be much more circumspect.

Look him dead in the eye and go, "Bless your heart!"

To add even more impact, make it, "Bless your little heart!"

Adding "little" takes it to another level.

Possible Use Number 2

Another colleague walks up and asks, "What is a selfie?"

Look at him and just go, "You don't know what a selfie is? Aww, bless your heart!"

Isn't that much better than asking him what rock he lives under?
This use also works well for those friends who take forever to get a joke.

Make sure to add "little" in this instance.

Possible Use Number 3

Yet a third colleague tells you he lost his dog over the weekend. This time, you want to show empathy.

"Bless your heart," you tell him.

Let it drool with sincerity.

I have learned a great deal in my years in the South, but nothing impresses me more than this phrase. I feel like understanding it means I have arrived, that I am finally part of this society.

So, if you think I am not because of who I am — well, bless your little heart!

The Last Great Meeting

As the man turned to leave, the little boy called out, "Dad, could you tell me the story of the great meeting again?"

The man stopped, turned around and smiled at the boy, who was by now sitting up in his bed.

"Didn't I just tell you the story last week?" the man asked his son.

"Yes, you did, but I want to hear it again. Please, Dad," the boy implored.

The man walked back to his son's bed and sat beside him. The boy rested his head on his dad, a broad smile on his face. His dad smiled down at him, cleared his throat, and started the narration:

"The old Great Priest called the meeting. It is said he was nudged to do so by one of the greatest chiefs and warriors in all the land — the One Who Blows the Big Horn.

The meeting was held in the great city in the Land-between-the-Great-Lakes. The city that is smiled on by the great Gods who live in the mountains that protect it.

They came from far and wide.

The great seafarers from the West, who traded with the men who drank tea slowly and with those who lived in the land with the huge wall.

They came — the great hunters from the North. The men who fought bears and buffalos.

The seafarers from the East came too. They who traded with the dark ones.

The Southerners were there too in their sunny bright colors and with wonderful music.

Even a few islanders who survived the devastation on the islands in the South Sea were there.

The great warriors of the Plains were there too. They rode in on their mighty horses.

The wise men from the Northeast came.

So, did the wonderful craftsmen from the Southwest.

It was a great meeting.

Not since the death of the last Great Priest of the Gods and Ancestors had there been such a meeting. It spoke to the importance of the occasion and the respect the old Great Priest commanded.

By sundown on the first day of the week, all were in town.

On the evening of the second day, the great assembly was held on the grounds of the Battle of the Spirits.

It was a great assembly indeed. The din that rose was heard

by the great spirits themselves.

The assembly was arranged in a semicircle around the tent of the old Great Priest. In the middle of the circle burnt a fire, its glow illuminating the intense faces of the men.

The old Great Priest rose up and rang a bell. A silence fell on the assembly. The old Great Priest started to speak.

'I thank you all for coming. I thank the Great Spirits for guiding your journeys here. We stay strong as a people if we show such unity. Now for the chant to the Spirits.'

The Great Priest picked up a bag, walked to the fire, and scooping a dark powder from the bag, sprinkled it into the fire. A plume of white smoke arose as he began the chant. The voices of the men rose in unison with him as they chanted.

After the chant, the One Who Blows the Big Horn got up. A hush fell on the assembly. The One Who Blows the Big Horn was one of the fiercest fighters and most courageous warriors his generation had seen. He was also a great hunter and had fashioned a horn from a great animal he fought and killed during a hunt in the North. It was said he killed the animal with his hands. He blew the horn during battles and on hunts. Hence his name.

He put his horn to his lips and blew a long, haunting note that sent chills down the spine of every man at the assembly that evening. There was a deep silence.
'My friends, I greet you!'

A response rose from the men, deep and guttural.

The One Who Blows the Big Horn continued, 'We meet here today as a people facing a grave danger. A grave danger indeed. Our land is in danger. Threatened by strangers. Strangers from over the sea. The strangers with the firestick.

Their numbers are ever increasing. They've been seen in the North, they are all over the East, and have caused devastation among our people on the islands in the South Sea.

They are taking our lands, killing our buffalo, and sleeping with our women!'

A gasp went up from the crowd.

'Open your eyes, my people,' he continued. 'Stop giving them our turkeys. Stop offering them food and help. Stop trading with them. They don't mean well. They have decimated the population of our brothers on the islands. They aim to do the same on the mainland. We have to stop them!

Let's burn their ships at the ports. Let's build tall fences along the borders so we can keep an eye on who enters our land. Let's hunt down those who are here already and remove them.
That is the only way we are going to ensure we keep our lands and we are not overrun by these firestick brandishing strangers!

Who is with me?' the One Who Blows the Big Horn bellowed.

A huge roar rose from the assembly. Most of the men stood up and started stomping on the earth with their spears. The din was thunderous. After a while, the One Who Blows the Big Horn put his horn to his lips and blew another long note. The stomping ceased, and the men sat down. He also sat down.

The old Great Priest walked up and rang his bell.

'Does anyone have anything to say to that?' he asked.

Almost everyone knew who was going to respond — He Who Treads Lightly. Another great warrior, but very wise and philosophical in his views. He was the water while the One Who Blows the Big Horn was the fire. While the former always preached caution, the latter always wanted action.

He didn't disappoint. He Who Treads Lightly stood up. He was tall and skinny. He had a goatee and a weathered, thoughtful face. When he walked, it was like his feet didn't touch the ground — hence his name.

He nodded to the Great Priest. He nodded to the One Who Blows the Big Horn.

'Our lands have always been very welcoming to strangers. For as long as we can remember, the great spirits have not turned anyone away from these lands. Why should we?

We travel to the land of the Dark Ones, to those who drink tea slowly, and to the land of the big wall. They have never asked us not to return, have they? Why should we do that to other strangers then? Is that in the spirit of friendship to do such a thing? I say, let's trade with the strangers with the firesticks. Let's welcome them. Let's teach them our ways so they know how to live with us. Maybe we can learn from them too. That is how a society grows.

Who stands with me?' he asked.

There was an even bigger roar from the assembly. Again, the men stood up and stomped the earth with their spears.

A haunting note from the horn of the One Who Blows the Big Horn brought an end to the stomping. The men sat down.

The One Who Blows the Big Horn spoke up, 'You speak of these other lands we travel to trade - the land of the Dark Ones, of those who drink tea slowly, and the land of the big wall. Do we go there to hunt their buffalo or to take their land and their women? No, we do not, and neither do they. That is why for as long as the spirits reign, we have traded with them and dealt peacefully with them. They always have meant well. The stranger with the firestick does not mean well. He does not come in peace. He comes to take and to kill. Beware my people, beware.'

The vote took place the next evening. The two antagonists sat side by side in front of the tent of the old Great Priest. The men filed by and depending on whose side you were on, you dropped an arrow in front of him. This went on for most of the evening.

At the end, it was clear who the winner was — the One Who Blows the Big Horn!"

"That is not true, Daddy!" the little boy piped up. "He did not win the vote! Do I have to remind you each time?"

"I know, son, but I wish he had," his dad said.

"I know, Dad. Like you always say, 'Our history would be so different today,'" the boy said.

"Yes, son, yes," the dad replied mournfully.

"Anyway, it's late. Get some sleep. Good night again and see you tomorrow," the dad said and kissed the boy on the cheek.

"Good night, Daddy. Don't be sad! Like Grandpa always said, 'the Spirits know best,'" the boy said wisely.

"I don't know, son; sometimes I don't know," the dad mused.

He turned the light off in his son's room and walked out. He went down the stairs and at the bottom, made a right turn into his study.

In the corner to the right stood a pedestal. On the pedestal was a glass case. In the case was an old horn. The man opened the glass case and touched the horn. He stood there with his hand on the horn and his eyes closed. He could swear in the distance, he heard a long haunting note.

What Do You Have to Offer?

It was around 1996 and the specter of the Clinton Health Plan was scaring U.S. doctors and medical students alike. A lot of programs in specialties like anesthesiology and internal medicine couldn't find residents to fill the needed slots. So, several top U.S. programs got together and headed to Europe to find young doctors.

I had finished medical school in Germany two years earlier and couldn't find a job after my internship. No one wanted to hire an African! Returning to Ghana was not yet an option, as I wanted to finish residency.

One winter night, as I left the genetics lab where I was working on a project, I saw a flyer. It offered the chance to doctors to go work in the U.S. if one had passed the USMLEs. There was a meeting scheduled for the next evening in an auditorium in the building where the lab was. I made it to the meeting. I met the head of the agency who was organizing the search by the top U.S. programs for residents in Europe. I registered for the interview.

Sometime in the summer of 1996, I headed to Munich for the interview. It was an overnight trip from Berlin. I changed into my only suit in a restroom stall at the train station when I got to Munich. I headed to the venue.

I entered a large hall with lots of people. Each program had its table. I registered again, got my name badge, and headed to the first table.

For the last two years, I had traveled all over Germany begging and groveling for a job. Somehow, my transcript from medical school was just not enough. Somehow, what I had to offer was not good enough.

I stood there at the first table, hopeless and expecting disappointment. The words I heard changed everything.

"Dr. Ghansah, what do you have to offer our program? Sell yourself!" the gentleman behind the table said.

I was dumbstruck!

Me? What did I have to offer? Me? A poor African doctor no one wanted, but who had a thousand dreams? I was dumbstruck!

"Dr. Ghansah, we are waiting!"

Right then, I knew the U.S. was different. Right there, I got hopeful.

I've been thinking of this a lot lately as I listen to two very distinct depictions of this country. One is dark and cynical. The other is bright and hopeful.

This country is different. The U.S. hasn't always done right by all, but man, is this an amazing experiment!

It is a given that there are many for whom life is a daily struggle. It is a given that there are many who are shut out from reaping the opportunities this country has to offer.

It cannot be denied that racial bias is still an impediment to some.

Despite all that, I'll go with the vision of hope. No other country offers it in spades like the U.S. does. I'll go with hope, because cynicism and darkness never helped anyone.

As an immigrant, I am always grateful for what this country has given me, and I can say that about all the immigrants I know. Like me, they all heard that question:

"What do you have to offer?"

That day in Munich, my answer was, "Hard work."

That is the answer of all immigrants — hard work. You see, when you offer hope and opportunity, you get a lot back. Hard work, perseverance, creativity, new businesses, entrepreneurs, artists, and on and on.

Maybe Americans born and bred here in the U.S. do not see what I see. Maybe they expect more. Maybe their standards are higher. That is fine. However, if you would indulge me, I would like to ask a few questions:

What does cynicism and darkness get you?

What do they have to offer?

Brünnhilde hasn't sang yet

The last part of Richard Wagner's Opera "Der Ring des Nibelungen" (Ring of the Nibelung) is titled "Götterdämmerung" (Twilight of the Gods). In it, the Valkyrie, Brünnhilde, a rather voluptuous lady, sings her aria to end the opera, even as she rides into flames.[48]

Hence the saying, "It ain't over 'til the fat lady sings."[48]

The German word "Götterdämmerung" is a translation of "Ragnarök" (Old Norse), which in Scandinavian mythology refers to the destruction of the Gods in a battle with evil, resulting in apocalypse![49]

For any Falcons fan, it feels like "Apocalypse Now!"

Let's rewind to February 8, 2008. Super Bowl XLII. The undefeated New England Patriots were playing the 12-point underdog New York Giants. It was the 4th quarter, and the Patriots were up by 4 with 75 seconds to go. The Giants had the ball on their 40-yard line for a third-and-five. Eli Manning, the Giants quarterback, avoided a sack and floated the ball to Tyree — who made

[47]Schwarm, Betsy. "Der Ring Des Nibelungen." Encyclopædia Britannica, Encyclopædia Britannica, Inc., 4 Apr. 2016, www.britannica.com/topic/Der-Ring-des-Nibelungen.
[48]Martin, Gary. "'It Ain't over till the Fat Lady Sings' — the Meaning and Origin of This Phrase." Phrasefinder, www.phrases.org.uk/meanings/it-aint-ove r-until-the-fat-lady-sings.html.
[49]"Götterdämmerung." Wikipedia, Wikimedia Foundation, 25 Feb. 2018, en.wikipedia.org/wiki/G%C3%B6tterd%C3%A4mmerung.

an improbable catch against his helmet for the first down. The Giants went on to win. It was an improbable upset!

Just before the ball was snapped by the Giants on the third-and-five, the Patriots players (who already thought they had the game won) were talking smack to the Giants players on the field. They were so sure of their win, they even invited the Giants to their after-game party! They had forgotten one important lesson in sports:

It ain't over 'til the fat lady sings!

The Falcons were up 21-3 at the half. Somehow, they relaxed. They lost their fire. Sure, the Patriots played better in the second half, but did the Falcons have to play worse? Did they forget the cardinal law in sports? Did they forget, "It ain't over 'til the fat lady sings?"

That is a lesson Tom Brady hardly ever forgets. Sure, his team forgot that in 2008, but in his 16- year career with the Patriots, this has not happened often. It is an unfortunate human tendency to get complacent and let one's guard down when victory is nigh. Brady has this uncanny ability to recognize this weakness in his opponents and exploit it quite well. He did tonight and has done it all through his career.

Also, he was picked in the 6th round in the 2000 draft. He has the mentality of an underdog. Underdogs pick their chances and never, ever give up, because they know it's never over 'til the fat lady sings.

Events this past year or so seem to drum this lesson home — Cleveland pulling the upset over Golden State, Brexit, the Cubs win, Trump, and now this. In my home country Ghana, 72-year-old Nana Akufo-Addo's landslide win in this past December elections fits in this category too.

For the winners as well as the losers, the lesson is clear:

It ain't over 'til the fat lady sings!

However, it is like all of humanity is being taught this one important lesson — DO NOT GIVE UP! Do not give up on peace, love, and empathy. Do not give up on this Earth, on one another, on making things better for all. Do not give up on fighting bigotry, racism, poverty, disease, inequality, and homelessness. It is like humanity is being told to fight and keep fighting, even if things look so dark and bleak.

Then, the fat lady hasn't sung yet. As long as that hasn't happened, humanity has one more play to win it all.

DO NOT GIVE UP!

As we walked....

He took me to the town square. It was early, so the square was empty. We sat on a bench perched on the side of a knoll that overlooked the square. It wasn't long before two men walked into the square. They both wore brightly colored clothing. Simultaneously, they both started taking to each other. As I watched, I made an observation — they were both talking, but neither was listening to the other. I turned towards him, hoping for an explanation, but he seemed lost in his thoughts — so I stayed silent.

Gradually, more men in brightly colored clothing streamed into the square. Like the first two men, they also started talking. Each man seemed to direct his speech to all, but no one seemed to listen to another. By now, the voices had reached a din and I could make words out. Surprisingly, all I heard were words like "black," "white," "red," "brown," and "yellow." All I heard were descriptions of color!

I strained to listen more closely — and over and over, all I heard were the names of colors.

Baffled, I turned to him again. His eyes were on me with a wistful smile on his face.

Before I could utter a word, he said, "All they do is speak. No one listens to the other, so all they see is each other's color."

I Told You So

When the first president, George Washington, was sworn in as president in April of 1789, no political parties existed.

About three years later, bankers and businessmen in the North, supportive of the policies of the then Secretary of the Treasury, Alexander Hamilton, started the Federalist Party. The Federalists believed in a sound fiscal policy and nationalism, and really reflected the interests of the commercial North.[50]

In 1793, Thomas Jefferson, then Secretary of State, formed the Democratic-Republican Party. Jefferson was against the centralizing policies of the Federalists. He wanted "state's rights" for the agrarian South.[51]

Even though Washington didn't belong to either party, he tended to be sympathetic to the Federalist positions.

Over time, a deep animosity developed between the two parties based on ideology. This animosity really reared its head during the French Revolution (1789-1799) and in Washington's second term.

The French Revolution ultimately led to a war between

---

[50]History.com Staff. "Federalist Party." History.com. A&E Television Networks, 2009. Web. 10 Feb. 2018.
[51]"Democratic-Republican Party." Wikipedia. Wikimedia Foundation, 09 Feb. 2018. Web. 10 Feb. 2018.

France and Great Britain. Hamilton wanted the U.S. to support the Great Britain, while Jefferson supported the French revolutionaries. Washington stayed out of the fray, keeping the U.S. neutral. However, when Britain captured U.S. ships trading with France, Washington was forced to negotiate with Britain. This galled the Democratic-Republicans.

The rancor that ensued forever tainted the view Washington had about political parties. Even though he was asked to lead the nation for a third term, he refused. He wanted to escape the hate in the capital to the solace of his farm in Virginia.

In early 1796, with the help of Hamilton, Washington started working on his Farewell Address. It was published in The Daily American Advertiser, a Philadelphia newspaper, in September 1796.

In it, he advised American citizens to view themselves as a cohesive unit and avoid political parties. He also issued a special warning to be wary of attachments and entanglements with other nations.

These words from the address are quite poignant even today, even prophetic:[52]
"They (political parties) serve to organize faction, to give it an artificial and extraordinary force; to put, in the place of

---

[52] *Avalon Project — Washington's Farewell Address 1796.* N.p., n.d. Web. 10 Feb. 2018.

the delegated will of the nation the will of a party, often a small but artful and enterprising minority of the community; and, according to the alternate triumphs of different parties, to make the public administration the mirror of the ill-concerted and incongruous projects of faction, rather than the organ of consistent and wholesome plans digested by common counsels and modified by mutual interests.

However, combinations or associations of the above description may now and then answer popular ends, they are likely, in the course of time and things, to become potent engines, by which cunning, ambitious, and unprincipled men will be enabled to subvert the power of the people and to usurp for themselves the reins of government, destroying afterwards the very engines which have lifted them to unjust dominion."

I wonder what the first President would say if he visited 2018 America. He would probably utter the same words the Lord Mancroft uttered in the British House of Lords in 1953. The words he termed ".... those happiest words in the English language, 'I told you so.'"[53]

---

[53]*Quote Investigator. N.p., n.d. Web. 10 Feb. 2018*

His Greatest Quality

Abraham Lincoln would have been 208 years old today. The 16th president is seen by many as probably one of this nation's greatest presidents. What made him remarkable was his empathy. In a lot of accounts about him, it seems to be the running theme.[54]

In a piece for Time magazine, the historian and biographer Doris Kearns Goodwin wrote:

"Perhaps the most important of his emotional abilities was empathy — the gift of putting himself in the place of others, to experience what they were feeling, to understand their motives and desires."[55]

In 1916, Lord Charnwood, a British aristocrat and Lincoln admirer, published a bio of the great leader. Among other things, he wrote this about Lincoln:

"For perhaps not many conquerors, and certainly few successful statesmen, have escaped the tendency of power to harden or at least to narrow their human sympathies; but in this man a natural wealth of tender compassion became richer and more tender while in the stress of deadly conflict he developed an astounding strength."[56]

---

[54]Goodwin, Doris Kearns. *Team of Rivals: The Political Genius of Abraham Lincoln*. New York: Simon & Schuster Paperbacks, 2006. Print.
[55]Goodwin, Doris Kearns. "The Master of the Game." *Time*, Time Inc., 5 July 2005, content.time.com/time/magazine/article/0,9171,1077300,00.html.
[56]Charnwood, Godfrey Rathbone Benson Baron. *Abraham Lincoln*. Charnwood. Grijalbo, 1970.

In his day, Lincoln recognized the evils of slavery, yet sought to understand the position of the slaveholders. He mourned the loss of his soldiers and gave speeches that comforted a nation at war.

His empathy is often attributed to his bouts of depression and the losses he suffered — the loss of his mum when he was nine, the loss of his first sweetheart, the 22-year-old Ann Rutledge when he was 24, and the loss of his 11-year-old son Willie when he was 53.

As a young man in Illinois, he often had to write letters for people in the community who couldn't write. Hearing the stories of these people may also have helped him developed the ability to walk in others' shoes.

Nowhere is this empathy more demonstrated than the letter he wrote to the daughter of his friend, William McCullough, who was killed during a night charge near Coffeeville, Mississippi during the Civil War.

Below is the letter he wrote to the then-22-year-old Fanny McCullough who was near a nervous breakdown after hearing of her father's death. Remember Lincoln had lost his own son 10 months earlier:[57]

---

[57] *Abraham Lincoln's Letter to Fanny McCullough, www.abrahamlincolnonline. org/ lincoln/ speeches/ mccull.htm.*

Executive Mansion,
Washington, December 23, 1862.

Dear Fanny,

It is with deep grief that I learn of the death of your kind and brave Father; and, especially, that it is affecting your young heart beyond what is common in such cases. In this sad world of ours, sorrow comes to all; and, to the young, it comes with bitterest agony, because it takes them unawares. The older have learned to ever expect it. I am anxious to afford some alleviation of your present distress. Perfect relief is not possible, except with time. You cannot now realize that you will ever feel better. Is not this so? And yet it is a mistake. You are sure to be happy again. To know this, which is certainly true, will make you some less miserable now. I have had experience enough to know what I say; and you need only to believe it, to feel better at once. The memory of your dear Father, instead of an agony, will yet be a sad sweet feeling in your heart, of a purer and holier sort than you have known before.

Please present my kind regards to your afflicted mother.

Your sincere friend
A. Lincoln

Fanny found inspiration in that letter and went on with her life. She fell in love with a soldier who unfortunately died in action too. She held up though and finally married, dying at the age of 80.

That letter from Lincoln was found among her possessions.

On this day like every other day, I pray this country would be touched by the Spirit of Empathy that possessed our 16th President and made him such a tower of humanity.

Water, water everywhere

August 3, 2017

Suffering and misfortune are as much a part of life as the air we breathe. The late Chinua Achebe, the great Nigerian writer, captured this fact superbly in a quote from his book Arrow of God.[58]

"When suffering knocks at your door and you say there is no seat for him, he tells you not to worry because he has brought his own stool."

In this quote, part of a speech by the character Moses to the elders of the town of Umuaro, he compared the folly of not accepting the fact the white man in the then-colonized Nigeria had all the power to not accepting the inevitability of suffering in life.

Just like the European showed up on the African shore with his own stool and took over, regardless of the fact the latter did not invite the former, so does misfortune sometimes intrude into our lives without an invitation and takes over.

I look at the misery imposed on the people in Houston and other parts of southern Texas, Sierra Leone, and Mumbai, and cannot help but think of how suffering

[58]Achebe, Chinua. Arrow of God. Penguin, 2016.
[59]Vidal, John. "As Flood Waters Rise, Is Urban Sprawl as Much to Blame as Climate Change?" The Observer, Guardian News and Media, 2 Sept. 2017, www.theguardian.com/world/2017/sep/02/flood-waters-rising-urban-development -climate-change.

walks around with its own stool.[59]
So, if we humans hate to suffer, why do we do things or make decisions that invite misfortune into our lives?

I've always wondered about this and somehow, the miserable images on TV in the last few days have amplified this deliberation.

All that musing brought to mind a verse from a poem by Samuel Taylor Coleridge, "The Rime of the Ancient Mariner."[60]

The story of the mariner in the poem contrasts greatly with the story of the people in Houston — he brought his suffering upon himself; the people of Houston did not. However, in both instances, water played a great role in the nightmare that ensued — a fact that is rather metaphorical, and we'll explore a bit more later.

A brief synopsis of the poem — a mariner, his crew, and their ship are headed on a voyage. A storm drives them towards the Antarctic. Lost, they get caught in ice. Suddenly, an albatross appears and with it a wind that leads them out of the icy debacle. All is well as they follow the albatross, but then the mariner shoots the bird with his crossbow and kills it.

Following that, it was as if the Gods and spirits had

---

[60]Coleridge, Samuel Taylor. "The Rime of the Ancient Mariner (Text of 1834) by Samuel Taylor Coleridge." Poetry Foundation, Poetry Foundation, www.poetry foundation.org/poems/43997/the-rime-of-the-ancient-mariner-text-of-1834.

conspired to punish them. The very wind that seemed to have led them out of the ice of the Antarctic led them into uncharted tropical waters. Lost, all of a sudden, the wind stopped. The ship just sat in these unknown waters, immobile. All his men blamed the mariner for their misfortune. It was in these dire circumstances that Coleridge wrote these lines:

Water, water, everywhere,
And all the boards did shrink;
Water, water, everywhere,
Nor any drop to drink.
Water, water everywhere indeed!

I'm sure the people of Houston look out and say that to themselves and wonder why such misfortune was visited upon them. Unlike the mariner in Coleridge's poem, they never shot an albatross!

Well, like Achebe wrote, suffering walks around with his own stool. He imposes himself even if you do not want him!

Going back to the poem, the mariner is forced by the death of his crew and him being alone with the corpses on that lonely immobile ship to learn to appreciate life and realize how senseless the killing of the albatross was. From the misery, he grew. He found the proverbial silver lining.

So, is that why suffering marches around with his stool? To force us to learn? Are those who make mistakes and dare misfortune the ones apt to learn faster? Is it most of us fail to grow, so suffering has to knock on that door and induce misery, so we can learn? Is suffering really the only way to sometimes learn the harsh lessons of life?

Is that why in both scenarios, water seems to be the common denominator?

You see, water is life — but in the case of Houston, Sierra Leone, and Mumbai, it has become the killer! How can life turn on itself? How can life connive with suffering? Could it be that life itself wants us to grow? That life itself thinks the only way for us to develop and be greater is through misfortune?

Water calls to mind the Christian custom of baptism, rebirth, renewal...

Water, water everywhere!

Maybe, when we open that door and suffering is out there, we should gladly invite him in. We should tell him, "As miserable as you look, I know there is a silver lining in you. I am going to find it, so set that stool in the corner and sit down."

In all this water and suffering, I hope Houston and the rest of Texas, Sierra Leone, and Mumbai find the silver lining.

Let's Jump Over Our Shadows

The Prophet Jeremiah in the Bible was one angry prophet, and he had every right to be. In his lifetime, he saw the Kingdom of Judea defeated and Jerusalem and Solomon's Temple destroyed by the Babylonians around 587 BC. For a prophet, the destruction of the Temple was a catastrophe.

In his mind, this calamity befell Judea because of the sins of the people and was a punishment from God.[61] His caustic rebuke of his people is evident in all three books that he wrote or co-wrote — the Lamentations, the Books of Kings, and Jeremiah.

Thus, buried in Chapter 13 of the book of Jeremiah is a verse that really captures his despair and maybe even cynicism. Verse 23 of that chapter reads:

"Can the Ethiopian change his skin, or the leopard his spots? Then may ye also do good, that are accustomed to do evil."

That verse has spawned the saying, "Can a leopard change its spots?", which means we are who we are and can never change. That our character decides our actions and we cannot be more or less than what our character is.

---

[61] Reiss, Moshe. "Bible Commentator." JEREMIAH, THE SUFFERING PROPHET, www.moshereiss.org/articles/09_jeremiah.htm.

The metaphor is quite powerful, as it teaches us the skin color of an Ethiopian (or Cushite as in some translations) and the spots of a leopard are just unchangeable. Maybe, with developments in gene technology, that might be a possibility in the near future — but now and at the time Jeremiah wrote, it is and was not a possibility.

There are many variations of this saying like, "You cannot teach an old dog new tricks," or like Popeye used to say, "I am what I am,"[62] or "Old Habits die hard."

My favorite of all the variations is the German version:

"Man kann nicht über seinen eigenen schatten springen" or "You cannot jump over your own shadow."

Being a very visual person, I have always imagined that vividly. It clearly illustrates the difficulty in overcoming oneself even more. One's shadow is basically a light-induced extension that is impossible to separate from, or even jump over. The shadow can also signify one's history, what one has done in the past, upon which others draw. Is this shadow so dark one keeps tripping over it?

Now, let's take this exercise a step further and apply the saying to not only humans, but everything that acquires an identity or develops a personality. To mind comes societies, groups of people, nations. These are entities that

---

[62]Brennan, John V. and John Larrabee (2008). "Popeye: The Black and White Cartoons". The Stuff You Gotta Watch.

over time acquire a distinctive identity and has moral and ethical factions. Thus, these groups can be said to have their own distinct characters that may arise from how the majority does things or in what the majority believes.

So, can we then ask if a nation, one such entity, can change its spots or even jump over its shadow?

If that nation is the U.S., can we ask if this nation can escape is dark history and jump over its shadow of racism and bigotry? Can black people be seen as humans who matter? Can we ask if whites can empathize with the lot of non-whites? Can we ask if Black America can escape the cycle of violence and poverty? Can we stop assuming all whites are racist, or all blacks are thugs? Or are we all condemned to being who we are?

The Ethiopian stays black, and the leopard remains spotted.

To continue on that tangent, let's go back to Jeremiah 13:23 and read the last part of the verse:

"...Then may ye also do good, that are accustomed to do evil."

As written, the statement is a bit unclear.

Did Jeremiah mean:

"Can you who are accustomed to doing evil ever do good?" or

"Even you who are accustomed to evil can find it in yourself to do good?"

This uncertainty in his meaning is evident in the way this statement is translated in the different versions of the Bible that are available. You'll find one of the three forms in different versions.

Yet, if we can remind ourselves how angry Jeremiah was and who he heaped the blame on for what befell Judea, then I am sure he meant:

"Can you who are accustomed to doing evil ever do good?"

He never believed in his heart the people of Judea were capable of changing their spots or jumping over their shadows.

Events of the past few days – a march by Neo-Nazis and Klansmen in Charlottesville, VA on August 12, 2017 that turned deadly —make me feel bit like Jeremiah when I look at the U.S. I despair and wonder if the leopard can change its spots. It does not help when one hears the unscripted words of the President.[63] His words confirm his dark spots and prove what kind of human being he is. One wonders if he speaks for the majority of White America and I

---

[63] *Shear, Michael D. and Maggie Haberman. "Trump Defends Initial Remarks on Charlottesville; Again Blames 'Both Sides'." The New York Times, The New York Times, 15 Aug. 2017, www.nytimes.com/2017/08/15/us/politics/trump -press-conference-charlottesville.html.*

wonder if the U.S. can ever escape its bitter history of slavery, Jim Crow laws, lynchings, and segregation — or will that past always find a way to tag along like a shadow? Is the national psyche capable of inducing the nation to jump over its shadow once and for all? It feels like the leopard is still spotted.

It is evident the President is neither going to be the leader nor the moral authority to champion such a cause. If one argues the President speaks for most of White America, then despair rolls like the waters and hopelessness like a mighty stream.

Ever being the believer in the good in humans, I choose to believe the majority, unlike the President, reject the bigotry and hate. If that is the case, maybe we have it in ourselves to attempt the jump over the dark shadow of our history.

As I pondered that possibility, I had a string of thoughts. Perhaps the leopard will never change its spots, but it will learn to live with what its spots make it. Maybe what really matters are not the spots, but what the leopard believes

.

Perhaps the U.S. will never be rid of those who believe in the supremacy of one race over the other or seek to subjugate the other race — of those who hate and discriminate. Perhaps there will always be pockets of racism and bigotry.

Yet, if the national psyche is one of a concerted effort to jump over this dark shadow that haunts us, then when Jeremiah asks, "Even you who are accustomed to evil can find it yourself to do good?" — we can all answer, "Yes, we can!"

"Hamilton" — the Musical

A Celebration of a Man and a Nation

Described by President John Adams as "the bastard brat of a Scottish peddler," the rags-to-prominence story of the immigrant Alexander Hamilton has always fascinated me.[64]

An illegitimate orphan born on the island of Nevis (Saint Kitts and Nevis), he would migrate to the U.S. at the age of 16, pushed by the power of his intellect and ability to write.

This immigrant would later become one of the seven Founding Fathers of the U.S.!

In his resume, Hamilton could also list the stint as George Washington's chief staff aide during the American Revolution, principal author of The Federalist Papers, America's first Secretary of the Treasury as well as the founder of the nation's financial system, the Federalist Party, the U.S. Coast Guard, and The New York Post newspaper.[65]

So, when my family and I visited the island of Saint Kitts in January of 2015, I made sure we took the ferry to Nevis,

---

[64] *"Founders Online: From John Adams to Benjamin Rush, 25 January 1806." National Archives and Records Administration, National Archives and Records Administration, founders.archives.gov/documents/Adams/99-02-02-5119.*
[64] *Chernow, Ron. Alexander Hamilton. New York: Penguin Books, 2005. Print.*

so I could check out his birthplace. Little did I know then that in a month, Lin-Manuel Miranda was going to take Broadway by storm with a musical based on Hamilton's biography written by Ron Chernow.

To be honest, I just couldn't buy into the hype. I had heard and read the stories — of how Lin-Manuel had used hip-hop and a mixed cast to tell the story of this amazing man I call the Patron Founding Father of Immigrants.

My daughter, however, bought into the hype and soon could sing each song from the musical. Literally. That is when I knew it was only a matter of time before I had to take her to see it.

The D-Day was today. To temper what my son and I thought would be like two hours of pain, we went to a Cirque du Soleil show last night. Nothing like clowns and acrobats to prepare you for a musical based on a political figure. Yet even that circus show took on a life of its own and was so aesthetically pleasing, we felt cheated (more on that another time).

We took our seats and when I looked over to my daughter, her excitement infected me too.

I was ready for some "Hamilton!"

Well, by the middle of the First Act, my son and I were just enthralled. He, by the music and lyrics; me by everything. Everything. Now, let me see if I can get it all out before I take another breath.

This musical is by a Puerto Rican mainly using a music form created by descendants of former slaves and featuring a mixed cast as diverse as the people who make up this great land celebrates the life of an illegitimate child born on the island of Nevis in the Caribbean, who becomes an orphan, migrates to the U.S., and turns out to be one of the seven Founding Fathers of this great country.

Whew!

How absolutely great is that?

This nation has not always been kind to those who are not Caucasian, but it doesn't stop us from loving this land all the same. We see the same promise and potential inherent in the dreams the Founding Fathers had, albeit a bit dim at times. We see it all the same. And we are glad to be part of that story. We celebrate it too. Given the chance, we celebrate it in our own way with style, rhymes, rhythm, and swag.

"Hamilton" is truly a celebration of the spirit of this nation and what it stands for.

However, that wasn't the only reason the show got to me so much and I sat through most of it with tears in my eyes.

Yeah, call me a sissy and I'll challenge you to a duel.

Hamilton's story, in part, kind of hit home. I guess immigrants share a certain bond due to common experiences. I feel the urgency Hamilton felt. I feel the need to not "throw away my shot."

I am haunted by the urge to "...write like I'm running out of time."

I bet he heard that clock I hear ticking all the time. That annoying clock that gets louder by the day. Tick, Tock. Hamilton's load was heavier, because he had a nation to build. Yet one thing stays the same, and it is that question. That question that haunts one day and night.

What will be my legacy when history is watching?

What story will be written about my life when it's all over – when history is watching?

That feeling of how fleeting time is and how much one still wants to do came through rather poignantly, gripped me by the scruff of my neck, shook me like a rag doll, and left me panting for breath.

When the curtain fell on that great performance, my son and I turned to my daughter and smiled at her.

I said, "That was awesome!'

She replied, "I told you it would be good."

We all laughed as we headed out of the theater.

Just before we stepped out of the theater I looked back, and I could swear I saw the ghost of Hamilton hovering over the stage with a look on his face that asked:

"Is it already over? I didn't want it to end!"

Tell me about it, Alexander! I felt the same way!

We are Just Guests

September 20, 2017

My heart especially goes out to the parents hoping against all hope that their kids survived the 7.1 magnitude earthquake that flattened, among others, the Enrique Rebsamen School in Mexico City's Coapa, this past Tuesday.[66]

Being a father with school-age kids, I can feel their pain and dread.

As immense as these parents' pain may be, they are not alone. Not even in Mexico. All around them in the Caribbean and parts of the U.S., in Southeast Asia and West Africa, Nature's wrath has left lots of hurt, pain, and broken homes.

We as humans may climb the Everest, fly to the moon, and dive to the greatest depths — but can we ever tame Nature? Can we ever predict its temper tantrums that can leave cities in ruins and lives broken?

In 79 BC, Vesuvius took out Pompeii and more recently, the 2004 Sumatra-Andaman Earthquake caused a massive

---

[66] *Semple, Kirk, et al. "Mexico Earthquake Kills Hundreds, Trapping Many Under Rubble." The New York Times, The New York Times, 19 Sept. 2017, www.nytimes.com/2017/09/19/world/americas/mexico-earthquake.html?action =click&contentCollection=Americas&module=RelatedCoverage&ion= Marginalia&pgtype=article.*

tsunami in the Indian Ocean that destroyed thousands of islands, including Sumatra. Even the mighty dinosaurs were destroyed!

Nature is unpredictable and is capable of a might that reminds us humans of our fragile mortality. She can unleash a power that tells us we are really guests here on this planet and Mother Earth tolerates us.

In case we forget, Nature has several reminders at her disposal to wake us up to reality — earthquakes, tsunamis, floods, droughts, tornadoes, hurricanes, fires, volcanoes.

So, as we prance around this Earth like we are overlords of all we cast our eyes on, let's bear in mind we may be unwelcome guests on this planet and she has the power to rid herself of us without any qualms. Let's remember the wise words of the Bard:

But man, proud man,
Dress'd in a little brief authority,
Most ignorant of what he's most assur'd—
His glassy essence—like an angry ape
Plays such fantastic tricks before high heaven
As makes the angels weep; who, with our spleens,
Would all themselves laugh mortal.

~ Measure for Measure, Act 2, Scene 2, 114-123, by William Shakespeare.

A Bottomless Void

November 14, 2017

The story I was told as a kid was that a little child fell into the well some years ago and if I didn't want the same fate to befall me, I should not go near the well by myself. That didn't stop me as a little boy from wandering over to that abandoned well and peeking over the short wall that surrounded it. The few times I did it without getting caught, I looked down the depth of that well and was struck by a darkness that seemed endless, even bottomless. It felt like a deep, dark void that threatened to suck one into it. I used to wonder if the ghost of the child was still down there, and that thought frightened me more than me falling into the well.

This past weekend, as I stood by and then stared into the pools that make up the 9/11 memorial, I couldn't help but think of that abandoned well from years ago and of that sensation of a void it emanated.

For those who haven't visited it yet, the 9/11 memorial is made up of two large square pools, 192 x 192 feet and 30 feet deep. They are made out of black granite and set into the footprints of the Twin Towers. From the top of each pool, water cascades down like a waterfall and flows into central square drainage basins.

The vision of the architect, Michael Arad, for the memorial was driven by the concept of voids. He imagined "two voids tearing open a surface of water and the river failing to fill it up". The "inexplicable" image captured "a sense of rupture and continued absence" that intrigued him."[67]

Even though he could not create two sunken pools with the names of the victims written on the walls as he envisaged, what he finally built conveys that feeling of emptiness quite starkly.

Interestingly, I had no idea of his vision as I stood by the pools and thought back about that well.

The childhood memory did not come that easily though. As I stood by the first pool reading the names of the victims from that fateful September day inscribed on the parapet that surrounds it, I kept stealing glances, not so much at the pool, but at the collecting basin in the middle of it. A thought kept nagging me. However, it was when I finally framed that basin through a lens that the memories flooded back.

As I looked into the darkness of where the cascading water escaped, I couldn't help but think of a void. A dark emptiness. The kind of dark emptiness death and loss create. Somehow, the more senseless the death, the bigger the void. And that seemingly bottomless emptiness can only be filled with tears that never seem to stop, cascading endlessly into a hole that has been torn into our souls.

---

[67]*Gonzalez, Susan. "Architect for 9/11 Memorial Tells the Story of Its Creation." Yale News, 8 Jan. 2018, news.yale.edu/2012/11/28/architect-911-memorial-tells-story-its-creation.*

Michael Arad really captured the sentiment.

Yet, should we allow this void to stay unfilled forever? Sure, its presence is a constant reminder of our vulnerability as humans, or in the case of 9/11, even as a nation. It is also a good repository for tears of loss. Even with these seemingly valid reasons, I posit we should try to fill the voids in our soul and our lives that come from great loss. Be it 9/11 or the death of a loved one, each human should strive to fill that void. And we do. We humans grieve but then somewhere along the line, we dry our tears and fill that void the best way we know how — by living. By appreciating the life, we have and making the most of it. We fill the void with life.

One day, a friend of my grandmothers caught me snooping around the well and told on me.
The spanking was swift, deterring and effective. I never went back to the "first monument to loss" that I saw. Yet, I never forgot the dark emptiness of it. That bottomless void.

Tech Day in Taylorsville

A Short Story

For the last 10 years, Richard Keene always drove over to the Jameson Technology Park on this day. Where his house used to stand was now a giant parking structure. He usually drove all the way to the top of the parking structure. That was no different on this day.

When he got to the top, he got out of his car and walked to one of the low walls that surrounded the topmost deck. He looked around as his eyes misted over. It was 10 years ago, but the memory was still fresh in his mind.

The area now known as "The Jameson Technology Park" used to be the Royalty subdivision in Taylorsville, Kentucky. It was one of the oldest subdivisions in town. Once upon a time, Royalty stood outside the town limits of Taylorsville, exclusive and sought after. Then the town grew and grew until soon, it had enveloped Royalty. A mall was built across the street from Royalty's entrance about 15 years ago and it quickly become a center of commerce in the town.

Richard and Elsa Keene had lived in Royalty forever. Even though both their kids had moved out, they still lived in the same home they bought several decades ago.

Twelve years ago, a young lady moved into the small ranch across from their home. Her name was Lisa Jameson. A few months after she moved in, her house caught on fire in the winter. She was not home, and it was Richard who saw the smoke and called 911. Homeless and with her parents out of the country, the Keenes invited her to stay with them till she sorted things out.

Her parents came to see her the following weekend, and the Keenes hosted them too. They had dinner together at the Keene home each evening.

While visiting, Lisa's dad, Pete Jameson, one of the most successful real estate developers in the state, fell in love with the Royalty neighborhood. It was not a love driven by a desire to own a place there. No! It was the desire to take ownership of that whole subdivision and turn it into a technology park.

Due to all the research being done and the patents being filed by the students and professors at the Taylorsville Institute of Technology (TIT), several technology and biotechnology companies wanted to open offices or even relocate there. Pete Jameson knew that if he could offer an optimal landing spot in Taylorsville, most of those companies would rent or even buy from him. With the proximity to the mall and the TIT campus, the area could become a great commercial, technological, and research hub, which he thought would make Taylorsville grow in leaps and bounds. The Royalty homeowners could easily move elsewhere after being paid for their homes, he surmised.

Jameson saw the idea of the tech park as a great business opportunity. From that point on, nothing or nobody was going to stop him from taking possession of the Royalty subdivision.

As the Keenes dined with Pete Jameson over those four days, little did they know he was going to have them removed from their homes the very next year.

Using all the pull he had in the state capital and in Taylorsville and standing on the principle of eminent domain, he got his wish. About a year after Lisa Jameson's house caught fire, the town ordered all the homeowners to move from Royalty. They were paid adequately for their homes, but almost all of them hated the ruling. Six months after that, the bulldozers moved in. Exactly a year ago to this day, the Jameson Company broke ground on the construction of the tech park where Royalty used to be. About 18 months later, it was done and filled up immediately with tech companies.

Just as Pete Jameson thought, it turned Taylorsville into a tech hub, and this day had been dubbed Tech Day in commemoration. Over the last few years, it had become so popular, the City Council decided to make it a holiday.

So, on each Tech Day, Richard Keene would go over to where his home once stood and reminisce.

He knew thousands of people in Taylorsville were thankful for the tech park and the jobs it had brought into town. Yet, how could he be happy?

As he stood there, he thought of all his former friends and

neighbors. Some had died. Others moved out of town. A few, like him, moved to other subdivisions.

His new home in the southern part of town was nice, but it did not have the sentimentality and history their old home in Royalty possessed. He sighed as his shoulders slumped.

He will always curse the day he opened his home to the Jamesons. He regretted that greatly.

Yet, can one cry over spilt milk? He took one last look at what was once home, got into his car and drove off to his new home in the subdivision called "The Reserve."

HAVE A HAPPY THANKSGIVING!

Cynical Me

When on October 3, 1863, Abraham Lincoln signed the Proclamation of Thanksgiving, he wanted Americans "...to set apart and observe the last Thursday of November next, as a day of Thanksgiving and Praise to our beneficent Father who dwelleth in the Heavens."[68]

Remember this was in the middle of the Civil War. Lincoln felt in spite of all the death and horrors of war, the nation had prospered.

He stated, "No human counsel hath devised nor hath any mortal hand worked out these great things. They are the gracious gifts of the Most High God..."

And thus, he saw it fit that Americans set aside a day to give thanks.

One can argue about the genesis of the custom itself and how it is somewhat tainted by the way the Native Americans were treated, but that is the topic of another discussion.

In the confines of this piece, the discussion shall be about the concept of being thankful!

So, every year in November, Americans celebrate probably the greatest holiday of this nation.

---

[68]*Thanksgiving Proclamation by Abraham Lincoln, www.abrahamlincolnonline. org/ lincoln/ speeches/ thanks.htm.*

One can even say, based on Lincoln's argument, every soul that wanders the earth should set a day apart every year to be thankful and pray for "...widows, orphans, mourners or sufferers...."

Yet, I keep wondering if everyone, even in this here United States, can be thankful each time November rolls around. Definitely at the time Lincoln wrote the Thanksgiving Proclamation, there were thousands who could not possibly find a reason to be thankful — the soldiers fighting the Civil War, the orphans and widows, the slaves, and Native Americans.

Today, think of families who have lost children to the opioid epidemic. How can they be thankful?

I think of the homeless and the poor and destitute. How can they be thankful?

How can a child who is being physically or sexually abused find it in his or her heart to be thankful?

How can that abused wife be grateful?

I knew a cleaner at a hospital I worked at who lost his wife and only child in one year. He spent that Thanksgiving crying.

Strife, disease, imminent death, and great loss make it tough to be thankful. They cover the soul and shut out the light of hope that confers thankfulness. The constant pangs of hunger chase away thoughts of gratitude. Fear devours the expectation of something better and makes one cower.

Maybe we need to allow people whose lives are a living hell to yell out like Mafala does in the musical "The Book of Mormon:"

"When the world is getting you down, there's nobody else to blame

Raise your middle finger to the sky and curse his rotten name!"[69]

They may need that as a form of catharsis instead of feigning thankfulness.

Sometimes, thankfulness has to wait its turn for the dark clouds to pass. Sure, there is something noble in smiling through the pain, but well, that is why it's noble. Mere humans do not do that well. Mere humans cry in anguish, curse the heavens, wail about their lot in life, and despair.

Mere humans tough it out though, hoping it will be all right. When the sun finally appears, they smile and are thankful.

---

[69] *"Book of Mormon (Ft. Andrew Rannells, Brian Tyree Henry, Darlesia Cearcy, John Eric Parker, Josh Gad, Lawrence Stallings, Maia Nkenge Wilson, Michael James Scott, Michael Potts, Nikki M. James, Rema Webb, Ta'Rea Campbell, Tommar Wilson & Tyson Jennette) – Hasa Diga Eebowai." Genius, 27 May 2011, genius.com/Book-of-mormon-hasa-diga-eebowai-lyrics.*

And you know, I'm sure God understands.
I'm sure He doesn't care if come that third Thursday in November, one cannot smile and say, "Thank you!"

I'm sure He knows when the dark clouds recede, He'll see a smile. For He knows we are mere mortals.

Coloring in the Corner

December 4, 2017

One morning several years ago, I had to help in the care of an 11-year-old boy who had a very rapid heart rhythm and needed an electrophysiological study to figure out the source and hopefully treat it. Since these cases take a while and the patients have to be still the whole time, the boy's pediatric cardiologist asked that he be placed under general anesthesia for the procedure.

Around 7 a.m., I went to see him in the cardiology perioperative unit. He was in one of the cubicles preoperative patients wait in with their parents, spouses, or a family member. When I entered the cubicle, I was immediately struck by his mop of red hair and his restlessness. He wasn't really sitting on the stretcher — he was all over it. The other thing that struck me was his mother. She sat calmly at a table in a corner of the cubicle coloring images on a sheet of paper. The kids usually got those sheets of paper with images and geometrical shapes to color as a way of keeping them occupied. Some kids did not color and this boy was probably in that group. Thus, the mother had access to the images and crayons.

I finished my preoperative interview, examined the boy, and left.

The nurses were going to attempt to gain intravenous (IV) access in the boy, since he was big and that would make our anesthetic induction easier. I asked them to give him an oral sedative to help calm him down before they attempted to get access.

About 15 minutes later, I heard my name over the PA system, asking me to go the cardiology preoperative area stat. I rushed over, expecting the worst. I swung the door open, and the first thing that hit me was the yelling. It sounded like an Apache battle cry. Then I saw him — the red-haired boy. He was running in circles around the nursing area, which was shaped like a large rectangle. Behind him were two middle-aged nurses trying to keep up. At that point I was so taken aback by the scene, I remained standing in the doorway.

The boy ran past me, still whooping, and close behind him were the two nurses huffing and puffing.

I took in the scene and realized one of three things could have happened. He could have been spooked by either the oral sedative or the needle used for intravenous access — or he had been given the oral sedative and was having an adverse reaction.

I watched as the boy finished three-fourths of the loop and headed back towards me. I moved from the doorway, stepped quickly into his path, and scooped up the kicking and screaming boy.

The nurses held his legs and with me hanging onto his torso, we got him back to his cubicle and onto the stretcher. With a nurse on each side of him, I tried to calm him down.

Reportedly, the marathon episode was set off when one of the nurses asked him to drink the sedative.

I was wondering where the mother was when I heard her voice.

"He does not like medicine," she said.

I looked up. His mother was still seated at the table — coloring!

Through all the ruckus, she had not budged. She just sat there and colored.

"You told me he has ADHD. Does he also have such frequent violent outbursts?" I asked.

She had not volunteered that information.

"All the time," she replied, still coloring, not so much as raising her head to look our way.

For a second, I felt anger well up, but then I looked over at the boy still carrying on; suddenly, I understood. For once, she did not have to deal with the son's violent episodes. She could escape into the peace and quiet of shapes, images, and colors and let others deal with him.

I asked the nurses not to give him anything and stay with him until the pediatric cardiologist scheduled to perform the procedure arrived.

The boy slowly calmed down and with the help of several nurses holding him down, we were able to put him to sleep later with an anesthetic gas in oxygen.

Now, even though coloring is not art therapy, it has benefits for the adult psyche. Like Marygrace Berberian, a certified art therapist and the Clinical Assistant Professor in Art Therapy Program at New York University (NYU) said in an interview with CNN in August 2017, "Coloring definitely has therapeutic potential to reduce anxiety, create focus or bring [about] more mindfulness."[70]

A clinical psychologist at the Mayo Clinic in Rochester, Minnesota, Craig Sawchuk, claims coloring reduces stress.[71]

However, this is not supposed to be a medical treatise on coloring or children with violent perioperative outbursts. It is rather a somewhat convoluted meditation on the sorry state of our political discourse in the U.S. today.

Bear with me.

I look at the current state of the U.S. political landscape

---

[70]Fitzpatrick, Kelly. "Why Adult Coloring Books Are Good for You." CNN, Cable News Network, 1 Aug. 2017, www.cnn.com/2016/01/06/health/adult -coloring-books-popularity-mental-health/index.html.
[71]Krug, Nora. "Here's How to Get into the Coloring Habit." The Washington Post, WP Company, 2 May 2016, www.washingtonpost.com/national/health-science/heres-how-to-get-into-the-coloring-habit/2016/05/02/697a9424-095e-11e6-a12f-ea5aed7958dc_story.html?utm_term=.000a9792d6e8.

and leadership and the pervasive storylines on sexual improprieties, tribalism, gun violence, Russian hacking investigations, threats of war, unwillingness to deal with the issues of climate change, the rise and rise of the Far Right and Nazism, the polarization, pseudo-Christianity, the ever-widening disparities in wealth and opportunities, and the rampant lies from the very top — and all I want to do is escape into the obliviousness of a coloring book with my kids' crayons.

I want to shut out the screeching voices of pundits, politicians, and liars — and I wonder if coloring can help me do that. It seemed to have helped the mother of that red-haired boy years ago.

This country seems lost when it shouldn't be. It seeks to be great again when it has always been mighty. It seeks to close itself off when its greatness is in its openness. It seeks to right non-existent wrongs but is blind to glaring problems and inequalities.

Yeah, I think I will do that. I'll head off into the corner and color. A little blue there, some red here, a dash of pink yonder, green at the edges, some brown down under, a splash of white overall, black into those spaces, and a dab of violet to accentuate burgundy.

Maybe in the peace and quiet, someone else will fix the screaming and yelling of a nation going around in misguided circles. Maybe I can color out the piercing screeches of a leadership-induced tumultuous, motion-sickness-causing merry-go-round.

What Good Can Come Out of There?

January 12, 2018

"Nathanael said to him, 'Can anything good come out of Nazareth? ' Philip said to him, 'Come and see.'" — John 1:46

It must have been 1991 or 1992 — my third or fourth year of medical school. I was walking home after totally acing a pathophysiology test, and I felt rather good about myself.

Most of my colleagues will agree with me that pathophysiology ranks right up there with embryology and pharmacology as probably the three toughest courses in med school.

To make it worse, testing at the University of Leipzig was oral. You sat across from a professor and his one or two assistants and were then handed questions like, "Discuss Virchow's Triad" or "Draw and Explain the Starling Curve for These 3 Conditions."

It wasn't just a narration from the student's part though. It was often a frank discussion of these medical topics where the examiners bored deeply to ascertain the student's grasp of the themes and their ability to apply them. And by the way, they were in German. Those tests were sweat-inducing ordeals.

And I had totally aced pathophysiology. I felt so good, I decided to do the 20-minute walk home instead of taking the tram. It was a cold fall day, but I was too pumped up to care. In a black suit with a burgundy tie and grey overcoat, I felt like Sidney Poitier in "Guess Who Is Coming to Dinner."

Then I came to the tunnel under Tröndlinring that led to my street. As I descended the stairs, I could hear voices. The three young German men came into view.

As I walked towards them, they burst out laughing, pointed at me, and said, "Ein Nigger" several times with other insults.

As they walked by me, one of them spat on the floor. They kept going and laughing.

Initially, I was relieved they did not attack me. There had been attacks on people like me. The sense of relief soon turned into one of sadness and deflation. I could feel my eyes moisten. My "A" in pathophysiology looked so inconsequential.

I looked back at them as the sadness slowly morphed into anger. In that moment, I vividly remembered the way they looked — their hair all disheveled, one had missing teeth, their clothing, their language, their unkempt appearance, their sallow-looking skin... My anger was slowly replaced by a smile as a deep realization set in.

You see, those young men were probably nowhere near what I had just accomplished. They probably could not tell you who Virchow even was. Yet, due to the color of my skin and where they imagined I came from, they saw it fit to treat me with contempt.

That incident taught me a great lesson. That in the eyes of some in the West, nothing good can come out of a place like Africa and the black man deserves nothing but contempt. That I could be the best and brightest and still be seen as nothing but "Ein Nigger."

Thus, when I heard what the President allegedly said yesterday, I was not really shocked.[72] Even though I am part of a group of doctors and nurses who are some of the nicest people I have met; even though in my day-to-day dealings with the surgeons, they are professional and friendly; even though among my peers, I am not rated by the color of my skin or where I come from but by my character and abilities; there are always going to be those who see me as nothing but a black man from a shithole. What good can come out of a shithole? They do not want you here, because they think you lower the standards and denigrate the gene pool.

Yet every human has an inherent right to seek a better life for himself and his family.

From the English-Somali poet Warsan Shire, comes this line from her poem "Home": "No one leaves home unless home is the mouth of a shark."[73]

---

[72]Davis, Julie Hirschfeld, et al. "Trump Alarms Lawmakers with Disparaging Words for Haiti and Africa." The New York Times, The New York Times, 11 Jan. 2018, www.nytimes.com/2018/01/11/us/politics/trump-shithole-countries.htm
[73]Shire, Warsan. "Home," Seekershub.org, 2 Sept. 2015.

When life in the place called home becomes unbearable, when dreams cannot be achieved, humans go seeking.

The Pilgrims did that. The European settlers did that. They fled religious persecution, feudalism, mercantilism, diseases, and wars to find a better life in an unknown land some 3,000 miles away.

At times, these terrible conditions are the work of one man and his ideas like we saw in Hitler's Germany, or an institution like the Church in medieval Europe, or the activities of an Islam-contorting group like ISIS. It could be the effects of a practice like slavery and colonialism, or rampant corruption like what's seen in a lot of African countries. It could be even be famine, floods, or an earthquake.

Whatever the cause, humans have the right to seek a better life — and the conditions they leave behind do not necessarily reflect who they are as humans or even the color of their skin. It is therefore sad there are people who believe that way and the President shares that sentiment.

The day I boarded a plane and left the shores of Ghana, I became an immigrant. Over the years, I have learnt a lot about myself, life, and humanity.

That fall day many years ago in Leipzig, I learned one cannot change the bigoted mind.
So, all I can do is be the best I can be in all I do with the few chances I get as an immigrant, take care of my family, continue to love this United States of America that has

given me so much, support my home Ghana any way I can, and just try to be a good human being every day.

Like it says in the Serenity Prayer, I pray for the serenity to accept that which cannot be changed, the courage to change that which can be changed, and the wisdom to know one from the other. Anything else would be a waste of time — and that is a lesson even someone from a shithole can grasp.

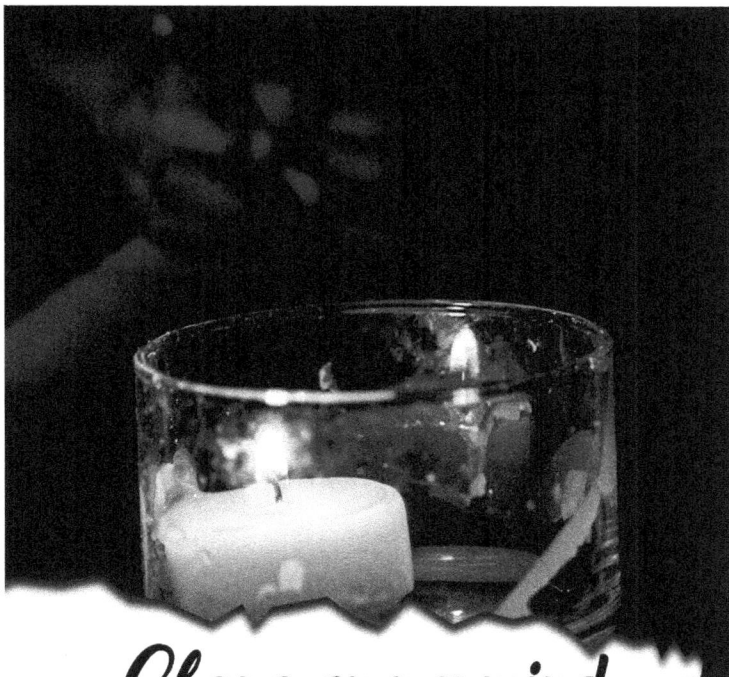

Ghana on my mind

"Sometimes we feel we straddle two cultures; at other times, that we fall between two stools."
— *Salman Rushdie*

Ghana is 60!

The road has been rough
Uneven, hard, and tumultuous
We had to hang tough
The times were tempestuous.
From the veterans who fell
Marching towards the Castle
To the Big Six made to dwell
Locked up in cells of hassle
A powerful black star was lit
Igniting in us the wish to be free.
May the spirit of that March permit
Us all today to sing with glee,
Ghana is 60, O what a day!
Ghana is 60, for greatness we pray.

He wished the nation well
Yet forever he wished to rule
That February when he fell
The gun was the main tool.
Twice we tried real hard
A republic to maintain
Each instance was marred
By a military refrain.
Yet a fourth time we tried
After twenty-four it still holds
So, with hearts full of pride
Our song today unfolds
Ghana is 60, O what a day!
Ghana is 60, for greatness we pray.

Why the Kalyppo Campaign is So Powerful

October 14, 2016

I don't know why the NPP flag-bearer, Nana Akufo-Addo, was drinking Kalyppo four years ago in that car. That picture, however, has resulted in a campaign that has drawn the members of the opposing party as well the general Ghanaian public together like not seen in a while.[74]

I found out about the boxed drink Kalyppo during my last visit to Ghana. My mother-in-law bought a pack for my kids, and my son fell in love with the Fruitimix flavor. Thereafter, there were days when we were out hunting for that flavor. That particular one was difficult to get.

So back in 2012, an occasion rose that made this grown man, an accomplished attorney and statesman, favor a boxed drink that kids love. Was it thirst? Was it curiosity? Was he reaching for a bottle of water and absent-mindedly grabbed a box of Kalyppo? Whatever the reason, at that point in time, Kalyppo was good enough.

So, it is in life. In a society like Ghana, where millions of people struggle every day to make ends meet or even get basic healthcare, most have to make do with what is available. For these millions, day in day out, the mantra is:

---

[74] *"Fruit Juice Stunt Turns Sour for Ghana's Ruling Party." Reuters, Thomson Reuters, 16 Oct. 2016, www.reuters.com/article/us-ghana-politics-juice/fruit-juice -stunt-turns-sour-for-ghanas-ruling-party-idUSKBN12G0OP.*

"Kalyppo has to be good enough. It just has to do!"

It doesn't matter it was made for kids or favored by kids — sometimes, Kalyppo has to do. The little ball of kenkey has to do. Not going to see a doctor has to do. The kids missing school to go sell water by the road has to do. Becoming a galamsey has to do. Their personal "Kalyppo" has to do.

So, to see minions of the ruling government, often blamed for the morass we are in now, deriding this powerful symbol — a symbol of Nana Akufo-Addo making do— was enough to ignite something. Those minions deriding Nana Akufo-Addo for drinking Kalyppo was like a derision of the millions who make do each and every day in Ghana.

Are you surprised at how widespread and popular the campaign became? Sure, there were the wags who saw (and still see) that as an opportunity to draw laughs. Yet underneath all that was a powerful message to those in power. The message was: "You may have your Voltics, chilled bottles of Coke, and freshly squeezed orange juice. However, most of us are lucky to even get a box of Kalyppo, and we are proud of it and make do with it. Just remember us when you are sipping on your bottled water, Coke, and orange juice in your mansions. Remember, because we put you there and we have the power to remove you."

Why I Rooted for the Black Stars

June 21, 2010

(I wrote this after Ghana eliminated the U.S. in the 2010 World Cup.)

I was born in Ghana, became a man in Germany, and made a home in the U.S. However, no matter how far I go, I never forget my origins – Ghana, Africa.

Why?

Because there is a bond that pulls all Africans together and to the continent.

It is a bond forged by pain and suffering, disease and hunger, exploitation and colonialism, tribal strife, and inept leaders.

This bond is not static. It waxes and wanes. It grows and sometimes looks like it's on its deathbed.

The bond reaches far. It reaches into the hearts of immigrants all around the world – living rooms in the U.S., England, and Australia. It reaches Darfur. It reaches the pirates in Somalia and the rival factions in the Congo.

This bond has stood the test of time, because it is nurtured. It is nurtured by family and friends, love and charity, the warmth of helping one another, and encouragement. We cry with each other and share the joys too.

Perhaps though, its strongest sustenance is hope. The hope of something great. The hope of rising above the impediments that litter our path. The hope it can be better. The hope that this time, it is different.

Like a clarion call, nothing gets this bond going more than hope.

So, when the Black Stars made it to Round 16 as the only African team, there was hope. The hope fed the bond, and the bond grew.

For the first time in its 80-year history, the FIFA World Cup came to Africa. It is really symbolic that it was held in South Africa. By the end of the first round of games, five of the six African teams are out, including the Bafana Bafana of the host nation, South Africa. The Black Stars of Ghana were left standing alone. That also by itself is deeply symbolic, for Ghana was the first sub-Saharan nation to win independence from colonial rule.

Before the games started, I am sure all the African teams hoped to make their countries as well as the continent proud. And all Africans, on the continent and abroad, hoped for the same. But only one team seemed to believe it more than all the others. The Black Stars. And with their performance so far, they have engendered a lot of hope in Ghana and on the continent...

...and are feeding the bond!
I rooted for Ghana in the World Cup match against the U.S., but not because I don't like the country I live in now.

Far from that! I love the U.S.! It's just Ghana and the continent of Africa needed this win more.

Many years ago, Kwame Nkrumah, Ghana's first president, said, "The independence of Ghana is meaningless unless it is linked with the total liberation of Africa."

Back then (and even now), that was a bold statement and many a critic berated him for it. Nkrumah, however, recognized how important and symbolic the Ghanaian independence was. It had spurned hope, and that hope was feeding the bond. He realized on this continent of pain and suffering, no one country was an island. We need each other. That is why the bond is essential.
That is why the success of the Black Stars is so important.

The continent needs proof we can measure up, even if just for a few weeks. Proof that if we set our minds and spirits to it, we can achieve success. Proof that given the chance, like the prepared, we seize it. Proof that in spite of wars, disease, hunger, famine, and bad leadership, we can rise above it all. The continent needs that spirit, even if just for a few weeks. This spirit can change and even save lives.

The U.S. has this spirit. It permeates every aspect of life here. This is a "Can-Do" nation. Africa could use a dose of that.

That is why I rooted for the Black Stars.

Who Will Watch Anas?

Sept 15, 2015

Anas Aremeyaw Anas is a Ghanaian investigative journalist and attorney whose work has garnered him a lot of praise and acclaim. Recently, his investigative work has exposed massive corruption in the Ghanaian Judicial system.[75] His modus operandi, however, worries me. His way of doing business brings to mind a very powerful man from another country and another era — J. Edgar Hoover.[76]

J. Edgar Hoover ran the FBI for 48 years — from 1924 till he died in 1972. He built the Bureau into a world-class law enforcement organization.

In his formative years, before he ascended to the leadership of the FBI, he had come to believe that Communists were trying to subvert the U.S. In the 1930s, he was instrumental in the Red Raids where about 6,000 people, mostly foreigners, were arrested on suspicion of being Communists. The majority were later released. The experience made Hoover decide to conduct such investigations secretly; this began his collection of

---

[75]Mark, Monica. "Ghana's Top Undercover Journalist Masters Disguise to Expose Corruption." The Guardian, Guardian News and Media, 24 Sept. 2015, www.theguardian.com/world/2015/sep/24/anas-aremeya-anas-ghana-corruption.
[76]"The History of The FBI's Secret 'Enemies' List." NPR, NPR, 14 Feb. 2012, www.npr.org/2012/02/14/146862081/the-history-of-the-fbis-secret-enemies-list.

information on anyone or any organization he thought was subversive. Soon, this ballooned into the collection of information on most public and influential figures. He kept secret files on more than 20,000 people! Using the information in these files, Hoover was able to control presidents, senators, and other very influential people.

One of his targets was the Civil Rights movement and Martin Luther King Jr. (MLK). He bugged MLK's bedroom, hotel rooms, and offices. Among other things, he found out about MLK's infidelity. Hoover tried to use the tapes to discredit him and knock him down as a moral authority. He sent the tapes to MLK's friends and colleagues. He sent one with a poison pen letter to MLK's home where his wife opened it.

"King, look into your heart," the letter read. "(The American people soon would) know you for what you are—an evil, abnormal beast...There is only one way out for you. You better take it before your filthy, abnormal fraudulent self is bared to the nation."

Hoover was trying to get MLK to commit suicide.

Hoover found out that JFK was having an affair with a divorcee who was also having affair with a mob boss in Chicago. He had a file on Robert Kennedy. Hoover even had the band the Kingsmen investigated for their song "Louie Louie," because he thought the lyrics were obscene. Recently, those files have been made public, and the information in them is astonishing. No wonder Hoover survived eight presidents!

This was a man who used his office to amass embarrassing information about his fellow countrymen and used this information to control them.

So again, if Anas may be watching you, who is watching Anas?

I am not saying Anas is going to be a Hoover, but the opportunity is there. What stops him from amassing information on all public figures? What stops him from using this information, if embarrassing enough, to blackmail or even control these men and women? If these figures are in government, what stops him from influencing policy? What stops those who work with and for him from doing the same? Who controls what Anas ultimately sees as right and wrong? How do we know if his moral compass changes? At the moment, he is amassing power and influence. How do we know that won't corrupt him? And if it does, WHO IS WATCHING ANAS?

Remember what the British historian, Lord Acton once said, "Power corrupts, and absolute power corrupts absolutely."

There are many things wrong with Ghana. Corruption ranks up there. A corrupt judiciary is rather demoralizing for a country and makes a mockery of the Rule of Law. In our bid to rid our dear nation of this cancer, let us be careful what we sacrifice. The willingness to accept the taping of private conversations without the consent of those involved is a very slippery slope that the nation does not want to get on. It is a civil liberty that should be near and dear to everyone's heart. Imagine a country where what you say and do in private is not sacred anymore. Anyone can record it and make it public without your consent. Imagine a government that can do that to its people. After all, Anas does it and it's fine. Do we want a 1984?

To end, I'll leave you with a quote from Friedrich Nietzsche, "Whoever fights monsters should see to it that in the process he does not become a monster. And if you gaze long enough into an abyss, the abyss will gaze back into you."

Heart Surgery in Ghana

Jan 15, 2012

Ever since I found out Kwabena Frimpong-Boateng, a German-trained cardiothoracic surgeon, had returned to Ghana and founded a cardiothoracic center at Korle-Bu in the 1990s, I have been intrigued. You see, I am what some people describe as a cardiothoracic anesthesiologist — I put patients who need heart surgery to sleep, so people like Dr. Frimpong-Boateng can operate on them.

I am intrigued because takes a lot to set up such a center, and the upkeep is rather expensive. My dear Ghana is not exactly wealthy, and the country has other pressing problems. Even though sub-Saharan Africa has its share of heart disease, especially congenital, I didn't see the leadership in Ghana backing him.

I am intrigued because knowing how Korle-Bu Teaching Hospital is, I doubted if anyone could set up something of that caliber and keep it going.

I am intrigued because if I ever decided to go back to Ghana, I might actually have somewhere to practice my craft.

Most Ghanaians and I looked on in shock as Dr. Frimpong-Boateng was removed as head of the Center last year by the government, in what most see as retaliation for him showing support for the opposition NPP party. The reason the government gave was his age. The retirement age for public servants in Ghana is 60. He was 61. I would understand if Ghana was crawling with heart surgeons and the dear professor was incapable of operating. There are less than 10 active heart surgeons in Ghana and the professor is NOT senile, demented, or has the shakes. He is neither on drugs, nor is he an alcoholic. In other words, HE CAN STILL OPERATE!

Anyway, I had always wanted to visit the center and meet the man. Imagine my excitement when a good friend, Albert Ocran, put me in touch with one of the surgeons who works at the center, Dr. Frank Edwin. We talked on the phone and planned to meet when I next visited Ghana.

I was in Ghana these last two weeks and took up Dr. Edwin on his offer. I walked into the center one morning, not knowing what to expect. I trained in Germany and the U.S., and now work in the U.S. My active practice since 2000 has involved working with cardiothoracic surgeons over 75% of the time. I think I am in the position to say what Dr. Frimpong-Boateng built, without any help from the Ghanaian government, is nothing short of amazing.[77]

My plan was to spend only about an hour with Dr. Edwin to look at possible collaborations.

I ended up staying close to four hours.

---

[77]Tettey, Mark, Martin Tamatey and Frank Edwin. "Cardiothoracic Surgical Experience in Ghana." Cardiovascular Diagnosis and Therapy 6.Suppl 1 (2016) : S64–S73.

I spoke with the other surgeons, cardiologists, and anesthesiologists.

There was a dedication that was palpable, contagious and refreshing.

I didn't get to meet Dr. Frimpong-Boateng, but I saw his work and I was impressed.

The center is no gleaming edifice of glass and steel. It is rather a bland-looking concrete structure with the bare necessities, run efficiently by men and women with dedication and vision.

There are two operating rooms with all one needs for cardiac, thoracic, and vascular procedures.

There is a six-bed intensive care unit, where an anesthesiologist or surgeon is available around the clock.

It is a 17-person team of surgeons, cardiologists, and anesthesiologists who care for the patients first and handle everything else later.

They use old, and I mean old, echocardiography machines to capture images.

They take the little they get and MAXIMIZE it — note: MAXIMIZE!

These are highly trained men and women who could earn six-figure salaries in the U.S. making about $2,000 a month in Ghana — and even that at times is subject to delays!

The rooms are clean and organized.

There is not the feeling of apathy and despondence that is pervasive in Korle-Bu.

The doctors order their own supplies, cutting out the bureaucracy and middlemen that is the hallmark of business in Ghana.

Therefore, they get their supplies when they need them and at much lower prices than the rest of Korle-Bu.

They take care of their equipment and keep it working.

They have a budget they stick to.

They plan for the future.

They are proactive.

To help out patients financially, Dr. Frimpong-Boateng started a foundation.

Some patients are brought in, fed for two weeks to get them strong enough for surgery, operated on, taken care of postoperatively, and even given money for the trip home!

Kidney failure requiring dialysis is a possible complication after some heart operations. When Dr. Frimpong-Boateng realized the renal unit at Korle-Bu couldn't help him out, he got his own dialysis unit!

Tetralogy of Fallot, lung cancer, coronary artery disease, carotid disease, valve diseases? No problem! Bring them over. Chest trauma? One patient in the intensive care unit survived gunshot wounds to the chest thanks to the center!

All this is due to the vision of one man — Kwabena Frimpong-Boateng.

If one man with a vision could get this done without any help from the government in Ghana, what excuse do we have as a nation? Did he overreach by wading into politics? Maybe.

However, can you blame him if in his heart he thought he could do more for the nation than the clowns otherwise known as leaders who are riding around in SUVs were? NO!

Was the way he was treated fair?

To answer that, I'll let every Ghanaian spend a day at the Cardio Center, hear its history, and let them answer that.

I have my answer.

As I left, I was filled with mixed emotions.

Happy that it is possible.

That as a nation, we can do it.

Sad that when we see someone do it, we don't even recognize it, appreciate it, emulate it.

Sad that a man could sacrifice so much for his nation and still be cast aside like an old shoe without a word of thanks.

May God bless Ghana with visionaries like Kwabena Frimpong-Boateng and bless Ghanaians with the ability to appreciate them.

To WeyGeyHey with Love

February 9, 2017

"Any woman who understands the problems of running a home will be nearer to understanding the problems of running a country." — Margaret Thatcher

Muhammad Yunus, the Bangladeshi social entrepreneur, economist, and banker, won the Nobel Peace Prize in 2006 for founding the Grameen Bank and innovating the concept of microfinance and microcredit. By giving loans to the poor, he managed to help thousands break out of poverty. Soon after he started the Bangladeshi bank in 1976, Yunus made some important observations.

The first was women who received loans used the money not only to generate income, but also to make the lives of their families healthier and better. For example, some women bought chickens — thus getting meat and eggs to feed the family. They generated income by selling the eggs and the chickens they raised.

The men, on the other hand, tended to use the loans for things that benefited only them — alcohol, gambling, and personal luxuries.

Yunus also noticed that women were more apt to repay their loans than men. While the repayment rate for women was about 97%, the men repaid about 77% of the time.

Then was the observation that women in Bangladesh were an untapped pool of hard-working entrepreneurs who could turn the smallest opportunity into significant gains. Small loans seemed to really empower the women to reach for more.

These observations soon caused Yunus to direct the bulk of his efforts towards women.

One hundred and seventy years before Muhammad Yunus won his Nobel Peace Prize, a woman named Harriet Wrigley, the wife of a Methodist missionary, must have known this too. That if you give women the smallest opportunity, they will build something great out of it. In a coastal town in the then Gold Coast (now Ghana), some 6,000 miles from Bangladesh and about 5,000 miles from her home in England, she started a school for young girls who were the least likely to ever receive an education. Mrs. Wrigley taught these girls housekeeping, religious education, writing, and reading.

Mrs. Wrigley would succumb to malaria a year later, but in 1837, another missionary's wife, Elizabeth Waldron, would take the girls under her care. Under her guidance, the brilliance of these girls would attract the attention of the Methodist Church. Using a core group of the girls being tutored in housekeeping, reading, and writing, a secondary school was founded — Wesley Girls High School.

From these humble beginnings in 1836 has grown a secondary school for girls that occupies one of the premier spots in pre-university education in Ghana. A school that epitomizes what secondary education should be. A school that year after year occupies the top spot in most rankings. A school that over the years has produced women who have contributed immensely to Ghana's slow but steady progress.

Wesley Girls High School! WeyGeyHey! Debu for us from Mfantsipim.

What is it about the female gender that allows them to make so much out of so little? What drives this wish to succeed? What is it about them that evokes such efforts to make the lives of those around them (their families, their friends, and the community) better even as they rise?

Maybe the answer lies in the time when humans were hunter-gatherers. The men hunted, and the women stayed home and raised a family. If the men did not return, the women still had to raise those children. They developed a survival instinct that is unmatched. Or is it that extra X chromosome? Does it give them extra power? Or the ordeal of carrying a child for nine months? Or is it the constant flux of progesterone ad estrogen waxing and waning? Maybe when God took that rib out of Adam, he took out the best rib!

Whatever the reason, the products of Wesley Girls, like the poor women of Bangladesh, epitomize this amazing trait to the highest degree.

Mfantsipim and Wesley Girls have histories that started

intertwining back in the 1880s. Not only have both schools supported each other, but there exists a healthy rivalry between them too.

Being a product of Mfantsipim School, it is coded into my DNA to always take digs at anything and anyone Wesley Girls'. However, beneath all that wisecracking is a deep respect and admiration for the school and its products. I should know — I am married to one of them. My sister, cousin, and several friends are products too. They are smart and classy. They do not suffer fools at all. They are hard-wired with the ability to lead and are visionaries. To the world, they proffer an aloof and polished veneer that hides wonderful and caring hearts of gold. Their desire for independence and autonomy runs deep, and this can often set them on a path of conflict in a society as misogynistic as ours.

So, as they celebrate 180 years of educating girls, let's all celebrate with them.

Let's celebrate the strength that allows a woman, in the words of the author Erick S. Gray, "...to make a baby out of a sperm, a home out of a house, a meal out of groceries, a heart out of a smile..."

Let's celebrate perseverance, strength, family, love, wisdom, opportunity and the future.

Let's celebrate the Woman.

Today let's all Live Pure, Speak True, Right Wrong, and Follow the King!

That Place Called Nambia

September 21, 2017

On Wednesday, President Trump delivered a speech to the Heads of States leaders of Côte d'Ivoire, Ethiopia, Ghana, Guinea, Namibia, Nigeria, Senegal, Uganda, and South Africa at the United Nations (UN).

This statement he made earned and still earns him a lot of derision on social media:

"Nambia's health system is increasingly self-sufficient."[78]

You see, there is no African nation named Nambia and everyone wondered if he meant Namibia, Zambia, or Gambia.

Yet like with everything that is Trump, within the web of lies, half-truths, and exaggerations, there often lurks a hint of reality on which his deck of cards is mounted.

The clue to all this is found in the first paragraph of his speech. He said:

"Africa has tremendous business potential. I have so many friends going to your countries, trying to get rich. I congratulate you. They're spending a lot of money. But it

---

[78] Karimi, Faith. "Trump Praises Nonexistent African Country's Health Care." *CNN, Cable News Network, 21 Sept. 2017, www.cnn.com/2017/09/21/africa/trump-nambia-un-africa-trnd/index.html.*

does — it has a tremendous business potential..."

So, Trump has a lot of friends who go to Africa to make lots of money.

They go to this continent racked with disease, poverty, and war to make a lot of money.

So, where do they go to make this money? Well, you won't believe it, but they go to...Nambia!

I can already see the looks of incredulity as you read this and can hear the question, "Where is this Nambia, Nana Dadzie?"

Well, Nambia is not a place per se. It is an institution. Nambia is an institution that allows a continent to be exploited to an unimaginable degree.

In urban parlance "nam" can stand for "a nothing," and one of the meanings of "bia" is weakling.

"Nambia" — "a weak nothing!"

Doesn't the continent often come across as a weak nothing?

Yet, it's not the whole continent that is a Nambia per se.

You see, the continent of Africa is blessed with resources. Like crazy amounts of gold, diamonds, oil, uranium, land, and human capital.

The institution of Nambia allows only a few access to these riches.

In the era of early European exploration and colonialism, they traded in everything, even humans! As the Indigenes languished, they amassed unbelievable wealth.

The whole continent was sucked into a giant Nambia.

The whole continent was a weak nothing!

These days, you see Nambias in Lagos, Accra, Abidjan, Nairobi, Lome, Luanda, or even Johannesburg.

The men and women who populate them are Nigerian, Ghanaian, Ivorian, Kenyan, or even Angolan. They wear thousand-dollar suits from Saville Row and Rolex watches bought in New York. They ride in Mercedes AMGs over potholed streets lined by hungry children begging for a morsel, yet these men and women do not see them through their tinted windows. They live in million-dollar homes far removed from the crumbling hospitals and dilapidated schools their poor constituents have to use.

You see, these are the men and women with the power and access to all the resources the continent has.

These are the men and women Trump's friends see when they go to make money. These are the men and women who cavort with the North Americans, Europeans, Japanese, and especially the Chinese, all of who want to reap the riches of the continent. These power brokers sell these foreigners access to Nambia and together, they get to enjoy this paradise. To assuage their guilt, they throw the masses a bone, like a health center, every now and then.

In this rarefied air, the masses who are afflicted with disease, racked with hunger, and killed in wars don't get to play. They hear their nations are rich, but they never see it. They hear of this place called Nambia and bide their time. If they ever make it there, they take as much as they can, propagating the cycle.

These men and women may have all the trappings of wealth — but due to their greed, they are weak nothings!

So, laugh at Trump all you want. He was right. His friends go to Africa to try and make lots of money. They spend a lot of money doing that, but only few of the Indigenes benefit from that.

The place they do that is called Nambia and unlike the rest of the continent, its health system is increasingly self-sufficient and those who populate it are far removed from the misery of life on a continent that is poor in the midst of riches.

Dr. Abdulai

August 10, 2016

"For I was hungry, and you gave me something to eat, I was thirsty, and you gave me something to drink, I was a stranger and you invited me in, I needed clothes and you clothed me, I was sick, and you looked after me, I was in prison and you came to visit me." (Matthew 25:35-36)

I dedicate today's post to an amazing man and physician I only recently heard about — and for that, shame on me.

Dr. David Fuseini Abdulai.[79]

Dr. Abdulai, born in the northern region of Ghana, is one of 11 children. He is the only one still alive. The rest and his parents died from poverty-related diseases. Hearing him describe it, they probably starved to death. His dad contracted leprosy (Hanson's Disease) and his mum was a beggar. After he lost his family, he lived on the streets where he often went without food. That experience proved critical in what he was going to devote his life to.

Through the help of the church, he managed to go to school and then to Ghana Medical School.

After graduation, Dr. Abdulai practiced at Korle-Bu and

---

[79] Blay, Kobby. "Inside Dr. Abdulai's Clinic, Where the Poor Are Cared for Free." Ghana Health Nest, 9 Aug. 2016, ghanahealthnest.com/inside-dr-abdallahs-clinic-poor-cared-free/.

37 military hospitals until 1989 when he decided to return to the northern region to give back.

And has he given back.

He founded the Shekinah Clinic for the indigent and the destitute. He founded the clinic to serve the Very Important People (VIPs, like he calls them) in his life — lepers, the mentally insane, the crippled — anyone society had cast out. In parts of Ghana, lepers, the mentally insane, and the crippled are often homeless. From his childhood experience, he remembered how hungry these people were — so he fed them. Dr. Abdulai still feeds them, houses them, clothes them, and treats them when they fall ill.

They willingly come to him in droves, and also, he goes out to find them. All the care is for free, financed by donations and volunteers. He hasn't drawn a salary in forever.

Dr. Abdulai also operates a "meals-on-wheels" service that feeds the destitute and homeless in a 65-kilometer (40-mile) radius. His targets again are the mentally insane who live on the streets and are often hungry, plus poor families who do not have enough to eat. He has been doing this since about 1992 and has never missed a day.

Every Christmas, he has a party for every destitute person in Gurungu, where his clinic is, and its environs.

He has since opened a second clinic.

Besides his VIP patients, Dr. Abdulai also takes care of the poor who need medical care — for free.

He is assisted by 27 volunteers and serves about 120 people daily.

What a man!

For his efforts, he was affectionately called "The Mad Doctor."

Life sometimes calls upon us to serve our fellow men. Few recognize this challenge and even fewer are able to rise up to this challenge. For the few who can, it is forever an honor and a blessing. For those of us who can only look on, it is a constant source of amazement and awe and it forces something out of us. It forces our better selves to the surface, forcing us to rise and be better people.

Dr. Abdulai, thank you!

P.S.: Shortly after I wrote this, Dr. Abdulai succumbed to thyroid cancer on October 2, 2016.

My Tribute to Dr. David Abdulai

October 3, 2016

My tribute to a Doctor, a Humanitarian, a Mensch...our own Ghanaian Saint...the man whose life reminds me of why I studied medicine...Dr. David Abdulai, fare thee well!

He fed the hungry every day
Never missing a single one.
The insane he didn't betray
Empathy when they had none.
Even the lepers got his care
Unafraid to reach out.
His love he did share
With those who lived without.
He healed without reward
He cured with so very little.
Honor and riches, he ignored
With selflessness as his mettle.
Dear Lord, did he really have to go?
We need David Abdulai here below!

You took him away
Removed a great one.
His smile lit up yesterday
Today there's no sun.
Let the example of his ways
Light up like a thousand beacons
That for us paths blaze
And us to service harken.
May we in selflessness toil

The poor and weak to serve
Our lives in efforts embroil
Humanity to show with verve.
So, Dear Lord, if he really had to go,
Let's be like David Abdulai here below!

Ghana Needs a Human Rights Memorial!

March 19, 2018

I recently got my hands on a copy of the Mike Adjei book Death and Pain: Rawlings' Ghana — The Inside Story.

Reading cursorily through it reminded me of the eight-week period last year when I got my hands on a copy of report of the National Reconciliation Commission of Ghana (NRC). The Commission was convened from January 14, 2003 to October 14, 2004. It was mandated to look at human rights abuses from 1957 to 1993.

The picture I got from reading the five-volume report was rather dark, and this book reminds me of that experience.

I could not help but conclude that we as Ghanaians really lost sight of what human rights were in those years. The degree of abuses and violations reported in that time period was really mind-boggling. They reached a zenith in the years of PNDC rule.

Human rights, however, are very important for the health of a nation. Knowing and respecting these rights by those in power prevents their violation that is expressed in deeds like extra-judicial killings, torture, detentions, and sexual abuse. Knowing and respecting these rights by all prevents the armed forces and police from brutalizing civilians. Knowing and respecting these rights prevents the lynching of suspected thieves. It prevents vigilante groups marching around and taking the law into their hands because their party is in power or they hate decisions made by the government.

A first step towards instilling the importance of human rights in the populace may be the raising of awareness about human rights. The serializing of the NRC report would help towards that. Books like Mike Adjei's also help.

Another important step would be a memorial to Human Rights in Ghana. A memorial that celebrates the dignity of each Ghanaian's right to a life devoid of torture, extra-judicial killings, detentions, and abuse. A memorial that stands to honor the lives lost through abuse of these important rights. Another reason a memorial will help is in acting as a reminder of those dark days.

So, what about an idea for such a memorial?

Imagine a calabash with a crack in it. The crack starts from somewhere along the lid and runs down midway to the base. Now imagine this cracked calabash built out of aluminum into a much larger bowl...maybe with a diameter of 10-12 feet and 6 - 8 feet deep, with the crack going through the side. On the outside of the bowl will be the names of all who were killed or vanished in those years. The bowl will sit in a pond of water. The bowl will have water in it that will flow out of the crack into the pond.

The bowl signifies Mother Ghana. She held us all in till she was cracked open by violence that led to our tears/blood flowing out.

The pond with the bowl will be surrounded by a small garden, all fenced in.

Sure, Ghana has more pressing needs, but such a project could be financed through private donations.

A copy of the NRC report is hard to get, but not the Mike Adjei book. Get a copy and inform yourself of what Ghanaians had to go through, once upon a time, and strive in all you do to prevent such a state from ever arising again.

To Kwabotwe!

After the saxophone, my next favorite instrument is the trumpet.

Whereas the tones that come out of the saxophone flow like honey, the trumpet has a bit of a halting feel to it — almost like the music comes out in pieces but gets put together before it hits the ear of the listener.

The difference in the way the instruments sound affect how I perceive the music that comes from them. Whereas notes from a saxophone speak of ease — the chill, lounging at the bar with a cigar kind of cool — the tones from a trumpet spark a different sentiment. A trumpet emits notes that can be haunting, exhilarating, and sometimes even beseeching. A trumpet has a soul that bares it all — the joys, the heartaches, the memories of broken hearts and sultry nights with nothing but sweat and moans. Yes, that is the trumpet for you.

So, the day I saw the video of the Ghanaian trumpeter, Frank Guildford, playing at the Mfantsipim School, it was more than just someone playing at Kwabotwe.

For those of you not in the know, the Mfantsipim School in Cape Coast, Ghana was established in 1876 as a school to train boys to be responsible men and leaders. Over the years, it has done that job admirably. We count as alumnus or as we term it "Old Boy" among other notable men, one Kofi Annan, former Secretary-General of the UN. It stands on the Kwabotwe Hill in Cape Coast and thus the boys in the school are affectionately called "Kwabotwe Boys."

As you might be able to tell, I am an Old Kwabotwe Boy and so is this trumpeter, Frank Guildford.

In 2016, the school turned 140. As part of the celebrations, Mr. Guildford performed. It was his performance of a song titled "Kwabotwe yɛwo skuul" (Kwabotwe is your school) that instigated this piece. I do not really know how many times I have watched the performance — but anytime I do, the sound of that trumpet encapsulates for me the soul of the time I spent on that hill.

Any Kwabotwe boy who hears the notes from that trumpet is going to feel a tug at the heart. Those notes flow like the wind blowing through those trees as you head up. They flow like Sunday night service. They flow like fans for Mr. Dontwi aka The Corrosive. They flow like sliding to Kenkey Down, like only a 'Botwe boy can flow — soulful, smooth, sultry, and touching. They flow with the fears, hopes, dreams, aspirations, and ambitions of those boys who climbed that hill and returned as men — a nostalgic flow that teems with memories and maybe even forces a tear. Yes, it does!

Hearing him play reminds you of those who came before us — the "Mfantsefo apem", Picot, Balmer, Mensah-Sarbah, Bartels, the Faithful Eight. We see where we have come from and strive to reach even higher.

It forces one to think of the school's motto — "Dwen Hwɛ

Kan" (Think and Look Ahead).

As one listens to those exhilarating notes blaring from his horn, the sentiment is not only nostalgia but also one of determination. A resolve to make sure that we as Old Boys can always look up to that hill and see where we came from. That means we must strive to hold up the school in all ways possible, so it survives even when we are no more. So that future generations will hear the haunting notes of a trumpet being blown by another talented Old Boy.

So, let's raise our school higher than we have ever done before. Let's raise Kwabotwe in words, deeds, song, and assistance.

Even as Frank Guildford's voice evokes memories and his notes tingle the spine, let those musical qualities drive us to never forget that "Kwabotwe yɛ yen skuul."

Issues Arising From the "Side Chick Culture"

February 26, 2017

"O curse of marriage, that we can call these delicate creatures ours and not their appetites."
- William Shakespeare, Othello Act 3, Scene 2

A Ghanaian writer who does a lot of work on all aspects of relationships recently published accounts of infidelity from a group of anonymous married men and women.[80] Reading through the rather graphic descriptions set me thinking. It made me want to explore the topic and so I started doing some searching.

The issue of infidelity in marriages, its causes, and its ramifications can fill a book of 1,000 pages. When I sat down to write my thoughts on the topic, I resolved to let a yet-unknown line of thinking guide me. Let's see what I can tease out.

There are events in life that can incite a lot of emotional turmoil — the death of a loved one comes to mind. Another is infidelity or adultery for married folks.[81] If you do not believe me, find a quiet corner, close your eyes and imagine your wife or husband making love to another.

---

[80]Krampah, Arthur. "Home to Unique Ideas from the World's Smart Minds." The Best Shoulder to Lean upon: David Papa Bondze - Mbir, adbays.com/around-ghana/218-the-best-shoulder-to-lean-upon-david-papa-bondze-mbir.
81 "Adultery." Wikipedia, Wikimedia Foundation, 26 February 2018, en.wikipedia.org/wiki/Adultery

See?

The chaos that ensues in the life of the cheated almost mirrors that seen in patients after trauma and has garnered the description "Post Infidelity Stress Disorder" or PISD [82]

Even though compared to married women married men are more prone to cheat (by a factor of about 2:1), both genders do stray. Cultural stipulations may dampen the infidelity of women, but it still occurs. [83]

To understand why we stray, one has to look back at human ancestry.

The man historically was concerned about sowing his seed and propagating his genes. His involvement in conception lasted anywhere from minutes to maybe an hour, so multiple sexual partners were possible — and thus that sexual appetite.

Women, on the other hand, could get pregnant only twice a year, irrespective of how many sexual partners they had. Since the woman was more concerned about her offspring and their well-being, her craving for sex was not as incessant and rabid.

---

[82]Ortman, Dennis C. Transcending Post-Infidelity Stress Disorder (PISD): the Six Stages of Healing. Celestial Arts, 2009.
[83]Buss, David M. The Dangerous Passion: Why Jealousy Is as Necessary as Love or Sex. Bloomsbury, 2001.

Yet throughout history, men's appetite for casual sex has found some reciprocation for it to last through the ages. This means that there were women throughout history until modern times who have also had the desire for casual sex.[84]

Sexual jealousy in men, stories of infidelity from all cultures, and the controversial theory of sperm competition (this occurs when the sperm from two different men inhabit a woman's reproductive tract at the same time) may point to the fact that women are also connoisseurs of casual sex.

So, whereas men are driven by a burning desire to pass on their genes, leading them to stray, women cheat for more solid reasons. These are all reasons that came about from our days as hunter-gatherers.

First is the economic benefit of liaising with a man wealthier and more powerful than one's partner. In olden times, this could mean more meat and yams in the dry season. Today, we see this driving infidelity in poor countries and families in the lower socioeconomic bracket of traditionally affluent countries.

Another reason is the genetic benefit. Women picked men who had traits their partner usually lacked.

Last is the need for a woman to have a form of backup in

---

[84] *"Sexual Jealousy." Wikipedia, Wikimedia Foundation, 26 February, 2018, en.wikipedia.org/ wiki/ Sexual_jealousy.*

case her partner no longer existed for whatever reason. Life then was short. An affair provided "partner insurance."

Thus, we see that both men and women have a propensity to stray.

That is why over the ages, the human has developed a rather powerful mechanism to protect against this insult. This phenomenon is jealousy. Even though jealousy can ruin relationships and even lead to men battering or killing women, in its benign form it is the one thing that helps us fight for our partners and ward off potential sexual challengers.

Interestingly, the behavior in women that evokes jealousy in men is totally different from that in men that makes women green.

Because of the basics of human reproduction, a woman is always sure that the baby that pops out after nine months is hers. The man, however, cannot be sure. How can he determine this baby was not sired by another man?

The woman, on the other hand, has a different set of worries. For her, a man's emotional involvement is the surest sign that he is still committed. If he starts showing emotional involvement with another woman, that is a dangerous sign. So, for women, it is not so much the one-night stand but that threatening emotional attachment to another female that is dangerous.

For the man, the thought of his wife involved in the

physical sexual act with another man evokes the most jealousy. It births the fear that he could be a cuckold — a man raising a child sired by another man or even the husband of an adulteress.[85] Being a cuckold can also be a fetish, but that is a discussion for another day. For now, let's stick with adultery.

The term "cuckold" comes from the cuckoo bird, a bird that lays its eggs in the nests of other birds, so they incubate, hatch, and raise the young cuckoo. It is a behavior termed "brood parasitism."[86]

Hence, adulterous women risk turning their men into the bird that "breeds the young cuckoo." It is this innate fear that drives the sexual jealousy in men. It is this innate fear that through the ages caused men to make female adultery a crime sometimes punishable by death.

The plight of the cuckold is depicted beautifully in the hilarious Miller's Tale from Chaucer's The Canterbury Tales.

So how rampant is cuckolding really? A UK study from 2009 puts it at about 1 in 25 children. However, could this higher in other countries. I have a feeling it might be.

In most Western societies, adulterous behavior can have dire economic consequences for the cheater or even the

---

[85] *"Cuckold." Wikipedia, Wikimedia Foundation, 26 February 2018, en.wikipedia.org/wiki/Cuckold.*
[86] *"Griggs, Mary Beth. "Cuckoos Don't Sneak Into Other Birds' Nests-They Barge Right In." Smithsonian.com, Smithsonian Institution, 30 June 2014, www.smithsonianmag.com/smart-news/cuckoos-arent-secretly-jerks-theyre-just-jerks-180951916/.*

whole family (including the kids) — especially when it leads to divorce. This may act as a deterrent in some instances against adultery.

In societies where divorces do not carry such an economic burden for the man, it is not uncommon to see rampant male adulterous behavior. I call this the "Side Chick Culture," where a "side chick" is whichever woman a man may be having an affair with at any particular time.
Besides the risk of disease, the emotional toll on the women and the neglect of the family, such behavior makes men in such cultures oblivious to the biggest fear of any man — to be a cuckold.

As an adulterous man is busy sowing his wild oats all over town, his wife may just well be
finding solace in the arms of another man. Women, as we discussed earlier, are wont to do that too. The interesting bit is an adulterous woman has the most desire to sleep with the other man when she is ovulating and with her husband at the other times.

In an interesting UK study from 2007, strippers were asked to keep a tally of their tips for two months. They also reported the beginning and the start of their menses, so the investigators could calculate their ovulation times. The strippers received an average of £42 per hour when they were near ovulation, but only £33 per hour at other times.[87]

---

[87] Hodgekiss, Anna. "Periods Make Women Smarter and More Likely to Cheat Claims University of Hertfordshire Professor." Daily Mail Online, Associated Newspapers, 31 Oct. 2016, www.dailymail.co.uk/health/article-3891172/Why-time-month-makes-TWICE-likely-CHEAT-Periods-make-women-smarter-sexier-tempted-stray.html.

So, guess who will impregnate the wife of that adulterous man who is also having an affair? And if she does get pregnant, guess who will raise that child if she stays married to the husband?

I think an active adulterous life prevents a man from picking up cues that his wife might be straying, a feat that under normal circumstances is close to impossible.
There are several reasons why the Akans of Ghana have maternal inheritance.[88] The one I subscribe to the most is because of cuckolding — a man can be sure that his sister's son is his kin but can never be sure that his own wife's son is really his.

So, to all married men who prance around enabled by a "side chick culture" to tick off their amorous conquests like Casanova; to all the married men who ascribe to the belief of Verus, that "Uxor enim dignitatis nomen est, non voluptatis" (a wife is for honor, not for pleasure)[89]; to all of you, I offer this old saying:

"Mama's baby, Papa's maybe."[90]

---

[88]Ferrara, Eliana La. "Descent Rules and Strategic Transfers. Evidence from Matrilineal Groups in Ghana." BREAD Working Paper No. 129, September 2006 | BREAD, Aug. 2006, ibread.org/bread/working/129.
[89]"Lecky, William Edward Hartpole. History of European Morals from Augustus to Charlemagne. G. Braziller, 1955.
[90]"Mama's Baby, Papa's Maybe." Servent - Wiktionary, en.wiktionary.org/wiki/mama%27s_baby,_papa%27s_maybe.

The art of healing

"As soon as healing takes place, go out and
heal somebody else."
— *Maya Angelou*

The Role of Disease in Sub-Saharan Africa (SSA) — Another Take

Sub-Saharan Africa (SSA) seems to be the crucible of disease. Most of our modern-day epidemics seem to emanate from this area — HIV, Ebola — to mention just two that have significant mortality.

Disease in SSA, however, is nothing new. The region has always had numerous infectious and vector-borne diseases.

I seek to argue that the prevalence of disease in SSA might have changed the course of its history.

Let's go back several hundred years to about 1490. This is the period when Columbus landed in what is now Central America and initiated the massive migration of Europeans to the New World, as it was called. Through the activities of the migrant Europeans and the diseases they introduced, millions of Native Americans were literally wiped out.

Now, SSA was "discovered" around this same time period. It ultimately became a source of manual labor for the cotton and sugar cane plantations in the so-called New World.

So, why didn't SSA see the same level of migration of Europeans like the Americas saw?

One argument is black Africans were seen as an optimal manual labor force, so their bodies were priced over their lands. Some have also argued SSA was more densely populated than the American continent. Yet another argument is the Africans mounted a much stronger resistance against the Europeans than the Native Americans.

The argument, which I tend to favor, is the role of disease — specifically, malaria. Malaria, a disease to which most indigenous Africans develop some form of immunity over time, is devastating for anyone contracting it for the first time. It killed quite a number of European settlers. This dampened any desire for an exploration of the continent. A glimpse of what could have been is seen in South Africa, a region with a climate and disease profile much kinder to the European settlers.

Malaria as a disease was known since the time of Hippocrates. In the ancient times, it was attributed to bad air. The term malaria was coined in Florence, Italy by the historian and chancellor Florence Leonardo Bruni in his Historia Florentina around 1400:

Avuto i Fiorentini questo fortissimo castello e fornitolo di buone guardie, consigliavano fra loro medesime fosse da fare. Erano alcuni a' quali pareva sommamente utile e necessario a ridurre lo esercito, e massimamente essendo affaticato per la infermità e per la mala aria e per lungo e difficile campeggiare nel tempo dell'autunno e in luoghi infermi...

(After the Florentines had conquered this stronghold, after putting good guardians on it, they were discussing among themselves how to proceed. For some of them it appeared most useful and necessary to reduce the army, as it was extremely stressed by disease and mala aria aka bad air...)

The term malaria was introduced in England in 1740 by Horace Walpole: "There is a horrid thing called the malaria, that comes to Rome every summer, and kills one." In 1827, John MacCulloch introduced it in medical literature.

So, Europeans knew of malaria and found out about other diseases that killed them in droves like dengue, yellow fever, and the bugs that caused dysentery. Even David Livingstone, the explorer and missionary, died from malaria and dysentery. The cattle the Europeans tried to raise also died en masse.

Unlike in America, Australia, the Polynesian islands, and part of South Africa where European diseases killed off the natives, the opposite occurred in SSA.

A true exploration of the African continent started in the mid-1800s, shortly after quinine was discovered as a cure for malaria. Then, you saw the true face of European colonization.

For Native Americans and Africans from the sub-Saharan region, the "discovery" of their respective continents by the European explorers of the 15th century has spelled nothing but misery. For most, the misery still continues.

Unlike the Native Americans, most Africans still have

control of their land, even if they are still massively exploited by richer nations and their own corrupt leaders.

Even as disease continues to be a major factor in the lives of most people in SSA, let's not forget that malaria might have been the one thing that saved us from extermination.

Who's Your Daddy?

"When the Grim Reaper comes to call, words fail — they're just too small." — Dixie Lyle, To Die Fur.

Harriet Tubman may be one of the most admired figures in all of American history. Her bravery is the stuff of legends. Besides my personal admiration for what she did, I'm also saddened that her ancestry goes back to the Akan people of Ghana. I am an Akan.

She will forever be remembered for her use of the Underground Railroad to free over 300 slaves after she escaped slavery herself. In about 19 trips, she never lost a single passenger.

I often think of Ms. Tubman when life rears its ugly head.

I also find myself comparing what she did to what I do. To what doctors and nurses who take care of critically ill patients in either the Intensive Care Unit (ICU) or the operating room (OR) do.

Please do not get me wrong. I am in no way setting the two jobs on the same footing. Not at all. I dare not. I wouldn't survive for a minute in the conditions she thrived in.

My aim here is to compare only an aspect of what she did to what we as critical care providers do.

Ms. Tubman used her wiles, intuition, courage, and the Underground Railroad to snatch men, women, and children from the clutches of slavery.

Doctors and nurses who work in the critical care setting, either in the operating room or the ICU, use their acquired skills, intuition, advanced monitors, and drugs to snatch men, women, and children from the clutches of the Grim Reaper.

Whereas Ms. Tubman never lost a passenger, we are not so lucky. Sure, modern medicine allows the most amazing stories of healing. A series of these successes makes one forget that, like Ms. Tubman, we are really trying save people from a very powerful enemy.

Her enemies were the slave owners and the states. Our enemy is the Grim Reaper.

We succeed not only because of our abilities, but also luck or chance or fate or providence — whatever you want to call it. Then every so often, just when you think you have reached a safe spot with your ward, the Grim Reaper shows up unexpectedly and snatches him or her back. That is when one realizes who really is more powerful. That our knowledge, monitors, intuition, and drugs are really feeble attempts to hold off the might of Mr. Reaper.

As the futility of the moment hits and the chest compressions are halted, a flat line on a monitor screen is all we are left with. In the silence that ensues, one can often hear Mr. Reaper's faint but powerful voice as he escapes with the soul of a patient who was alive only a few minutes ago.

One can usually hear his chuckle as he asks, "Who's your Daddy?"

No answer is needed, as those moments remind us all of the frailty of life and our powerlessness. One can then only sigh, get their composure back, and march off to the next battle, hoping this time to get the upper hand.

This dance with the Grim Reaper is as old as life itself; it is truly a macabre yet a rewarding dance indeed. We get better at it each day, and I'm sure Ms. Tubman would be proud.

Pain Pays the Income of Each Precious Thing

Of all the rotations I had to do as a resident, my least favorite was pain management. I never enjoyed that specialty. Pain being a rather subjective sensation, it is almost impossible to measure. What a patient says must be taken at face value unless there are circumstances and clinical signs that contradict his or her story. No matter how much empathy one has, there is always the feeling some patients are not being truthful and pain is being used as a bargaining chip to obtain narcotics and not work. Don't get me wrong — there were patients who were truly in chronic pain. But more often than not, those patients found a way to lead a life not totally ruled by their suffering.

It was during that rotation I learned the phrase, "Pain pays," and came to realize how true it is.

For some patients, pain brings attention, an excuse from work, doting upon by a loved one, and medications that often lend a high.

For the physician, it is cash from performing pain-alleviating procedures on these patients and the lure of a "pill mill."

For the drug companies, selling all those pain pills spells profits.

Pain pays !

Shakespeare uses the term in his 1594 narrative poem, "The Rape of Lucrece."

The poem tells the story of Tarquin, the son of Lucius Tarquinius, King of Rome. Tarquin was a soldier in his father's army, which was besieging Ardea. One night, all the men bragged about how chaste and virtuous their wives were. To prove their claims, they all secretly retuned to Rome to see if each other's wife was as described. The only wife who proved chaste, virtuous, and was also incredibly beautiful was Lucrece, the wife of the soldier Collatinus, whom was a friend of Tarquinius'. Lucrece's chastity and virtue sparked something in Tarquinius. When they all retuned to Ardea, he stole back to Rome and went to Collatinus' home.

Lucrece, seeing her husband's friend and the king's son, welcomed him and allowed him to spend the night. In the middle of the night, he entered her room, raped her, and fled.

Tarquinius debated whether he should commit the dastardly act. As he approached the door of Lucrece's bedroom, he said to himself:

"Pain pays the income of each precious thing;
Huge rocks, high winds, strong pirates, shelves and sands,
The merchant fears, ere rich at home he lands."

The next day, Lucrece summoned her father and husband back to their home in Rome. She asked them to avenge what had happened to her, told them the story, and then stabbed herself to death. Her husband and father carried her body to the public square and told the people of Rome what had happened. The Tarquinius family was chased out of Rome, ending the monarchy.

Did pain really pay?

For a while, Tarquinius may have enjoyed the bitter fruits of his act — but his win led to death and misery for all involved.

Before the 1990s, doctors used opioids rather sparingly. One can say pain was under-treated. Narcotics were mainly given to cancer patients.

Then in 1980, Hershel Jick published a study claiming that the use of narcotics in 11,882 inpatients led to only four cases of addiction.[91]

Six years later, R.K. Portenoy published his study looking at the use of narcotics in non-cancer patients. He claimed there were no adverse effects. He studied 38 patients on whom he based his claims!

Even though both studies were highly flawed, they dramatically changed medical thinking and then practice. Portenoy formed the American Pain Society and preached that the risk for opioid addiction was less than 1% — a number

---

[91] Zhang, Sarah. "The One-Paragraph Letter From 1980 That Fueled the Opioid Crisis." The Atlantic, Atlantic Media Company, 2 June 2017, www.theatlantic.com/health/archive/2017/06/nejm-letter-opioids/528840/.

he would later confess that he grabbed out of thin air! The society came up with the "pain as a fifth vital sign" slogan, and it caught on.

Purdue Pharma dropped the drug OxyContin into this fray in 1996. With aggressive marketing, they promoted this new drug.

The Joint Commission got behind pain as the fifth vital sign. By 2004, doctors who under-treated pain faced sanctions. Opioids were being prescribed to all, even outpatients. Later Endo Pharma and Johnson & Johnson would join the opioid party with their own portfolio of synthetic opioids.

Purdue Pharma claimed OxyContin was a slow-release formulation and would never lead to addiction. Well, we know better now. They had to pay $635 million in fines in 2007 for misbranding and also were required to reformulate the drug — but by then it was too late.

By 2012, sales of opioids were more than $9 billion a year. In 2013, opioid overdoses surpassed car accidents as the number one cause of accidental death.

It's 2017 and these created addicts are now not just sticking to prescribed narcotics, but also are using heroin and cocaine as well as illegally made fentanyl and carfentanil of unknown potency!

Like Tarquinius, pain did pay the income of each precious thing. The drug companies got rich. Doctors ran "pill mills" where they prescribed opioids like candy...and got rich. Whatever misgivings these players may have had was only like "the merchant who fears, ere rich at home he lands."

Like Tarquinius, doctors and the pharma companies took from these patients something really valuable. Almost as valuable as what was taken from Lucrece. They took away their will to not fall prey to opioid addiction. They took away their independence and sense of worth. They made them dependent. All those years of easy narcotics made all these patients highly susceptible to addiction to heroin and cocaine.

Lucrece killed herself shortly after her defilement. However, these patients are dying slowly yet still in large numbers. The misery their fading lives cause is as profound as what Lucrece's father and husband felt.

How is all this going to end?

Are the drug companies and doctors going to get banned from our cities?

Already, states like Ohio are suing the drug companies to force them to finance the care of all these addicts.

Will doctors be held liable too? Will our rule as arbiters of all things health end?

Whatever happens, I hope we all learn pain is not a means by which to amass wealth — but rather a sign that the sufferer needs help.

A Touch of Humanity

I try to see each patient before they come back for surgery. It is not easy in the fast-paced medical practice of today.

Each time I visit a patient, the reception is different.

Some patients are friendly, others indifferent and resigned.

Every now and then, some think I am an orderly coming to roll them back for surgery. Can you blame them? After all, I'm black and speak with a funny accent.

Then is the occasional, "Have you even finished medical school yet?"

Well, I cannot help my boyish, good looks. Hey, don't hate!

Then there are the really difficult patients who come in with their own treatment plan they pulled off the Internet and expect every doctor and nurse to follow it.

Some give us other commands:

"I don't want the IV until I am asleep!"

"I am leaving my dentures in!"

Then there are those who won't stop talking. God help you if you are pressed for time, and you get a garrulous one.

"So, have you had any problems during an anesthetic?"

"Doc, you wouldn't believe what happened in 1963, just after I came back from the war. Have you heard of Vietnam? Kate, how old was Emily then?"

My favorite ones are those with a sense of humor, the older patients with very interesting lives, and the old ladies who think I'm cute as a button. Again - don't hate!

I love to ask the older couples how long they've been married. Some of the answers are impressive. The record so far is 69 years. Is amazing how these old couples dote on each other. So, so heartwarming.

Then are the frankly scared-out-of-their-minds patients. The interesting bit is how each of them expresses their fear – flat affect, weepy, hostile, demanding, talkative, direct, unfriendly. Whatever the form of expression of this fear, you can see it in their eyes. It has that get-me-out of-here look. It is really easy to chalk it up to the patient being a horrible person. In my case, I could always pull out the race card. However, I think it's in those instances one should stop being a doctor and be a fellow human being. It is in those moments one should lose the impersonal tone and warm up to the patient. Break the ice.

I am rather direct and go, "You look worried. What is bothering you?" or "You look totally scared. Want to run away?"

The reactions are interesting. I always get a torrent - of

tears or words. The men are tougher to crack. You know us. We need to be tough and all.

Once the torrent starts, I just listen or wait with a box of tissues until they finish crying and then listen.

Listen to their fears. Listen. As you do, don't be disdainful, even if their fears sound silly to you.

Call up all the empathy you have. When they are done, try to explain in lay terms why each fear is realistic or not. If it is realistic, tell them what the surgical and anesthesia teams do to prevent such misfortune(s) from happening. A little expression of humanity is way better than any anxiolytic you can order for the patient, believe me.

A surgical procedure is very scary for most patients. It is at a time in one's life where one is totally at the mercy of other people (air travel offers a similar situation). These "I-am-at-their-mercy" people are supposed to be experts, but how good are they really? Are they rested enough? How many of these procedures have they done? A patient is supposed to have asked all these questions at the surgeon's office but for some, their fears were not allayed enough.

There is that element of chance. What if something goes wrong?

Then there are those facing terminal illness or the possibility of a terminal diagnosis.

Is it a surprise some patients are scared out of their wits?

We are doctors, highly trained in the art of healing. That is our job. We are pressed for time. We have to leave emotion out of it. Beyond all that, we are also humans. So are the patients. Sometimes, these patients want to see that human. Show it to them.

The Five Senses and You

"Half of us are blind, few of us feel, and we are all deaf." — *Sir William Osler[92]*

This incident occurred in my third or fourth year of medical school in Leipzig (outside the U.S., most medical schools are six-year programs). We were on a medical-surgical (med-surg) floor one afternoon with one of our instructors for a session on the physical exam. Before we went off to terrorize our patients, he warned us to pay attention and observe. He asked us not to be too distracted by what the patients said — to listen but also to watch. To use all five senses.

I marched off to my patient — a woman in her sixties who was in the hospital with an unknown-to-me cardiac condition. My job was to talk to her, examine her, and figure out her condition and the cause. The patients are usually asked by the instructors beforehand not to divulge their diagnoses.

Well, my patient was as garrulous as they come. She thought I was the cutest thing she ever saw, and I allowed her to pinch me cheek and pull my hair (I had a 'fro then!). Soon, she told me what her ailment was— atrial fibrillation (a condition where the heart beats irregularly) — and all the medicines she was on. Well, who was I to complain? I had my diagnosis and treatment. I stepped

---

[92]Osler, William, et al. *Sir William Osler Aphorisms. Iwanami Publishing Service Center*, 2001.

out, feeling like the second coming of Hippocrates. I had totally forgotten why I was in the room in the first place.

I presented my patient to my instructor, who promptly asked me what the cause of her atrial fibrillation (A-fib) was. Having neglected to examine her, I promptly responded it was idiopathic, a fancy term for "I don't know." He asked me to list the causes of A-fib, which I did. He asked me if the lady could have hyperthyroidism (an overactive thyroid gland and a cause of A-fib). I said no.

At this point, most of the other students were back. He introduced my case to the group and asked me to lead the group to my patient's room. The instructor was a tall man, and he was right behind me when I opened the door to the patient's room. From the door, one saw the patient resting in bed and she turned her head to look at us as we entered. From about 12 feet away, one could see the goiter (a large swollen thyroid gland) bobbing in her neck. I wanted to vanish!

It's a lesson I've never forgotten — to observe, to watch, to feel, to smell, and to listen. Do I do it well or all the time? Of course not, but I try.

The power of observation is as important to the practice of medicine as the power of taste is to a chef. A doctor needs to be able to notice that jaundiced skin, that throbbing mass in the abdomen, those engorged veins in the neck, those blue lips, the child who is always squatting instead of playing, those trembling fingers, that deviated tongue, that strange gait.

We need to listen to the patients' answers, but above all know what to ask. We need to examine patients and really listen to those breathing sounds and make out those murmurs. We need to be able to smell those almonds on a patient's breath.

The practice of observing the patient has been dealt a serious blow by the use of technology in medicine. In this age of CT Scans and MRIs, why even bother? Why not let technology do all the work? An echo will soon tell you if the patient has valvular disease, so why does one need to know what aortic stenosis sounds like?

First, it makes one a better doctor because it forces one to be interested in that human in front of him or her. You have to be truly interested in another person to observe them closely.

It also saves time and money. It cuts down on the number of useless tests. Sure, we do a lot of tests to cover our butts (Defensive Medicine) — but there are also cases where a good physical exam makes a huge difference.

Furthermore, it gives one a better picture of the patient. One may pick up other ailments the patient may not even know about.

Our colleagues who practice in developing countries will tell you most times, all you have are your five senses.

(At this point, a shout out to all the doctors in Ghana and to two esteemed colleagues — one who spends half his time working in Haiti and the other who volunteers with Doctors Without Borders.)

Recently, the practice of observation has been dealt another blow. Since electronic medical record-keeping became mandatory in most medical practices and hospitals, I often take time to observe other colleagues and nurses working. It is a sad sight. One sees extremely well-trained and dedicated professionals observing not the patient, but a screen. A culture that already suffered from a lack of observing the patient has been worsened by the need to chart electronically.

Then is the notion the practice of medicine is nothing but a series on protocols and best practices, and the best results are obtained when everyone sticks to these protocols and best practices. Well, the jury is still out on the wisdom and effectiveness of that. As most practitioners will tell you, no two patients or two cases are ever the same.

Finally, just the volume of patients one has to deal with plus production pressure make it sometimes very challenging to really observe well.

I look on in despair and wonder what William Osler would say if he was alive today. He aptly once wrote: "Learn to see, learn to hear, learn to feel, learn to smell, and know that by practice alone can you become expert."

We have all become experts, but are we in the process forgetting how to see, hear, feel, and smell? If we do forget, what kind of experts do we become then? I wonder; I really do...

You Are Because of What You Do

Human nature...a very interesting thing indeed.

After working with people for a while, one starts noticing little things that tend to be intriguing and interesting.

Who we are is a function of a lot of things, including our character, upbringing, and environment.

However, is there also the chance that we are what we do?

Let me explain by asking a question:

Would the stern demeanor a teacher has to assume around rowdy elementary school children every single day soon translate into a stern bearing?

In dealing with patients, I tend to notice certain tendencies that are peculiar to certain professions. Now, the following descriptions are purely observational and are not backed by any kind of science. These observations are also in no way a form a profiling, because they do not have any bearing on how I treat them. I just wonder if they somehow support the claim that you are what you do.

So, let's get started.

I have noticed patients who are teachers still maintain that stern demeanor even when facing surgery and anesthesia. Facing a teacher, I always feel like I forgot my homework. They seem to have assumed control, and I come across as being there to do their bidding. Even when they are asleep, they still look and exude that teacher look! It is an interesting dynamic.

Accountants offer a very straightforward kind of effect. Much like, "You are the doctor, I am the patient. You have the obligation to take care of me, so do your job already and stop the chit-chat!" If they are nervous, they never show it. It's almost like business as usual. I have had a few auditors as patients as well, and they seem to be a level more intense.

With lawyers, one always has the feeling like they are circling the wagons, looking, sniffing, ready to pounce. Almost like, "A-ha! I'll see you in court!" Everything one says to them is weighted, compared, and balanced against the scales of something unseen.

Veterans are an amazing bunch. (The few left from World War II and the Korean War are in a special class of awesome!) Describing them as stoic is an understatement. Most times, I expect them to say, "Doc, I don't need anesthesia for that amputation. Give me a shot of bourbon and a bullet to bite on!" If one ever asked, I wouldn't know where to get a bullet at the hospital. I wonder if the pharmacy stocks them.

Staying with the military, drill sergeants are a special breed. They cannot help just instilling fear wherever they are. At least in me they do. I always feel like I have to drop and give them 50.

Cops, firemen, and soldiers are sort of stoic to a level too, but not as much as veterans. They almost exude the feeling, "I need to be out there, so please hurry up!"

Probably the most challenging group to take care of are patients who are in the medical field. Those who do not work in the perioperative setting are the most interesting. A short read-up on the kinds of anesthetics and practices out there 24 hours before surgery is often enough for these colleagues to dub themselves specialists in anesthetic care. Some demands are, well, interesting.

"Are you going to do a spinal for my thyroidectomy?"

"Huh?"

Most of us in medicine tend to be attentive to detail and want to be in charge. Well, we seem not to be able to let go in the perioperative phase too.

So, what do my unscientific and probably biased observations really show? Do they support my initial claim that we are what we do? Probably not, but these observations show humans are a diverse bunch; hence, the reactions to the same set of conditions will vary widely. Whether what someone does affects how they react may well be true, but a real study may be needed to figure that out.

In the meantime, I'll keep adding to my observational sample size by listening to my patients, calming down their fears, and giving them the best care, I can.

Don't we all?

What if...?

Like life, the practice of medicine is filled with the highs and lows, the moments of heartbreak and the euphoria of success, times of hair-pulling (if one has any) frustration, and uplifting encouragement.

Losing a patient unexpectedly is very traumatic. It happens to every doctor, and it is a pipe dream to think it will never happen to you. Yes, some specialties are less prone to experience it than others. However, when it does happen, most physicians have no one to talk to. Fellow physicians are the worst group of people to seek solace from. The majority have their own professional and personal issues.

Then is the judgmental bit: "If you had done A instead of B, maybe..."

Which leaves our significant others, the majority of whom have already been overburdened with medical talk to the point where they are insensitive and frankly do not care anymore.

And then is there the small issue of, "Anything you say can be used against you when the family sues you!"

Would it not be great if there was a "listening ear" for physicians in such times? I am thinking a 1-800 number one could call to unload the disappointment and pain. Say 1-800-I-LISTEN.

A physician could call and talk anonymously about the

death one had in the operating room (or emergency room or cardiac catheterization suite or floor). About facts like: the team did all it could; the patient had undiagnosed SAM or carcinoid or an unknown tight left main; you were in the operating room for 15 hours; you bonded with the patient, his wife gave you a hug, and his kids shook your hand; the malignancy was inoperable. It would give us a chance to talk about all those things we are supposed to keep inside because we are supermen — but really aren't.

What if you could just open up without fear of judgment or medico-legal action?

What if...?

Then are those times where one out of pure frustration wishes to yell or scream or throw something.

My surgical colleagues, can I get an Amen?

Yet, you cannot yell or swear or throw anything. It is unprofessional and creates a hostile work environment. It is absolutely disrespectful to the team busting their chops to make it happen.

You may have done it in the good old days, but we are in 2016 and that kind of behavior will get you in trouble quickly. However, every doctor has had a day where frustration rolled down like waters and impediments like a mighty stream. Where that surgeon didn't understand that blocks sometimes don't work; where that anesthesiologist cancelled that case even though the best cardiologist in town "cleared the patient"; where that cardiologist wants you to do that CABG today and not on Monday; where you are stuck in the OR because the PACU is full; where you find out some administrator decided to pull your favorite suture or antibiotic because it's too expensive; when you have to work with that scrub tech you cannot stand...the list goes on.

You want to scream and yell and call someone names that would make Tony Montana wince, don't you? You want to do that because long before you became a doctor, you were a human with emotions and long after you cannot practice anymore, you will still be that human! And humans get frustrated and sometimes, just sometimes, want to yell and scream and hop up and down on one leg and then the other.

So, won't it be great if there was a Scream Room?

"Scream Room?" you're probably wondering. "What is a Scream Room?"

The Scream Room would be a soundproof room somewhere in the hospital where one could go and scream and throw things of one's choice for as long as one wanted to let out pent-up frustration. One could use as many four-letter words as one wanted and jump up and down like Rumpelstiltskin if one wished to.

The room would also have a 100-pound punching bag hanging from the ceiling. There would be boxing gloves available. One only has to pin a picture of the cause of one's ire on the bag, don appropriate size boxing gloves, and punch away.

What if there was such a room?

What if...?

Like I wrote earlier, before we become doctors, we were humans. Humans are strong but can also be weak. They can be wise, but sometimes folly reigns supreme. They can be patient and understanding, but occasionally brash and irritable. It's only in accepting our strengths and weaknesses that we become whole. Whole humans. Whole doctors.

What You Do Afterwards

"To err is human, to forgive, divine." — *Alexander Pope, from An Essay on Criticism.*

Probably, the most important lesson I learned in all of residency can be summed up in these words:

"It's not the mistake! It's what you do afterwards that matters."

These words have accompanied me all these years. I practice by them, taught that to my residents when I was in academics, and pass it on any chance I get. It is not only true in medicine, but also in the criminal justice system and even at home with our children and spouses. For this discussion though, we'll stick to medicine.

To elucidate, we have to take a trip back to 1999.

"To Err is Human: Building a Safer Health System" was a report issued in 1999 by the U.S. Institute of Medicine that detailed medical errors in the U.S. healthcare system and the human as well as financial toll it was exacting.[93] The figures were sobering. Between 44,000 to 98,000 people die each year as a result of preventable medical errors. They have been estimated to result in total costs of between $17 billion and $29 billion per year in hospitals

---

[93]*Institute of Medicine (US) Committee on Quality of Health Care in America; Kohn LT, Corrigan JM, Donaldson MS, editors. Washington (DC): National Academies Press (US); 2000.*

nationwide!

It was pointed out in the report that system failures rather than individual provider mistakes were responsible for most medical errors. The push since the report was issued has been to reduce medical errors and improve patient safety, and the results have been encouraging.

However, the fact remains physicians are only human and like the saying goes, "To err is human..." — and that is where my lesson comes into play.

Sooner or later, every physician is going to make a mistake. Show me a physician who hasn't made a mistake before, and I'll show you a doctor who hasn't practiced long enough or doesn't practice at all.

So, if we are prone to make mistakes, shouldn't there be a readiness to face and deal with these errors when they happen? Beyond the checklists and time-outs, beyond the constant threat of loss of accreditation and fines, shouldn't we as physicians on an individual level be ready to deal with mistakes?

That mentality of, "It's not the mistake! It's what you do afterwards that matters," takes away the fear that dogs someone when a mistake is made. It makes one communicate clearly with the patient if possible and explain what happened and what will be done. It allows one to keep a level head and work alone or with a team to reverse or limit any damage. It also reduces the incidence of lawsuits.

This mentality demands something from the physician. It demands a certain honesty and strength of character.

One should be able to say, "I screwed up. Now how do I fix it?"

It demands empathy with the patient à la, "If it were me..."

I know it is much easier to sweep things under the rug of unintelligible medical speak or blame someone else, but that only stokes the fire of trouble down the road and possible harm to the patient.

To help develop this mentality, a mantra that was drummed into me during residency helps.

It was, "What is the worst thing that can happen now, and what would you do about it?"

With that kind of mindset, one tends to be prepared for whatever happens — but most importantly, one tries to prevent that whatever from happening. One tends to see all those checklists on a personal level, and that readiness on a personal level ultimately translates to one on the team level too.

Most physicians do as Hippocrates said and try do no harm. However, since humans are plagued by fallibility, maybe accepting that and factoring it into our daily practice might help.

So even as you go about your day, remember, "It's not the mistake; it's what you do afterwards that matters."

Keep It Simple

Back in 1998, I heard a trauma surgeon talk about communicating with patients. His words have stayed with me all these years.

The gist of his message was:

Physicians are as a group, are highly educated. A lot of the patients we deal with do not understand medicine, surgery, anatomy, or physiology like we do. If we need to explain a procedure, the need for it or a disease process to a patient, we need to keep it simple.

Now that coming from a surgeon is deep!

It's one of those things I've never forgotten. To keep it simple.

One can tell a patient:

"I am going to place a central line in your right internal jugular, float a pulmonary artery catheter, and also place an arterial line in your left radial artery. You need that for your aortic valve replacement."

Or one can say:

"To better take care of you during your operation, I need to place a larger IV in that vein in the right side of your neck. It helps us give you blood faster if you need it. Also, we feed a tube through it into your heart that helps us measure how much blood is being pumped in and out. You also need a better way of measuring your blood pressure. Feel your left wrist. Feel that pulse? That is an artery. I'll put a small tube in there that will help measure your blood pressure better."

Sure, the latter takes longer — but you don't have a patient who stares at you after you are done speaking like you just dropped from Pluto! We must all try to talk to patients in terms that are understandable to them. Terms we take for granted may sound like Greek to most lay people. Even a term as simple as "colonoscopy" has befuddled some patients.

Some steps that help me are:

I imagine explaining a procedure or even a disease process to one of my older uncles or aunties or to my kids. I break it down to a level they can understand.

I use diagrams that I sketch. I find drawing out the anatomy and pointing structures out and what is going to be done helps immensely. A lot of patients in Kentucky believe epidurals are the number one cause of paralysis in the world. A small drawing of the layers a needle goes through to reach the epidural space and its relationship to the spinal cord helps allay a lot of fears.

I encourage questions. If a patient can repeat what you said and base a question on that, your work is done.

Do not look at patients with disdain. It is not their fault

that they do not understand what a myxomatous mitral valve is. I bet you do not know what Capital Structure Theory is either. A degree of empathy is needed to understand where patients are coming from. Without that empathy, it is difficult to relate to patients and explain things at a level they can understand.

That Nagging Feeling

"When you reach the end of what you should know, you will be at the beginning of what you should sense." — *Kahlil Gibran, from Sand and Foam.*

Some years back, a colleague asked for my opinion on a patient he was getting ready to anesthetize for coronary artery bypass grafts. Something about the patient bothered him. About a week earlier, said patient developed chest pain while helping his daughter move. A visit to the ER led to diagnosis of acute coronary syndrome. Soon, he was on a table in the cardiac catheterization lab where he was found to have three-vessel disease and scheduled for surgery.

Preoperatively, even though he was not having any chest pain, no shortness of breath, or EKG changes, something about his affect bothered my colleague. I took a look at the patient and concurred his affect was weird. There was just something we couldn't put our fingers on.

The patient was wheeled back into the operating room. Before the surgery started, my colleague placed defibrillator pads on the patient. There was no rhyme or reason for him to do that, but he did it anyway.

Well, guess what happened during the induction of anesthesia? The patient went into ventricular fibrillation! With the pads in place, he was shocked out of it and resuscitated. He went on to have his surgery and did well, allowing my colleague to look like the hero that he was.

That nagging feeling! Anyone who has been in patient care long enough has had it. Nurses and doctors alike. It is called intuition. A hunch. I favor the definition of the Oxford Living Dictionaries which is: "Intuition is a thing that one knows or considers likely from instinctive feeling rather than conscious reasoning."

As in the above scenario, instinctive feeling rather than conscious reasoning informed the decision to place defibrillator pads. I could give several truer scenarios.

Even though almost every physician has these episodes, the majority do not talk about them. How could we? Beside sounding like one wears tin-foil hats, insurance companies do not pay for decisions based on intuitions and most hospital boards do not take kindly to care based on hunches. So, we keep these hunches to ourselves and may occasionally base a clinical decision on it. It does not mean one always makes decision based on hunches. NO! These are rare occasions when something tugs at someone over a case that cannot be explained by the evidence.

In most situations, clinicians do not pay attention to their intuition. The inclination to act on a hunch increases as the outcome of a case or the prognosis for a patient worsens. In cases where death is imminent, clinicians have been known to act on intuition as acts of last resort, sometimes saving the day.

A group of physicians who use intuition quite often are older colleagues and family practitioners. I remember my days practicing with an older family practitioner (Dr. M) in Berlin. We had a diabetic patient whose blood sugar levels were uncontrollable. She seemed to take her meds and swore she followed her diet. We wanted to have her admitted, but she wouldn't hear of it.

One afternoon after lunch, Dr. M asked me to take a walk with him. We soon found ourselves before the door of an apartment about two miles away. From outside, we smelled freshly baked cake. Dr. M rang the bell. The diabetic patient opened the door and the smell of cake hit us in the face. The minute she saw us, she got this silly look on her face. We had our diagnosis from the hunch of an older colleague.

So, where do these hunches come from? It seems to be a function of age and experience.

In Mind over machine: The power of human intuition and expertise in the era of the computer, Dreyfus and Dreyfus wrote:

"The novice practitioner is characterized by rigid adherence to taught rules or plans, little situational perception; and no discretionary judgement.

The competent practitioner is able to cope with 'crowdedness' and pressure, sees actions partly in terms of long-term goals or wider conceptual framework; and follows standardized and routinized procedures.

The expert practitioner no longer relies explicitly on rules, guidelines, and maxims, has an intuitive grasp of situations based on deep, tacit understanding; and uses analytic approaches only in novel situations or when problems occur." (T. Greenhalgh, British Journal of General Practice, May 2002)."

There is also the factor of empathy — being able to understand one's patients and sense their needs. That is also often a function of time and experience.

So, what is one to do? I think one should not disregard these hunches. How one handles these hunches will definitely spend on the specialty. As anesthesiologists, I recommend finding a colleague who believes in intuition and running your thoughts by him or her. Often, they can offer another perspective. If the intuition demands a procedure that is not too invasive or expensive or will not delay or prolong care, one may consider doing it. It is surely another story if it could lead to say, a case for a surgery getting cancelled.

It is definitely possible to weave evidence-based medicine and clinical intuition to give the best care. If the majority of us aren't doing it, then maybe we should.

A Tincture of Time

"When things don't please you, the best medicine is to swallow a little tincture of time." — *Ken Alstad, from Savvy Sayin's.*

To make a tincture, one uses mainly alcohol to extract those chemicals from a plant that are deemed beneficial. The practice of making tinctures is a very old practice.

In the 16th century, Paracelsus found that alcohol did a much better job at getting opiates into solution than water and with that Laudanum or the tincture of opium was born.

Up until the 19th century, the tincture of opium was used to treat almost every ailment known to man — from coughing, diarrhea, and pain all the way to insomnia and menstrual cramps. In Victorian times, a bottle of laudanum was cheaper than a bottle of gin! As one would guess, there were many laudanum addicts, among them, First Lady of the U.S. Mary Todd Lincoln and the English poet Samuel Taylor Coleridge[94]

In light of the sequelae of addiction, more and more physicians started recommending not using laudanum for every ailment but to just watch and wait. So, instead of a tincture of opium, the patients were treated with a tincture of time.

---

[94] Cock-Starkey, Clare. *"The Lure of Laudanum, the Victorians' Favorite Drug."* Mental Floss, 29 Nov. 2016, mentalfloss.com/article/89268/lure-laudanum-victorians-favorite-drug.

And thus, was born the phrase, "A Tincture of Time."

In these hectic times of medical practice, falling reimbursements, demanding administrations, a population of discerning patients, the internet, and social media, can a physician even dare to recommend or even consider a tincture of time?

I dare to say, yes! That old prescription is as effective today as it was in the heady days of laudanum.

I see it borne out daily in my practice as a cardiac anesthesiologist. I put patients who need all manners of heart surgery to sleep, so a heart surgeon can work his magic. Most heart surgeries are facilitated by the heart-lung-machine (cardiopulmonary bypass or CPB), a machine that takes over the pumping and oxygenation of blood as the heart gets fixed and blood is diverted away from it and the lungs. The beating of the heart is also stopped with a solution quite high in potassium (cardioplegia).

After repairing what needs to be repaired in the heart, the potassium solution is washed out of the heart, the heart resumes its pumping action, and it's made to assume its function as it's gradually separated from the heart-lung-machine.

All hearts are not the same. Some hearts have, despite their diseases, maintained optimal pumping function. Others not so much. Once these sicker hearts are taken through the rigors of surgery, cardioplegia, and CPB, their willingness and ability to resume their intrinsic pumping function takes a huge hit. These poorly functioning hearts have to be supported to help them regain their function. One way is to assist these hearts with a drug like epinephrine (adrenaline) that gets these poor pumps going again.

Another way is, you guessed, the tincture of time.

I cannot profess my wonder at how many times I've watched a poor, ailing heart, sitting all alone in the open chest, struggling to beat again and being given time, finally do just that. I cannot express my amazement enough at those hearts that I thought had no chance, come back like Cinderella in March. All these poor hearts needed was time. A tincture of it.

We as physicians always feel we need to treat. Patients need to feel like something is being done. Do we always need to prescribe that antibiotic? Those opioids? That back surgery? Those expensive tests? Do we? Could it be that if we let things be, time would fix it? Could it be that maybe what a patient needs is just a tincture of time? Your time?

Practicing as a GP in Berlin many years ago, I learned one thing. Most patients were not really sick. They didn't want any medications or EKGs. All they really wanted was a tincture of my time. A tincture of my attention, so they could share what was on their hearts and minds.

I am not advocating not doing anything in the face of real pathology. Of course not. I'll be the first to give you a lecture on taking care of yourself. However, in those instances where time is the best option, are we able to recognize that?

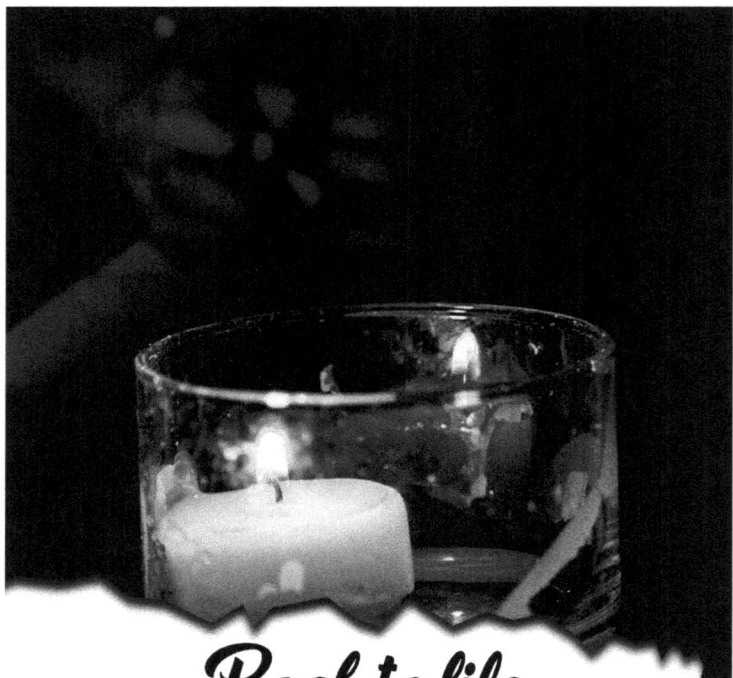

Back to life

"I seem to have run in a great circle and met myself again on the starting line."
— *Jeanette Winterson,*
from Oranges Are Not the Only Fruit

Back to Life

A Short Story

I did not survive the stroke.

A big clot occluded the blood supply to the left side of my brain one night, a few months shy of my 81st birthday. Death was sudden, and my wife found my cold body beside her the next morning.

By then I was walking down this long, white corridor that was very well-lit. There were hundreds of us walking down that path. I do not even know how I got there. One minute I was sleeping by my wife, the next minute I was in a white corridor. There was just this sense of peace that pervaded my being or whatever was left of it.

I looked around as we walked and that is when I noticed another corridor to my right. There were people walking down that corridor too, but in the opposite direction. I wondered where they were going. Then I wondered where the hundreds of us walking down that hallway were going.

Suddenly, everyone started branching off into little cubicles to either the side of the hallway. It felt like each person was attracted to a particular doorway and cubicle. It was fascinating to watch. Soon, I found myself enter one of those cubicles too. The door closed behind me.

Inside was a rather comfortable looking bed. I lay down and felt the need to close my eyes. As I did, I saw a pregnant woman enter a hospital. The next scene showed her in labor. I looked at her again. She was my mother. She delivered a baby boy. I saw the baby grow up to be me. I continued watching as my life played up before me. It ended with me dying that night beside my wife. Funny enough, there was no sadness watching the playback of my life — but a persistent and deep sense of peace.

I opened my eyes to see the door reopen. I felt the urge to get up and walk through the door into another hallway. I looked around me. I was alone this time.

The man with the piercing dark eyes appeared beside me out of the blue. If he surprised me, I did not show it.

"Welcome back," he said.

"Thank you," I replied.

A door opened ahead of us and we entered a large room with a table and two chairs on either side. He sat in one and signaled me to sit in the other.

"How do you think you did?" the man with the piercing dark eyes asked me.

"I made the most of the opportunities I had," I answered.

"Did you learn any lessons?"

"A lot of them."

"What was the most important lesson you learned?"

I thought for a minute about all the life lessons I had accumulated in my 80 years of life.

"Nothing lasts forever," I finally replied.

I swear I saw a smile flash across his face.

"Did you discover any talents?" he asked.

That question threw me. It brought to mind the exhortations of my dad to use my musical talents. It reminded me of my artistic abilities I never really explored...

"Yes, I did," I responded — haltingly.

"Did you use any of them?" he asked.

"Not really."

"Why not?"

"Well, I worked hard to get a good education, so I could get a good job and be able to provide for my family — which I did," I pointed out.

"So how come both your kids were not talking to you?" he asked.

That question threw me.

I believed in working hard, keeping your eye on the ball,

and not taking it off for the frivolities of life. My parents had been poor so as I got older, I resolved not to end up like them. I guess that made me a bit harsh and unyielding.

I thought my son should have become a doctor. He wanted to be a sculptor and defied me to become that. We had not talked to each other in years. I did not want my daughter to marry the man she did. That was after she refused to do corporate law and instead became a public defender after law school. I talked to her maybe once a year.

"We saw life differently," I finally replied.

That is when he smiled.

"They wanted to explore the talents they had been given. You wanted them to work hard, save money, and live comfortably," he said.

I nodded.

Suddenly, I could see my son. He was with a group of inner-city kids, working on a large sculpture in a park. The look on the kids' faces exuded pure joy. Then my daughter appeared. She was reading a newspaper. The story was about her. She had just got a man freed who was in jail for a murder he did not commit. She looked so happy.

The images vanished.

"You worked hard and made a lot of money. What did you do with it?" the man asked.

"My wife and I traveled. We used to travel with the kids. We lived well," I answered.

He lifted his eyes and stared at me, his look piercing.

Then he launched into a speech:

"Each time you are given life and made human, you are given a set of talents to help you learn a lesson or lessons. Each lesson learned helps you grow towards immortality at which point there is no more need for life as a human. You are repeatedly failing to learn the lesson that you are meant to learn. Life is short which make it precious. Each minute on Earth should be used towards leaning the needed lesson or lessons. It almost always involves exploring your given talents. They lead you to the lesson or lessons.

The demands of life can obscure the need to tap into your talents and learn these lessons — but that is no excuse.

You disregarded every help that was sent your way to prod you to explore your talents. Your parents, your best friend growing up, all your girlfriends, your wife, your business partners, and your children.

So, you have to go back to learn those lessons."

I gasped.

"Back to life? Start all over again? Childhood, teenage years, adulthood, kids...oh no!", I exclaimed.

"O yes! Do not worry — you won't remember your previous life," he said.

"Do I get to pick where I go?"

"No!"

Suddenly, that sense of peace was gone, replaced by a raging turmoil of fear, foreboding, and sadness. It raged like a fire.

"Is this my hell?" I asked.

He looked at me again with those piercing eyes and said, "You can call it what you want."

Then he was gone as quickly as he appeared.

I looked around the room.

Images appeared again. I was watching my funeral and listening to what my wife, kids, and friends were saying about me.

I heard "harsh" and "not compassionate." I heard "hard-working," "wealthy," "disciplined," and "principled."

It struck me that I never heard the word "love."

I felt sad.

The images vanished as soon as the room began to move. Then I started moving too. Slowly, I drifted into a hallway. It looked familiar. It looked like the one that I had been walking down not too long ago. There were hundreds of people in there with me. I looked to my right and saw another hallway. Those in that hallway were walking in the opposite direction.

It slowly sank in.

They were the souls returning to learn their fate.

We were the souls going back with the gift of life to learn lessons to help us reach immortality.

I prayed that this time around, I would be able to learn that lesson or those lessons.

About 4 months later
Kumasi, Ghana

Kwame Andoh and his wife Essie were at the gynecologist. Afia lay on the stretcher, belly exposed and covered with ultrasound jelly. The doctor moved the probe around, speaking as she did.

"Mrs. Andoh, you have a healthy baby boy in there. Congratulations! I see no defects this time," she said.

Essie started weeping silently, tears of joy rolling down her pretty, chocolate-brown face. Finally! A child! She had miscarried twice in the first month each time. Then two years ago, she carried the baby until the third month only to find out that he had so many birth defects that he would not survive after birth. She decided to carry it anyway, only for her to have a stillbirth. Now, finally, a healthy-looking fetus. She kept crying.

Her husband Kwame took her head in his hands and wiped away her tears with a handkerchief. He was tearing up too.

Somewhere in another realm, a man with dark, piercing eyes was smiling to himself. He wished them and their soon-to-be son well. Then he went back to see to those souls returning...and decide who got to stay and who needed to go back to life.

Walking Away

*"One day you will ask me which is more important? My life or yours?
I will say mine and you will walk away not knowing that you are my
life."* — **Kahlil Gibran, from The Treasured Writings of
Kahlil Gibran.**

We all need to walk away sometimes. From that bad
relationship, that god-awful job, that half-baked deal, or
even that date from hell. The choice we have to walk away
from these negative scenarios signifies our independence,
sense of self-worth, and announces to the other party that
we think we deserve better. It also helps us to grow because
we hopefully move on to a better relationship, find a nicer
job, negotiate a better deal, or go on better dates — thus
improving our lives. The inability to walk away from these
adverse conditions restricts our happiness and impedes
our growth.

At times, unlike in the previous examples, we have no
choice but to walk if we want to stay alive. I think of the
woman who flees an abusive marriage in the middle of the
night, passengers disembarking in a hurry from a plane
that crash-landed, or a family evacuating a home in flames.
In all these cases, the people have to walk away. They really
have no choice. It did not matter what they were leaving
behind — lives and limbs were in danger and those were all
that mattered.

Then are those times that we do not want to walk away but
have to. Those are moments when walking away breaks our
hearts and tears a hole in our souls...

The year was probably 2000, I was still in residency, dreaming of becoming a pediatric anesthesiologist. The boy was eight-years-old. He choked on peanuts, could not get air for several minutes, and ended up with irreversible brain damage.

When a peanut accidentally ends up in the airways, it absorbs the moisture from that milieu and swells up, occluding the passage for air. This is especially notable in children. It also releases acids that lead to inflammation, worsening the picture. If the peanut is stuck in the trachea of a child, brain damage can ensue quickly, even with help. Attempts to fish out the peanut by endoscopy often lead to the peanut crumbling and the pieces just worsen the picture.

The parents agreed to donate his organs and he was brought into the operating room for the harvesting procedure. Even though the brain at that point is dead, the body can be supported to maintain the other organs in a viable state. Thus, he got anesthetic care until blood flow to the heart was clamped off to allow the heart to be removed. At that point, I turned the respirator off and walked away.

Now you should note this very important fact — an anesthesia provider never walks away from a patient. We only do if another provider relieves us or we drop off the patient, awake or still sedated, in the Post Anesthesia Care Unit or an Intensive Care Unit. We never walk away. I walked away. He was eight. I found an empty restroom to lock myself in and cry.

I also walked away from my dreams of ever becoming a pediatric anesthesiologist.

Dad died 10 years ago. I "zombied" through the funeral ceremonies, not wanting to believe and refusing to accept the fact that he was gone for good. After all, every time I looked at his face, he wore than tranquil look. We buried him on a Sunday after mass. I stood around the grave with the family as the coffin slowly descended down into that gaping hole. Even then, I refused to accept it. I continued in my denial as the dirt hit the coffin and that hole quickly filled up.

As we turned to leave, my brother Kojo remarked, "So, we are really leaving Dad in there!"

That is when it hit me. We were walking away from our Dad. We had no choice. It tore a hole in my heart, but we continued walking.

Walking away is protective. We all need to do is sometime. We may hate to on occasion, but it is the only way to say goodbye to someone we love dearly. Sometimes, that is all death leaves us — a quiet and heavy-hearted walk away.

Yet, are there times when we really cannot walk away?

I had this question on my mind this morning when I went to Kroger. When I got to the check-out, I noticed the young man packing the groceries was rather slow. His eyes looked blood-shot and swollen. I watched as he absent-mindedly packed my groceries.

"So, when did it happen?" the cashier asked.

"Last night," the bagger replied.

"I am so sorry," the cashier said.

I got nosy.

"Lost a loved one?" I asked.

"Yes, my aunt," he said.

He was tearing up.

"I am sorry. Why didn't you stay home?" I asked.

He forced a smile.

"I need the money," he said wistfully

I could only maneuver, "It will be well. My condolences."
I helped him pack up my groceries.

So, sometimes, no matter how much we want to, we
cannot walk away. Then in spite of the pain and sorrow,
we stay and do what has to be done even as we cry silently
and hope the hole in our hearts will heal.

However, no matter the reason for walking away, we do it
to preserve life, save life, or even as we mourn the loss of a

life. And if we have to stay, we do so hoping for a day and hour when we can walk away. Hopefully by then, the hole has healed, and the soul is whole.

Lost Along the Way

"We've all lost something along the way." — *Po Bronson, a novelist.*

Invariably I will ask, "So how long have you been married?"

It always makes both of them smile, maybe recognizing the importance of the answer they are going to give me.

"Forty years!"

"Fifty years!"

"Sixty years!"

The longest I've heard so far is 80 years. That was an old couple! They were both in their 90s and the man held the hand of his sick wife with so much love and care, it touched my hopeless romantic soul.

I always congratulate these couples on such an amazing achievement and will sometimes ask what the secret was.

The answers have differed. The men usually say things like, "I did what I was told" or "I let her be the boss." The women will reply, "We still love each other." The one answer that I found to be an outlier was, "We never had kids."

In spite of the answers, I have never felt like meeting these amazing couples has taught me what the secret to a long and happy marriage is. Then earlier this week, I met two different couples who I think have brought me closer to an answer.

The first couple had been married for 60 years. They still finished each other sentences and laughed together at their stories. When the wife looked at the husband, there was genuine affection in her eyes and the husband just looked like he adored his wife of 60 years. They looked like they fell in love yesterday in high school.

I basked in the moment with them as they told me how they met and congratulated them on having such a beautiful bond.

Whenever I walk away from these older couples who have been married forever, I feel quite uplifted. It's an experience that droops with what is great about humanity. Marriage is not easy and to see two people who have done it for so long infects one with hope. So, I walked away, feeling grateful that I got to meet such an amazing couple.

About an hour later, I met the second couple. They were in their late forties and had been married less than five years. The both came from previous marriages that did not work out. They found each other and after dating for three years, decided to tie the knot.

As I talked to them, it struck me that they exhibited the same mannerisms of the couple that had been married for 60 years. They finished each other's sentences, looked lovingly at each other, and shared a certain joy that was remarkable.

It hit me that this younger couple was exhibiting the same traits as the older couple.

I congratulated them and left but could not chase the two meetings out of my mind.

The more I thought of it, the more I had a nagging feeling that I might be on to something.

Once, a wife from one of those long-lasting marriages told me their secret was that they had stayed friends all these years.

In looking back at the two couples from earlier this week, I thought they really liked each other.

They treated each other as lovers, but more so as friends.

Could it be that in marriages that last a lifetime, the participants never lose their friendship?

Could it be that instead of treating each other as husband and wife they treat each other as friends?

Could this be the secret ingredient of the long marriage sauce?

We treat friends differently than our spouses — and sometimes we give friends more leeway than our spouses. From our spouses we may expect a lot more, are more judgmental, and less forgiving. On the other hand, we may be very forgiving of the foibles of our friends.

Maybe it is this very leeway, this ability to be forgiving, that gets lost in a lot of marriages. Perhaps those couples who stay married for so long learn to see their spouses as that good friend who they should accept for who he or she is. Could it be that these "marriage marathoners" never lose their friendship?

This sentiment is probably best elucidated by a quote that is attributed to the actress Marilyn Monroe, but whose source I cannot verify:

"Experts on romance say for a happy marriage there has to be more than a passionate love. For a lasting union, they insist, there must be a genuine liking for each other. Which, in my book, is a good definition for friendship."

The fire of passion burns out ultimately. Kids grow up and leave the home. The job or profession is not the answer. There should be something that a couple should be able to fall back on. Is this nothing else but good old friendship?

I will continue my probable hopeless search for that elixir that blesses us with long and happy marriages — but I have a feeling that when I do find it, friendship will be in that mix.

So, in the meantime instead of the proposal — "Will you be my wife?" — maybe men should fall on their knees and ask, "Can we be friends forever?" And once we have it, we should try not to lose that friendship along the way.

The Best Window into Our Souls

This is a theory I have been working on for a while, so bear with me.

We as humans are a potpourri of emotions, thoughts, ideals, intrigue, hopes, aspirations, dreams, and regrets. Most are able to hide all these sentiments behind a veil of normalcy and go about the chores of daily life. Others find it hard to mask the turmoil that boils in them and are sometimes seen as antisocial.

So, we plod through life, never really getting a full glimpse of what lies behind that veil as we try to conform and adjust ourselves to fit a norm. Those outside our immediate families and those we do not work with daily have a hard time knowing who we really are. Sometimes it takes years for people we are in a relationship with to figure us out.

Yet, there are occasions in life that tear through this veil and expose what lies behind. It's in those moments that those non-family members who have gotten really close to us get a sense of what makes us tick. It is on these occasions that one's personality really comes across. One such instance is at a time of illness. For example, if two people are dating, the way the man reacts to the woman getting seriously ill or vice versa says a lot about who they are. Empathy and compassion, the unwillingness to help, callousness, apathy, fear, strength, support, and/or kindness are all traits that become quite evident in such a moment.

Another such instance — and perhaps the most powerful — is when people make love.

I posit that the way a person makes love exposes one's true nature. Whether one is kind, greedy, controlling, mean, selfish, or a submissive pushover cannot be hidden during sex.

This is because in that act, two people are interacting at the most intimate and open level — and this removes all barriers that we subconsciously put up in daily life.

This pertains to both sexes and might actually cross cultures.

So, a Type A personality may not necessarily make love like a typical hard-driving, competitive, and overachieving man if underneath that veneer is a scared person who really wants to belong and seeks approval.

Conversely, the calm taciturn type might exhibit a strength and control in bed that is not evident in daily life because he was taught to mask his abilities.

We've all heard expressions about "the choir girl who is a tiger in the sack." Could this be a woman who tries to conform to the norms of society by being meek and mild, but shows her strength once it's time for intimacy?

Why does this even matter?

Well, as one enters into a relationship, there is always that question about the true character of one's partner. One might not fall ill at the start of a relationship, but sex is something that sooner or later will come up. If one can pay attention to how one's partner makes love, it might help in exposing the true nature of said partner and help in the decision-making process when it comes to making deeper commitments.

Yet, who has the wish or even strength to think of anything else when the rush of ecstasy breaks down the dam of our will? No one really.

However, when it's all over and you are reminiscing, just think back...Did he give or just take? Was he selfless or selfish? Was she submissive or took control? Was he gentle or brusque? Was she curious or stuck in her ways?

You see, the most pleasurable act known to the human may also be the best window into our souls.

The Bet

A Short Story

March 14, 2018

"However difficult life may seem, there is always something you can do and succeed at. It matters that you don't just give up." —Stephen Hawking in an Oxford University Union speech given in November 2016.

This piece is dedicated to the memory of Stephen Hawking, the amazing theoretical physicist who passed away earlier today at the age of 76.

What an inspiring life! May he RIP!

Stephen was alone in the compartment on the train. He sat with his eyes closed trying to recollect all that had happened but could not stand the overwhelming feeling the memories came with. The last 49 years had been especially challenging, but he had risen above all the hurdles that came his way.

The thought reminded him of that day many years ago when he sought them out. It was just before his departure to his new life. Even then, he knew what he was going to be. So, he sought them out to pick their brains.

He found Isaac, Galileo, Ernest, John, and Marie at the cafe where they almost always hung out.

He walked up to them and introduced himself.

"Hi! I am Stephen. I am heading out next week and plan to be a physicist. Any tips for me?" he asked.

Even then, he was confident, bordering on cocky.

"Beware of black holes," John replied.

They all laughed.

"Actually, I think I'll take a whack at those holes and develop some laws...like your laws," Stephen said, nodding at Isaac.

"Ah! We have a cocky lad here, don't we?" Isaac asked.

"Not cocky, just confident and quite smart," Stephen pointed out.

"You know there is a war out there right, young man?" Ernest asked him.

"I do, but I can thrive anywhere and in any circumstance. It's all in the mind," Stephen replied.

"Well, unless the Church threatens to take off your head in which your mind is," Galileo quipped.
They all laughed.

"Or maybe an apple will fall on my head and I'll figure black holes out," Stephen said.

That made Marie laugh, but Isaac frowned.

"I like this young man," Marie said.

"And I like you too, Mrs. Curie," Stephen said, blushing.

"Your brashness will only take you so far, my lad. You have to learn to stand on the shoulders of others and realize that the world out there can be unforgiving, even for someone as brilliant as you claim to be," Galileo advised.

"Thank you but I believe, like you all, all one needs is the mind. I bet that even if I was to lose all my limbs, I could still use only my mind to achieve greatness and answer a lot of questions that still dog the world of physics," Stephen said.

"That Is a wager I'll like to make," Isaac said, smiling.

"I'm in on it too," Ernest added.

"Count me in," Galileo added.

"You know what you wish for yourself now will happen out there in the world right?" Isaac asked Stephen.

"Yes, I am aware of that," Stephen replied.

"Young man, you do not have to do this. You do not have to prove anything to these old men," Marie cautioned.

"I agree with Marie. The fact that you believe in black holes warms my heart. Forget them and go out and conquer the world," John added.

Mrs. Curie, Father Michell, thank you — but I have already thrown down the gauntlet," Stephen said.

"You have one wish. You are going to use it to wish for a life without limbs and still achieve greatness only with your mind. If you fail, on your return, whenever that is, you'll be a page for a year. If you succeed, we'll serve you for a year," Isaac explained.

They shook hands over the bet.

The blaring horn of the train woke him up from his reverie. He was back. It had been 76 years, but he was back. He got up and headed for an exit. The train came to a stop and the doors opened. He gasped. Outside were hundreds of people.

He wondered what was going on, until he realized they were all there to greet him. They were all clapping.

He heard some whistles and one person call out with a German accent, "You showed those old men! You won the bet."

He looked over and it was Albert with his shock of white hair, smiling.

The crowd parted for him to walk out and everyone tried to shake his hand. He saw Dickens, Tolstoy, Bach, Leonardo, and even Cleopatra. The warriors were even there, looking grim, especially that African Shaka and Genghis.

Somehow, Albert found him in the crowd and steered him towards a big hall.

"First, you need to register and then we'll go and find them," Albert said.

Albert led him to the cafe. The same one he had met them in those many years ago in space time. Albert was effusive in his praise over the work he had done with black holes and his apparent horizon concept. Stephen nodded appreciatively.

"And today was my birthday," Albert added.

They found Isaac, Galileo, and Ernest in the same cafe. Marie and John were there too. John was so excited to see him. He hugged Stephen.

"Thank you for proving me right. I knew they existed," John said.

Stephen turned towards Marie and gave her a kiss on each cheek.

"Welcome back, Stephen, and well done. You made us all so proud — even those three grumpy losers," she said, laughing.

"Thank you and it is good to see you again," Stephen replied.

He turned towards the men he had made a bet with so many years ago.

"Welcome back, young Stephen," Galileo said.

"You did well," Ernest said.

"Show off," Isaac muttered under his breath.

"So, are you guys ready to be his personal servants?" Albert asked with glee.

"Shut up, Einstein! Why don't you go off and play a violin or something?" Isaac growled.

"Someone is touchy," Albert said.

"Isaac, Galileo, Ernest, good to see you again. It seems as if I won the bet, but I did not," Stephen said.

The men gasped.

"Of course, you did, so don't rub it in," Ernest said.

"Let him speak," Marie said.

"You were right," Stephen continued. "I learned to stand on the shoulders of others. I realized that the world out there could be unforgiving, even for someone as brilliant me. Only with the help of technology, the love of my wife and kids, and the help and support of a lot of people was I able to have the peace of mind to think. So, I did not achieve all this with my mind alone — but with the help of others. I guess one cannot be an island out there, no matter how brilliant one is."

"So, what are you saying?" Isaac asked.

"What I mean is, if you agree, the bet is off. I was able to be who I was because of who you were," Stephen said.

The clapping that erupted all around him made him spin around. That deserted cafe was now overflowing with physicists. He shook the hands of Isaac, Galileo, and Ernest. Then, he began to walk around the cafe shaking the hands of the men and women who paved the path on which he walked to glory.

The Cameras Are Rolling

March 18, 2018

On Friday, I watched "Three Billboards Outside Ebbing, Missouri."

A few hours ago, I watched "The Darkest Hour."

Both movies, though riveting, are great for slightly different reasons.

Now before I get to that, I must say that movies are the ultimate storytelling tool. A bibliophile might claim otherwise — but, in spite of my love of reading and books, a good movie is a really great experience. The mix of moving pictures, dialogue, and a matching soundtrack can really bring a story with all its characters to life.

The two elements that seems to make or break a movie is the one thing every writer or narrator knows — how good the story is and how it is told.

The first element is a function of the script. The last encompasses everything else — acting, directing, cinematography, the soundtrack, and so on.

So, I am always reminded of the movie that launched Spike Lee's career. The title was "She's Got to Have It" and he shot it in 1986 with four actors and an actress. The budget was about $175,000 and it grossed $17 million. It was all filmed at one location and has no frills — but the story of a very beautiful woman dating three men in Brooklyn is so compelling and well-told that it makes up for the lack of catchy visuals.

The story really matters and that is what makes "Three Billboards Outside Ebbing, Missouri" such a great movie.

Sure, Frances McDormand and Sam Rockwell give some compelling performances, but the story wins the day. I always marvel at the imagination of writers who twist stories around like pretzels and take moviegoers on a roller coaster of a journey with a nuanced narration. I just love it and wonder what goes on in such minds.

I want you to watch the movie, so I am not going to spoil it with any kind of synopsis.

"The Darkest Hour" on the other hand, is a movie about a historical occurrence and personality — how Winston Churchill guided the UK into World War II. What makes this movie so good is the acting of Gary Oldman, who plays Churchill. His acting is so compelling that it is the story of the movie! So, if the story is known, great acting is what takes a historical movie to the next level.

We may all not get the chance to make a feature film in Hollywood — but with our lives, we create a reel of action, missteps, bad decisions, love, hate, loss, and friendship that can rival the biggest blockbuster.

One thing people who have had near-death experiences speak of is an almost complete visualization of the life that was — from birth to the near-death experience. I can imagine how that will play out like a movie. If we all had the chance to experience this footage of our lives play before our very eyes, what impression would we walk away with?

Would it be, "That movie sucked" or "That was a great story"?

Would we be impressed by the story of our lives and how we told it, or will we realize that we resorted to good acting to carry us through?

Would it be all action and no story, or just catchy special effects that leave us empty?

Would it be a comedy, tragedy, drama, or pure fantasy?

When the alarm goes off each morning, that is the clap of the slate and the voiceless director soundlessly yelling "Action!"

The cameras are rolling.

Tell your story and tell it well.

Reflections from the Ringside

"In life and in a boxing ring, the defeat is not declared when you fall down. It is declared only when you refuse to get up" — *Manoj Arora, from Dream On*

I was excited when I finally got her on the phone. I had spent the previous night watching good boxing — ringside. I could have literally taken six steps and grabbed a boxer's leg. That's how close I was to the action.

In my excitement, I forgot she hated boxing. She found it senseless and violent. She refused to buy my argument that it was a metaphor for living. She asked why an activity that led to brain injury could be a metaphor for living.

"You know I do not care for boxing," she said.

The air escaped my bubble with a hiss that I masked with a chuckle and an "Oh, I forgot."

The conversation turned to other things less violent and not metaphorical.

Long after the conversation was over, I could not help but wonder why I found a violent sport like boxing so reminiscent of living.

As I thought this over, I saw the fighters from the night earlier float before my eyes - how they walked into the ring with so much expectation and confidence...each felt that they were the better fighter...going at each other on the ring of the bell. There were those fighters who took almost a whole round to size each other up and those who went at each other right away.

I thought of how it did not matter how a boxer started a fight, but only how he ended it. I thought of the one boxer who tried to fight with a cut over one eye that got worse with each round and led to the fight being stopped, of the one fighter who let his guard down just as the bell rang and got knocked out with a left hook to his jaw, and the one who looked so tired that it looked like he was just fighting on pure instinct towards the end.

There were the fast boxers and the slow ones; the deliberate ones and the hasty ones; the thoughtful fighters and those who seemed to fight on instinct.

They overcame their fears, egos, bad habits, and tapped into all the training done before the fight to win.

Once the boxer stepped into the ring, he had no way out but to fight till the bout was over, or the trainer threw in the towel, or he was knocked out, or got injured. A boxer just did not walk away because he lost interest in the fight.

Boxing!

It is not all pugilistic. A great deal of strategy, patience, and timing is needed to be successful —and those prerequisites remind me of living, how living is a bout that lasts one's entire presence on this Earth with an opponent called Life.

Preparation helps. Patience, timing, and strategy gives one a good chance — but the problem is the unpredictability of Life. He does not always fight fair and has no mercy. Sometimes, even when you are down, he keeps raining a barrage of blows on you. Life scoffs at your preparation and strategy, testing your patience and making you tap into the greatest of all qualities — hope. Hope that you can withstand this terrible round, that you can get off the canvas and punch back, that the bell will save you. Like the tired fighter, sometimes all we have left are our instincts and a deep sense of survival.

Somewhere along the line, something happens. We figure Life out somewhat. We learn his footwork and sense when that left jab comes into play. We figure out when to duck, when to put up our hands, and when to dance away. We learn to land our blows when an opening arises and go in for the kill when all looks right.

As we dance around in the ring, fighting with Life, we figure out how to live.

As the fighters floated away, I remembered her question. Why could I not find a metaphor for living that was less violent? I could. I really could. Life is full of metaphors, but I really like boxing as one that depicts living.

Imagine two fighters in the ring for a 12-round fight. The arena is full of fans expecting a 48-minute event. The boxers do too. They both have so much promise. Then in the second round, one boxer knocks out the other. Poof! The fight is over. Just like that! All that promise meant nothing! Now if that is not a metaphor for living, I really do not know what else can depict the transient nature of life.

Moreover, just like a fight can lead to brain injury, the very act of living can lead to a breakdown of our bodies, relaying the subtle but present nature of the violence of daily living.

So, listen! I heard my bell ring. I did. It's Round 52 for me. My legs feel rubbery and my head is pounding. I do not want to leave my corner, but I just caught the eyes of those people who depend on me and they want me to go out there and slug it out. Wish me well.

What about you? Do you hear the bell? I bet you do. Life is waiting. Go out there and knock him out!

Is There Really No Love?

April 22, 2018

I just finished two episodes of Christiane Amanpour's "Love and Sex Around the World" on CNN[95] and all I can say is "Wow!"

It only further reinforces my argument that we Africans need to tell our own stories and should never let any Westerner do that for us. They hardly ever get it right. For some unknown reason, they can never reach the true essence of our story and the great Amanpour was no different.

Having the chance to see the episode she shot in Shanghai, China before watching the one she filmed in Ghana allowed me to compare and contrast how she told the stories of two very different cultures regarding love and sex.

In the Shanghai episode, she started off by explaining how the conservative and rather emotionless nature of the Chinese society greatly affects love and sex. She then went on to weave her story around that central theme and in a very humanistic way. She succeeded even in making the perpetuators of these rigid cultural practices look good and acceptable.

---

[95] *"Christiane Amanpour: Sex and Love Around the World." CNN, Cable News Network, 12 Feb. 2018, www.cnn.com/shows/sex-and-love-around-the-world.*

The episode from Accra followed the Shanghai one. Ms. Amanpour opened by describing Ghana as "one of the most religious countries in the world." While that could be true, it is not the true basis of why love and sex are seen and practiced the way they are in Ghana.

However, it is from this perspective that she painted Ghanaian men as hypocrites who hide behind the religion to practice infidelity and oppress their women.

A much more fitting background would have been what a friend suggested:

"A society struggling with two opposing cultures — the monogamous dictates of Christianity and our long-lived culture of polygamy."

Based on such a background, the words of the older businesswoman Ms. Amanpour interviewed later in the show makes sense:

"Love is love. As love means in your country, love means the same thing in our country. As the man wants to be with one wife, the love has to be shared."

Those words are almost an ode to polygamy and the old way of life.

Without that background, then Moesha Boudong statement at the end of her segment carries the hour and the narrative: "I don't think true love works in Ghana."

However, it is on this latter statement by Ms. Boudong that the whole documentary comes to rest. And thus, depicts Ghanaian men as selfish, hypocritical, sex-obsessed male chauvinist Neanderthals!

Truth be told, some Ghanaian men may fit that bill — but there are also a lot of men trying to do right by their wives.

Amanpour even throws in the Trokosi culture to further sink us into that pit of depravity.

Ghana, like most other places, has its faults as well as strengths. The way of life of the people, like most places in Africa, is subject to a culture that is often a blend of the traditional and the colonial. These cultures are frequently not complementary and are loggerheads with each other. The dictates of a traditional polygamous culture clash with the demands of Christianity.

In telling the Ghanaian or African story, it is always important to tease out these nuances in order to give a close-to-true representation of the reality. Failure to appreciate these nuances often leads to the rather negative depiction of the African and in Ms. Amanpour's case, the Ghanaian.

Human behavior is a very difficult thing to change. Thus, the Southern states in the U.S. still struggle with the history of slavery and Arab nations struggle to allow women equal rights. Is it any surprise that Ghanaian men struggle to get over a long history of polygamy?

Do not get me wrong. I am in no way condoning infidelity or polygamy. All I am saying is if one wants to explore sex and love in a nation with a long culture of polygamy — a country now trying to adapt to a culture of monogamy — an explanation of the background helps tell the true story. That will also allow space to tell the stories of the men who have successfully made the transition and respect a monogamous relationship. That will help tell the stories of women who are in such marriages and relationships and how they see love and sex. After all, they are Ghanaians too.

In that, Ms. Amanpour failed. In that, like most Western journalists, she failed to appreciate the nuances of our land and ended up doing what the Western media does best — portraying us in a negative light.

In Shanghai, China, she was able to do that. Why could she not do that in Accra, Ghana? Is it because she did not take the time to understand our culture and is it because she could not appreciate our humanity?

Whatever the reason, the fact remains — we need to tell our own stories!

It is time!

The Traders are Kidnapping My People

Between 1400 and 1900, the continent of Africa saw four waves of slave trading that ultimately decreased the continent's population by 50%.[96]

The Trans-Saharan slave trade saw people taken from south of the Saharan desert and shipped to Northern Africa.

In the Red Sea slave trade, people were taken from the area around the Red Sea and transported to the Middle East and India.

The Indian Ocean slave trade had people taken from Eastern Africa and shipped either to the Middle East, India, or the plantation islands in the Indian Ocean.

Compared to the Transatlantic slave trade, the above three paled in scope.

Beginning in the 15th century, men, women, and even children were shipped from Western, Central, and Eastern Africa to the European colonies in the Americas. Slaves were captured through kidnappings, raids, and warfare. None of them went willingly into the slave ships. A conservative estimate is that 20 million Africans were taken away as slaves.

---

[96]Nunn, Nathan. "Understanding the Long-Run Effects of Africa's Slave Trades." The Industrial Revolution as an Energy Revolution | VOX, CEPR's Policy Portal, voxeu.org/ article/ understanding-long-run-effects-africa-s-slave-trades.

Then there are the countless men, women, and children who died during the raids, during the marches to the slave castles, in the slave castles, and during the Middle Passage.

Even though the institution of slavery has existed worldwide for centuries, the fact that slavery existed in Africa turned out to be catastrophic.

Slavery as an institution is inhumane, but the slavery that was present in Africa was benign and adaptable compared to what the Europeans established in the Americas. Slaves in Africa were prisoners of war, payments for family debts, criminals, or part of a dowry payment. No one went on raids to capture slaves or kidnapped others to enslave them.

Most won their freedom by the next generation, could marry, and were often part of the extended family. Even though there was some viciousness towards slaves, what happened to slaves in the Americas paled in comparison to that.

When the Europeans arrived in Africa, the age-old practice morphed into a frank holocaust.

A good example of this complex dynamic is happened in the Congo after the Portuguese arrived in 1493. The kingdom of Congo was about 300 square miles and had been in existence over a century before the Portuguese showed up. It was ruled by a king called the ManiKongo.[97]

[96]*Hochschild, Adam. King Leopold's Ghost: a Story of Greed, Terror, and Heroism in Colonial Africa. Pan Books, 2012.*

Diogo Cão was soon followed by other Portuguese merchants and priests from the Catholic Church. Schools and churches were built. Copper, ivory, and textiles were traded. The people of the Congo also wanted to acquire the skills of masons and carpenters, so they could build European style buildings. They also wanted education and literacy, so they could communicate directly with Europe.

In the interim, the Portuguese had discovered the value of African labor and were interested in acquiring slaves. Initially, only war captives were traded — but the Portuguese wanted more slaves for their plantations in Brazil. They started colluding with Congolese noblemen and chiefs to kidnap Congolese people and sell them as slaves. By 1500, the trade had hit a frenzy.

Hochschild reports how "men sent out from Lisbon to be masons or teachers at Mbanza Kongo soon made far more money by herding convoys of chained Africans to the coast and selling them to the captains of slave-carrying caravels."

Even the Catholic priests got into the act. They "abandoned their preaching, took black women as concubines, kept slaves themselves, and sold their students and converts into slavery."

Interestingly after the Reformation, these Catholic priests turned slave traders refused to sell to Protestants.

It is into this melee that Nzinga Mbemba (or Afonso I) became the king of the Congo or the ManiKongo in 1506.

A very smart man, he was a provincial chief and, in his thirties, when the first Portuguese missionaries arrived in 1491. He studied with them for 10 years. In the process, he converted to Catholicism and gained a great command of the Portuguese language.

Afonso, I sought to modernize his kingdom by harnessing the knowledge the Portuguese had, held back prospectors who wanted gold, and tried to control the slave trade that had gotten out of hand. In his despair, he even wrote to two Portuguese kings and to the Pope for help .[98]

This from a letter Afonso I wrote to King Joao III of Portugal in 1526:

"Each day the traders are kidnapping our people — children of this country, sons of our nobles and vassals, even people of our own family...This corruption and depravity are so widespread that our land is entirely depopulated...We need in this kingdom only priests and schoolteachers, and no merchandise unless it is wine and flour for Mass...It is our wish that this kingdom not be a place for the trade or transport of slaves."

Later, Afonso I would also write:

"Many of our subjects eagerly lust after Portuguese merchandise that your subjects have brought into our domains. To satisfy this inordinate appetite, they seize

---

[98]*Andrea, Alfred J. and James H. Overfield. The Human Record: Sources of Global History, Volume I: To 1700. Houghton Mifflin, 2011.*

many of our black free subjects... They sell them...after having taken these prisoners [to the coast] secretly or at night...As soon as the captives are in the hands of white men they are branded with a red-hot iron."

The king also wrote about the issue of the priests turned slave traders:

"In this kingdom, faith is as fragile as glass because of the bad examples of the men who come to teach here, because the lusts of the world and lure of wealth have turned them away from the truth. Just as the Jews crucified the Son of God because of covetousness, my brother, so today He is again crucified."

If Afonso I was expecting sympathy from King Joao III, he got none. This was part of King Joao III's reply:

"You...tell me that you want no slave-trading in your domains because this trade is depopulating your country...The Portuguese there, on the contrary, tell me how vast the Congo is, and how it is so thickly populated that it seems as if no slave has ever left."

Due to Afonso I's efforts to rein in the activities of the Portuguese slave traders, an attempt was made to assassinate him. It was unsuccessful. However, when he sent 10 of his young nephews and grandsons to Lisbon to study, they were captured en route and sold off as slaves in Brazil.

In the meantime, the slave trade went on — turning wide

swaths of the once-populous kingdom into wastelands as countless people died in war or as they marched to the slave forts or fled the advance of the raiders. One can imagine how the livelihood of millions all over sub-Saharan Africa was destroyed in this fashion.

After the death of Afonso I in 1542 or 1543, the power of the Congo continued to decline until it finally became a colony of Belgium in the 1800s and suffered further under King Leopold's atrocities.

Thus, we see how the trade in slaves morphed from its small beginnings into a terrible institution that the locals could hardly control.

By all measures, the trade had a huge impact in reshaping the continent. Quoting from a paper by the economist Nathan Nunn from 2017:

"The evidence suggests that it (the slave trade) has affected a wide range of important outcomes, including economic prosperity, ethnic diversity, institutional quality, the prevalence of conflict, the prevalence of HIV, trust levels, female labor force participation rates, and the practice of polygyny. Thus, the slave trades appear to have played an important role in shaping the fabric of African society today."

In spite of all the evidence a lot of people — even smart and well-meaning Africans and African-Americans — discount the impact of this holocaust on our continent. Some even blame it all on Africans.

Even a world geography book from the famous publisher McGraw Hill included this sentence: "The Atlantic Slave Trade between the 1500s and 1800s brought millions of workers from Africa to the southern United States to work on agricultural plantations."

The slave trade has been over for ages, but Africans and blacks in the Americas and even Europe have to live with the consequences. The least that the part of the world that benefited most from the trade can do is study the heinous practice and the circumstances that led to it, learn from it, and try to help those whose lives are affected by the consequences of slavery to overcome the impediments that litter their way.

By studying the slave trade intensely, we as Africans can better understand some of the socio-pathology that plagues our societies and find ways to combat it.

We need that to understand who we are.

Like Charles Siefert's wrote in his 1938 pamphlet, "The Negro's or Ethiopian's Contribution to Art"[99]: "A Race without the knowledge of its history is like a tree without roots."

---

[99] Seifert, Charles C. The Negro's or Ethiopian's Contribution to Art. Black Classic Press, 1991.

The Most Hallowed Right

Maybe it is because life is so serendipitous and unpredictable. Like the old adage that the Persians claim the Sufi poet Attar of Nishapur[100] wrote or the Jews attribute to King Solomon, "This too shall pass." The problems or the joys we face in life are fleeting and nothing is really as it seems.[101]

Maybe it is because some see a Deity as the Creator of life. Life is then seen not as a gift, but as a loan from this Deity that we are supposed to treasure, protect, and make the most of. Then one day, we will be called upon to account for that loan called life and will be punished if we misused it and rewarded if we treasured and made the most of it.

Maybe it's because the State sees life — all life — as something sacrosanct that falls under its purview to protect.

Maybe it is because there is the feeling that we are all in this together and turning one's back on the experience is a betrayal of a common cause.

Maybe it is the loved ones one leaves behind...loved ones whose love was just not enough?

Or is it that life is seen as being so precious that no matter how terrible and unbearable one's circumstances are, its

---

[100] *"Attar." Love Poems of Rumi, www.khamush.com/sufism/attar.htm*
[101] *"This Too Shall Pass." Wikipedia, Wikimedia Foundation, 1 May 2018, en.wikipedia.org/wiki/This_too_shall_pass.*

sanctity should be upheld?

Is that why the issue of taking one's life is so controversial?

Most consider life a truly great gift. That this fleeting, ephemeral experience on this crazy planet is a wonderful thing. Or could be a wonderful thing.

If life is a gift, then each of us has the right to do with it what he or she chooses. That is a right that comes with life. No one else can decide for a mature adult of sane mind what he or she can do with his or her life.

Even if it is the decision to end it.

Which brings me to one of those questions without a right answer:

"Does any human have the right to end his or her life?"

The issue of suicide is a controversial issue. Is it wrong, or right? Why does it carry such a stigma? Why do some societies criminalize it? If one has a right to live, should that same right not pertain to death?

You might feel strongly about it being right or wrong, but your point of view is not inviolate and that is the aim of this exercise — to present a stand unlike the conventional that sees suicide as a very bad thing, even criminal.

Surely, there are diseases of the mind, like depression, that cause one to think of ending it all. Since one is not of sound mind, it can be argued that this is an exception.[102]

On the other hand, the desire to live is such a strong phenomenon that very few people who have all their mental faculties intact think of ending it all.

The WHO estimates that about 1 million people die from suicide each year (the world's population is 7.7 billion and is growing by about 83 million people per year).[103]

The majority of these people are believed to have major depression. However, substance abuse like alcoholism, financial woes, debilitating disease, and societal pressure can lead to suicide.

The highest number of suicides are seen in Europe and Asia (Lithuania and Japan come to mind), with Africa having the least. This raises another question that I ponder often: Do Africans value life or are we just afraid of death?

Anyway, I digress. Let's go back to the matter at hand.

This means that those who are not depressed or suffering from other mental illnesses who commit suicide do so because they cannot handle their lives at that point in time anymore. They see death as the only way out.

---

[102]Joiner, Thomas. *Why People Die by Suicide.* Harvard University Press, 2007.
[103]*"Suicide Data."* World Health Organization, World Health Organization, 20 Dec. 2017, www.who.int/mental_health/prevention/suicide/suicideprevent/en/

As ill-informed as that decision might be, is it not in their right to do so?

Should a patient with terminal cancer with metastases all over and who suffers from indescribable pain not have the right to end his or her life? If that person continues to live in pain and suffering, what does that achieve?

A slave who jumped off a slave ship to his death in the churning waters of the Atlantic during the Middle Passage saved himself the horrors of bondage that befell Africans in the New World. Did that slave not have the right to make that choice?

A banker who loses it all when the market crashes and thus jumps out of a 30th-floor window to his demise chooses death over life. This is similar to what the Japanese pilots of the Tokubetsu Kōgekitai who flew kamikaze missions against Allied targets in the Pacific during World War II did. They all at that point in time had a similar mantra in mind — like the quote from 1775 that has been immortalized and is seen as one of the catalysts of the American War of Independence. The famous words uttered by Patrick Henry, but probably written by William Wirt:

"Give me liberty or give me death!"[104]

---

[104] *"Give Me Liberty, or Give Me Death!" Wikipedia, Wikimedia Foundation, 14 Apr. 2018, en.wikipedia.org/wiki/Give_me_liberty,_or_give_me_death!*

Most people respect that and see valor and patriotism in those words. However, how is that different from the other scenarios I painted earlier?

The African slave leaping into the churning waters of the Atlantic made a decision to die rather than be in bondage. The terminal cancer patient wants death rather than pain. The banker might well have screamed, "Give me wealth or give me death" and the kamikaze pilot, "A victorious Japan or death."

What underlines all these scenarios is the freedom to make that choice between life and death. Society may hail one but condemn the others. Why?

The issue of suicide has bedeviled mankind forever. Camus put it best when he wrote, "There is but one truly serious philosophical problem and that is suicide."[105]

In ancient Greece, in Massilia and Ceos, a man who could convince the magistrate why he needed to die was handed a cup of Hemlock and bid farewell.[106]

Pliny the Elder wrote[107]:

"Life is not so desirable a thing as to be protracted at any cost. Whoever you are, you are sure to die, even though your life has been full of abomination and crime. The

---

[105]Camus, Albert. Myth of Sisyphus. Vintage, 2018
[106]Plato and W. D. Geddes. The Phaedo of Plato. Macmillan, 1885
[107]Schopenhauer, Arthur. Studies in Pessimism. Kessinger Publishing, 2008.

chief of all remedies for a troubled mind is the feeling that among the blessings which Nature gives to man, there is none greater than an opportune death; and the best of it is that everyone can avail himself of it."

Sure, there were also philosophers like Camus, Kant, Locke, and Sartre as well as writers of Christian-leaning and the Church itself who opposed and continue to greatly oppose suicide.

Hobbes' position is probably the most revealing. He claims that natural law forbids every man "to do, that which is destructive of his life, or take away the means of preserving the same."[108]

Breaking this natural law is irrational and immoral.

Religions like Hinduism support suicide while Christians abhor it, citing the suffering of Jesus on the cross as an example of how tough life can be and how we are called to bear it.[109]

However, even Jesus prayed for strength to carry that cross and ultimately made a conscious decision to bear it (from the New Testament of the Bible, read Matthew 23:39).

---

[108]Hobbes, Thomas. Levianthan; or, The Matter, Forme, and Power of a Commonwealth, Ecclesiasticall and Civill. https://ebooks.adelaide.edu.au/h/hobbes/thomas/h681/contents.html

[109]"Religion and Spirituality." Death With Dignity, www.deathwithdignity.org/learn/religion-spirituality/

So, if one cannot carry this burdensome cross, can one just end it? To cull from the Herodotus quote, "Does death not become for man a sought-after refuge, when life is burdensome?"[110]

Maybe the person who looks at life, finds it unbearable, and decides to end it does not commit "the greatest act of cowardice", but rather uses his or her most hallowed right — the right to live or not, the right to be a person or a memory.

---

[110] "The Internet Classics Archive | The History of Herodotus by Herodotus." The Internet Classics Archive | Antigone by Sophocles, classics.mit.edu/Herodotus /history.7.vii.html.

Aren't We All Broken?

They always look so frail, like they will break if you pick them up the wrong way. In a way, they are broken.

There is that persistent look about them — a look of want. They seem like they want something all the time. Something that they cannot get or something someone is denying them — and when they look at you, their eyes implore. They beseech. They almost beg you to give them what they want.

That look tugs at one's heartstrings and can pull you into that orbit of insatiable wanting.

And it does, especially if it is one's first time dealing with one of them.

Even if they get what they want, it is never enough, and their craving knows no end.

Their faces are often gaunt with eyes sunken in and they look much older than their biological age. If they smile, there are often missing teeth or if the teeth are present, the state of the them is quite bad.

They appear fidgety like they have something to do or somewhere to be. They look like they do not have enough time.

In those who inject their scourge, there might be track marks. Sometimes, they line the arms like a path that leads to nowhere. At times, one even sees them on the neck, the chest, and on the legs and thighs. Even the penis is not spared in the men and in females, the breast has been an opportune target too. Some even go for the spaces between the fingers and toes.

They are usually very sick when they show up, especially those whose choice is an injectable substance. Pneumonias from aspirating their own vomit. Pneumonias that lead to empyemas of the pleural space. Infected heart valves that need to be replaced. Strokes caused by clots that are loaded with bacteria from dirty needles. Hepatitis. HIV.

In spite of being deathly ill, they keep making bad decisions. They get friends and sometimes family to bring them what they want in the hospital. They refuse procedures. They leave against medical advice.

Their habits have a progression to it. They start abusing those pain medications — Oxycontin, Percocet, Tramadol. They swallow the tablets in quantities that would kill most normal men and women, but no quantity is ever enough. The body craves more. Soon they are found crushing and snorting these tablets to get a faster and more intense effect. Then they learn to liquefy them so they can inject these medications directly into the bloodstream to shorten the distance to the brain. The switch to cocaine and heroin is fluid. These days, the heroin is laced with fentanyl and carfentanil.

Or it might be methamphetamine (aka meth, aka Tina) cooked in an abandoned barn somewhere in the Bluegrass that is their scourge.

Whatever the poison, the addict is a broken human being whose life is a vicious cycle revolving around an insatiable want for a drug, or a habit like sex or gambling, or for alcohol, cigarettes, or marijuana.

For today, let's think of those hooked on drugs.

We are taught that the pathogenesis of addiction is multi-pronged — nature, nurture, availability, friends, and purpose in life or lack thereof.

Yet at the end of the day, even all the training in the world cannot block that feeling on seeing them that they are truly broken. Broken by urges that to the non-addict are unfathomable. Broken by the inability to fight a craving.

However, aren't we all as humans broken in one way or another? Aren't we all craving one thing or another? Fame, wealth, companionship, sex, power, influence...Aren't we all, with our deep desire to live forever, addicted to life? Aren't we all addicts with cravings that are insatiable? Don't we sometimes beg, borrow, and steal to make that dream we've had for years come true? Don't we have the track marks on our psyche as evidence of our addiction?

An addict is truly broken and sometimes there is nothing we can do to fix them. Their habits burden not only their families and loved ones, but also the immediate community and even the nation. They get sick and need care. They need rehab. They need a second or even third chance. That burden they place on others is the last thing on their minds, because the craving occupies every fiber of their bodies and every neuron in their minds.

Life is a gift and each of us is called upon to make the most of it. Being a gift, one can do pretty much whatever one wants with it. Even if it is being an addict. Even if it leads to a broken life.

You see, that is the beauty of choice for the one making it who thinks of nothing but himself or herself.

But then again, aren't we all selfish?

Aren't we all broken?

Epilogue

"If life gives you a lemon, squeeze it!"
– Drew Selby Ghansah

It Might Have Been

"For of all sad words of tongue or pen, the saddest are these: 'It might have been.'" — From the poem *"Maud Muller"* by John Greenleaf Whittier(1807–1892)

I met him the first time about six months ago. I walked up to his stretcher, introduced myself to him and the woman who was in the room with him, and said I was going to be his anesthesiologist.

"Archaeologist?" he asked.

"Anesthesiologist," I corrected him.

"Archaeologist," he repeated.

"Anesthesiologist," I corrected him again.

Once more he said "archaeologist "and for the third time I corrected him. At this point, the woman, who I assumed was his wife, was laughing her head off. That is when it slowly dawned on me — the old man might be yanking my chain. The woman confirmed it.

"He is messing with you," she said.

I glared playfully at the old man and said, "Oh, now it's on."

He laughed, a full, throaty laugh.

I took a liking to him at that point.

He asked me where my funny accent was from.

I replied, "Ghana, Kentucky."

It was his turn to glare.

"And where in Kentucky might that be, young man?" he asked.

"You don't know where Ghana, Kentucky is? Moonshine Capital of the World?" I asked, feigning incredulity.

"Oh, no! The best moonshine? You don't know what you are talking about!"

The conversation veered into which county made the best moonshine.

The woman was indeed his wife. She was laughing so hard, I thought she was going to choke on her spit.

As we talked, I examined him. He had a loud heart murmur. That brought us down to reality. It turned out, the murmur was the least of his cardiac problems. I ended up calling a cardiologist to work him up and cancelled his procedure for the day.

As he was rolled off to the cardiac catheterization suite, he shouted, "It's not over, my archaeologist. We'll have to figure out whose moonshine is the best!"

I patted his shoulder and told him to just accept the inevitable. He went through the door laughing.

As it so happens in life, the days and weeks rolled by and those special moments are relegated to the back of one's memory bank. So, a few days ago, even though the name on the patient's chart I picked up around noon looked familiar, I didn't think much about it.

I walked into the cubicle the patient was in and greeted the old man I found resting on the stretcher. There was an elderly woman in the cubicle with him. The moment had a déjà vu feel about it.

"There is my archaeologist," the old man said.

Suddenly, I knew who he was.

We shook hands and picked up from where we had left off, verbally sparring about moonshine and where Ghana, Kentucky was.

Then suddenly the conversation took a turn I had not expected. He started complaining about how weak and miserable he felt. He lamented he hardly had any more strength to do what he wanted.

I sensed there was more, so I decided to shut up, listen, and only make the occasional necessary remark. The day had slowed down somewhat, so I knew I had time.

He continued griping about how he could not take the walks he used to take regularly anymore.

I knew his history and was aware of the hurdles he faced, yet he had never complained when I had first met him, and he was sicker then.

That is when I remarked, "It is particularly frustrating when you still have a such a sharp mind."

"Me? Sharp mind? I did not even go to college."

Out of the corner of my eye, I noticed his wife suddenly looked disinterested and was fiddling with her phone. I wondered about that.

"Why didn't you go to college?" I asked him.

"I didn't want to. I got a basketball scholarship to UK (the University of Kentucky), but I refused to go. My father wanted me to, but I didn't want to. I wanted to be my own boss."

"So what did you end up doing?"

"I became a farmer."

"Were you a good one?"

I wasn't expecting his wife to talk, but she piped in at that juncture.

"He farmed 450 acres. Tobacco, then cattle, and some horses. He did well and took good care of me and the kids," she said.

"Going to college would have been great, but you apparently did not need to. You found success in life without it," I pointed out.

"You do not understand. I was a very good ball player and I dreamt then of becoming a basketball coach like Rupp," he confessed.

Something in his tone and eyes communicated how serious he was about the dream he once had. It wasn't just some whimsical desire that arose and vanished soon after it was birthed. It was not from a midlife crisis. This was remorse from an unachieved dream.

"So why didn't you go to UK?" I asked.

He thought for a while and said, "Because I was defiant and stubborn."

"Sir, so once upon a time you made a decision that has taken your life on a different path. However, on that new path, you did great. You farmed 450 acres. I doubt you made any decent moonshine..."

He laughed as I continued, "But you were, according to your wife, a very successful farmer. So, it's not like you refused to go to college and became a bum. You made something awesome out of this life, so why the regret?"

He wasn't going to give in that easily.

"Maybe if I had gone to college, I could have done both," he remarked dryly.

"Well as a coach, you would never have really been your own boss. You would have had to answer to the athletic director and the fans as well as deal with the players."

The old gentleman thought for a minute and then said, "You may have a point there."

Yet his eyes could not hide that he was going to spend the rest of his days on this Earth obsessing over what could have been.

My phone rang. Duties were calling. I walked off, promising to return. The next time I saw him, he was resting after his procedure. The next few hours got so insanely busy that he left before I could talk to him again. He left with that deep regret.

It could be something you should have done and did not do or something you did but should not have done; it could be a loss or a missed opportunity...a behavior, an event, a decision...all these can generate regrets that can be haunting. For some reason, the regrets due to omissions (things we did not do) seem to gall more so than those of commission (what we did).

Often, we can make amends for actions taken that we

regret, but with the passage of the time it tends to be more difficult or even impossible to catch up on what should have been done once upon a time. Thus, regrets due to inaction seem to last forever. Time also allows for more introspection (like we saw with the old man), making the inaction seem worse. Physical disabilities or health conditions that impede one's mobility compound the problem.

Yet, regrets have a place in our lives. They can force us to correct wrongs and make amends for mistakes made or hurt caused. They can make us reconsider our life's trajectory and take measures to change for the better.

However, if we spend each passing day wallowing in regret and do not do anything about it when we can, then we are letting precious time fly away. If we let regret weigh us down — even though there is very little we can do about that road not traveled — we cheat ourselves out of what is now possible. There comes a time when one just has to accept what is and move on.

As I think about the older gentleman and his one regret, I cannot help but feel a twinge of guilt.
Here I am judging him for feeling remorse over what he should have done and not appreciating what he had achieved. Somehow, I have a nagging feeling I met him for a reason. I have a feeling that his referring to me as an archaeologist and even our banter about moonshine may have served a purpose. Somehow, his detour into his one regret in life seemed not coincidental.

Maybe Life wanted to tell me to stop digging into the past

like an archaeologist, let my regrets peel away like the worries of a drunk after several shots of moonshine, and avoid clouding my last days with regrets like the old man was doing. Maybe like those distillers during Prohibition, Life wants me to create something in the moonlight if I cannot do it when the sun is up.

Life's lessons do really come in different ways.

Reviews & Blurbs

I

Reflections is a must read. It conjures vivid imagery that take you right into the moment. It is very captivating and appeals to one's best sense of imagination. At the same time, it is so well put together, it makes such an easy read. Like the proverbial walk along the garden path, this collection leaves you mesmerized, bedazzled, and at the same time so relaxed that you levitate into the zone. The author brings his deep sense of recollection and extraordinary analytic skill combined with poetry that is genius.

Whether waiting to catch a flight, hanging out in the coffee shop, sleeping in on a weekend or savoring some me time, "Reflections" is a good fit. This book comes in handy for those moments you need a good companion.

Eugene Sangmuah MD
Internist, Charlotte, North Carolina

II

There is a mesmerizing way drama and prose start to feel like life being played out right in front of your very eyes. Nana Ghansah's woven tales from the USA through East and West Germany of yesterday, the Opera house with Brünnhilde and even further back into Greek mythology and Cassandra. This page turner will have you reach for a tissue as you dab your tears of both joy and sorrow. A juxtaposition of feelings only Nana Ghansah can bring out.

Enjoy the read and be prepared for a late night...

Emmanuel Dadzie
Entrepreneur,
Woodbridge, Virginia

III

As a small boy in Ghana, he would write by the glow of a candle. He grew up to be a talented physician, photographer, poet and writer. He has produced a compelling collection of essays, musings and poetry. Covering a broad range of topics and woven with threads of self-revelation, his work draws on his life as a physician, as well as his myriad interests, experiences and curiosities.

Suzanne Shewcraft
Certified Nurse Anesthetist
Lexington, KY

IV

In this fascinating collection of memories, dreams, musings and all that a creative mind can conjure, Nana Dadzie Ghansah takes the reader on very descriptive journeys across time, as he sweeps his grandfather's compound to perfection (the creation and beginnings of the meticulous scientist and clinician he is today), and as he contemplates the meaning of life and dignity, meandering through mundane family meals and surreal appreciation of art. Nana writes across generations and zigzags us across the world from Ghana to Paris, France to Kentucky, Cincinnati, Namibia and more. In these journeys, he shares thoughts and some quotes of great men and women, and through his eyes, we meet Dr. Seuss, Bob Marley, Jesus Christ, Chinua Achebe, Abraham Lincoln and others who bring life to his narrative. This is by all measures, an energizing outburst of thought and a simultaneously sober reflection of the past, present and future through multiple lenses, and if you're looking to go on a thought-provoking and yet humorous journey that leaves your mind enriched, then this collection is a great pick.

Dr Esi E. Ansah
CEO, Axis Human Capital
Lecturer, Ashesi University

V

Reflections In A Ring Of Light, by Nana Ghansah, harkened back to a lonely boy in Ghana writing to his mother in the big city by lantern light at the end of the evening once the tasks of the day had been accomplished. Somehow the author suffered from existential nihilism with its inescapable darkness and started recollecting his life from a village in Ghana to a creative genius with words and light as a photographer/videographer. Incidentally, he became an exceptional cardiac anesthesiologist. As he unfolded specific moments in his life, I became part of his story.

Studying medicine in Germany breaking up with his girlfriend finding solace in Whitney Houston's music on a dreary day or raging against the lack of health care for a friend, I connected my emotions with his.

Existential nihilism this was not. This scattered autobiography brought light illuminated by each unique story along his life's way. The profusion of life in the variegated adventures affirmed the light amidst the darkness.

Judson Chalkley MD
Staff Anesthesiologist, St Joseph's Hospital, Lexington, KY
Volunteer Anesthesiologist, Samaritan's Purse

VI

If a good book must be as voluminous as the dictionary, then one will quickly dismiss Nana Dadzie Ghansah's second book Reflections In A Ring of Light but thank God the beard does not make a philosopher.

Considering the variety of topics that Nana tackles in this book one cannot help but to be genuinely impressed. A cursory look at the table of contents is a look at life itself. The author, a physician by trade, has a polygamous or polyandrous association with all disciplines and in this book strolls through all these corridors like a colossus. Indeed, his knowledge of 'life' and his wisdom and industry are finely and superbly distilled in words to bring this wonder of a book into fruition. Nana cannot be compartmentalized as a specialist in this or that alone since he is a specialist in all things earthly as seen through the eyes of his books. Even so he does that with such humility which only the great can exhibit. He has become that giant octopus whose tentacles reach into many professions – engineering, philosophy, psychology, psychotherapy, religion, music, history, poetry, painting, photography, cinematography etc. These go a long way to enrich his books. Indeed he is a 21st century 'polymath'.

A good book is for all times and for all people; even race, culture and creed cannot defeat its purpose and that is the shelf one finds Nana's latest child of his brain. It is so crafted and so woven that a single narrative on its own will be worth the entire price of the book.

Right from the prologue, the writer takes the reader to his grandpa Maapa's compound in the village. Here, one does not encounter Maapa but his qualities. He demanded excellence in everything and never settled for 'almost perfect'. Matching this with his narrative "DO IT WELL", a story told by his mother that has all the ingredients of 'any task must be done well or not at all', one is quick to know the source of the writer's trait of excellence. Therefore, in treating this book too, as usual, one finds him most meticulous as he examines issues with greater perspicacity. He makes sure at the end of the day the reader's breadth of vision and view is widened and his experience is enhanced. This is where 1 find myself now after going through the pages of this book. He who follows the compass is sure of his bearings.

The writer's love for nature, which brought him into photography, dates from his short stay at the village. This is seen in his description of the village scene. A true ornithophile and a shepherd boy too! As a shepherd boy like biblical David, he is more than ready, literary, to take on the world by rescuing 'a lamb' – by significance the reader, from the mouth of 'destructive philosophy' by raising the reader's moral conscience.

With his style, Nana Dadzie just like his camera, captures the picture so distinctly for the reader. Very descriptive and so picturesque that the reader yearns to be at his 'Abbey'. Like Achebe's description of the village setting in Things Fall Apart during the bright moon, 'it makes the cripple hungry for a walk'. His description of events makes the reader hungry to devour and also dizzy with the frequent and fast-flipping pace of the pages.

In one volume the writer puts together a total of 95 narratives under different headings titled 'On Life', 'Far from Home', 'Ghana on My Mind', 'The Art of Healing' and 'Back to Life'. Needless to say, all the narratives under these headings are stoutly built and come from his unrivalled funds of commonsense, wisdom and high intelligence which easily manifest themselves when you physically come into contact with him. It's worth noting that the daily neatness in his physical appearance is a reflection of the tidiness of his fertile brain.

His 42 narratives under 'On Life' are so inspirational and

soul-searching. His is a style that only few authors can hardly emulate. He doesn't leave the reader orphaned. He provides the reader with both the firewood and the meat for the burnt offering. This is how he does it. He opens each narrative with a classic quotation. Then he introduces the topic and smoothly and unhurriedly like the movement of a heavily pregnant woman, lead you on. He then hammers on his theme to pulp. By doing this, he provides the reader with very interesting life examples like 'Olympiosis', 'The Curse of Cassandra' etc. all to make the understanding of his theme so ordinary. This he does so convincingly with such authority, such grace and such finesse. After he gains the reader's attention he succeeds to sustain his interest until the reader finds himself sliding into the depth of the pages and then he is jostled by some of his deep-seated rhetorical questions, 'when we take the road less travelled in life, do we sometimes fail because we are not well prepared for what we may face?'. More of these rhetorical questions slap the reader at every turn of the pages.

If Nana Dadzie treats hitherto more-battered topics like life, death and wisdom as in 'Dignify Death', 'Memento Mori', 'An Audience with the Father', he brings some level of freshness to it. Here it is no longer hackneyed. He even bullies the much-feared death in such a way that the reader is bound to hold opinion with the poet John Donne that 'Death be not proud, though some have called thee mighty and dreadful, for thou art not so'.

While at it, his sense of humour is never lost on the reader as one sees in 'This Thing' etc. His beautiful anecdotes like

'Mother's Love' and allegories like 'The Story of the Praisers', 'Feeling Contemplative' etc. could all get under the reader's skin and fester like a boil until one gives it a reflective attention.

In examining religion, especially Christianity, this time he does not put it in the crucible, to be subjected to the severest test, but openly displays it for the reader to see that life on earth too is equally important just like life after death and that we need to place emphasis on life here too as in 'The Bitter Cup'.

When he makes an argument in the book it is very 'distin'. He is able to win over his reader into his boat by strong reasoning and ratiocination and not by coercive attempts. The treatment of Plato's Symposium in Nana Dadzie's 'In the Praise of Eros' will excite every reader. Many including yours truly, may not have seen the 'Symposium' being handled in such-like manner. So simple and so appealing, filigreed with his usual keen sense of humour. And if you yearn to know that after all Nana Dadzie is also given to romance then do not skip 'Good Bye, Whitney' where you get to know Nana Dadzie at age 21. He leaves his 'sweetheart' in Ghana to study in faraway Germany with lines like 'I was head over heels in love...' Tempting as these may be, do not take my words. Get on board and read it for yourself.

'Far From Home' comes with 19 different topics. It starts with a poem same as 'On Life'. As the meaning suggests it is mainly based on the writer's nostalgic moments like his experiences from his days of studies in Berlin and professional life in America; Philly, Atlanta, Kentucky etc. Often times there is a departure from this to other interesting, researching topics since Nana Dadzie can never be tagged. With 'What Do You Have to Offer' he comes into contact with his destiny and when he departs from that narrative he tackles interesting personalities like Abraham Lincoln and his inspirational letter and spirit of empathy, 'Brunnhilde hasn't sang yet', a true lesson in perseverance well couched to appeal to the reader. These and many others like Samuel Coleridge's poem, 'The Rime of the Ancient Mariner' is cleverly pitched against that of Houston's flood by the writer and then draws a nice analogy and beautiful lessons in his narrative 'water water everywhere'. The poem is successfully appreciated much to the envy of any English Literature student. After Houston's flood and its lessons he tackles another natural disaster, Earthquake in Mexico. Going further he draws interesting analysis from Prophet Jeremiah's quotation from the Bible, explains it so convincingly and further stretches it to significance and robes in Trump and his style of leadership in 'Let's jump over our shadows'. He then returns to his nostalgic self as we see the writer being derided by three young Germans after a classic performance in a pathophysiology test. While the reader is enjoying himself he has more reserved for him in 'Bottomless void'. Here the stubborn child Nana Dadzie at the village is flogged for peeking over a short wall of an abandoned well and masterfully make useful philosophic contributions from what he saw. A real good read!

'Ghana on My Mind' takes care of 12 equally interesting short narratives. It is a must-read for every Ghanaian everywhere. Being that thoroughbred scholar, he starts with an 'award winning' poem 'Ghana is 60'. What runs through this particular section is a refrain that needs fair and honest introspection so that our shortcomings as a people are not glossed over nor are our achievements underrated. He throws light on Nana Akufo-Addo with Kalyppo and Ghana's exploits in 2010 World Cup. The reader is really taken aback with what the writer does with these pieces. Not satisfied, he moves on to compare the controversial Anas Aremeyaw Anas' style with J. Edgar Hoover who ran the FBI for 48 years. He doesn't really favour their modus operandi and even further holds opinion with Friedrich Nietzsche that 'who ever fights monsters should see to it that in the process he does not become a monster . . .' But in Mfantsipim 1984 Year Group Whatsapp forum the writer digladiates saying ' Even though l find sting operations unfair, if that is what it would take to expose the rot in our society, so be it.' The writer is also seen meddling in human rights abuses in Ghana in those dark days of the revolution and without being biased as a physician, pays glowing tributes to Dr. Kwabena Frimpong-Boateng and Dr. David Fuseini Abdulai who had a clinic for the destitute. One can never bring the curtain down on 'Ghana on My Mind' without pointing out his admiration for Wesley Girls' High School and its contribution to the progress of Ghana and the positive exploits and qualities of its old girls. Equally, he puts Mfantsipim School too on its right pedestal but forgets to refer to it as THE SCHOOL. One may be tempted to think that Ginero (the writer's nickname in Mfantsipim) uses all the positive superlatives to describe these two schools because his wife Kuukua attended

Wesley Girls and he himself a dye-in-wool Mfantsipim old boy but this is not a case of 'one will eat ripe fruit once his brother is up the tree'. Theirs are solid achievements worth capturing. Isn't it worthy to 'Think and Look Ahead'?

'The Art of Healing' and 'Back to Life . . .' are the concluding sections which comprise of 22 short but powerful and captivating narratives. It happens to be the writer's professional field and therefore his 'baby project'. He clears the curtain for the reader to peep through the medical world. 'Does any human have the right to end his or her life', Do you know one million people commit suicide in a year and Africa though poor, is the continent with the least occurrence? Do you also know that the term malaria was first coined by a historian and chancellor named Florence Leonardo Bruni in 1400 in Florence, Italy? Do you know what a myxomatous valve is? One needs to read "A Touch of Humanity' and such a person will NEVER be the same. The reader is captivated by the writer's description and dialogue with all caliber of patients; young and old, male and female, rich and poor, those who are scared of surgery and those who just want company etc. In there the writer has cogent advice to young and would-be physicians. 'Five Senses and You' is another of his composition; solid and educative. Here, Nana Dadzie is 'floored' for once – to the best of my memory and one cannot escape the humour. Just as he starts with a prologue the writer ends with an epilogue.

In conclusion, though one knows Nana Dadzie Ghansah as an omnivorous reader this time one is left too mesmerized when he comes to examine the rich-fitting quotations that Nana Dadzie Ghansah easily drops like confettis in the book as well as the references and the names of writers he referred to in his narratives and at the footers. They are nothing but a veritable who-is-who in all disciplines. With the writer's permission I wish to quote one of them as I leave the stage, 'Gentlemen, we will chase perfection, and we will chase it relentlessly, knowing all the while we can never attain it. But along the way, we shall catch excellence' by Vince Lombardi Jr. I am glad to say with *Reflections In A Ring of Light,* Nana Dadzie Ghansah has caught excellence. The book joins the host of good books out there bearing in mind that when the Pope gets to town even the Bishops (the other good books in town) become mass servers.

Leslie Ampiah-Bannerman
Council for Law Reporting
Accra, Ghana

VII

In *Reflections In A Ring Of Light* Nana Dadzie Ghansah shows a keen sense of observation that picks on the mundane to the extraordinary events in his and other people's lives as well as everyday occurrences in the world as an invitation to the reader to share his thoughts and lessons learned in this journey call life.

He literally uses all his senses which go way beyond the traditional 5 attributed to Aristotle and uses talents that spans knowledge in the sciences and the arts to weave stories that thrills, educates and exhorts in the 94 short stories authored in this book.

Nana is a veritable raconteur as he draws on his life experiences as a cardiac anesthesiologist, a poet, a photographer and a writer.

As a man who earns his living by putting people to sleep before major surgical procedures, he gives ringside narratives of the highs and lows of the art of healing. That miracles still do happen in the surgical wards. And that life is fleeting, and death is inevitable. What you put into it is what counts.

Nana writes on life lessons and shares his views on finding, developing or creating your talents which are relevant to all (but especially to parents and teachers in Crawl, Turtle, Crawl) Death, Excellence and Character. He celebrates womanhood and believes that the African is best placed to tell his own story. On religion he shares the belief that "we are not human beings who go through a spiritual experience but that we are spiritual beings that we go through human experience.

Reflections In A Ring Of Light is a thoroughly enjoyable read.

David Osae-Akoto
Private Health Insurance Practitioner and Lawyer

I have known Nana'adze since we entered High School in our pre-teens in 1979. Established brainiac, irreverently and irrepressively naughty to the core. I have not known any medic who is as fascinated with the arts as Nana is. He finds or makes time from his day job of "administering propofol" (which is how I have chosen to define his profession as an anesthesiologist), to dabble in photography, prose and poetry. On occasion he even tries to dabble in something that we may imaginatively call 'music.' When he sent me what he called his first recorded 'song,' what I heard is best describes as a mish mash, jumble, hotchpotch, hodgepodge, assemblage, ragbag and potpourri of uncoordinated sound, something I could not call a 'song,' no matter how kind and generous I was feeling at the time. That was irrefutable evidence of him having, not precious little, not zero, but negative music skills. But it doesn't stop him. He still assaults my ears with such auditorily macabre productions. Being sensitive to his feelings, I always beg him to have them played on radio... so I could turn the radio off.

Right from the Prologue where we are introduced to the 'Ring of the Light' Nana shows us that he is about to take us on a journey into epiphany. And he is relentless. In essay after essay, story after story, line after line, precept after precept, Nana takes us from one moment of sudden revelation into another moment of unexpected insight.

We meet his grandpa, Maapa, who demanded excellence even in the most mundane of activities – sweeping the compound. But Nana's admiration of this man is buried in imagery and a simile. Maapa inspected work like "inspected it like a jeweler inspected a diamond." Attention to detail. Clearly rubbed off Nana. Thus, whether his epiphanic trip takes us to Besease or Lexington through Leipzig, he shows great attention to detail.

We meet his Dad from who made death look and seem welcome to Nana. Dignity in death, a lesson learned from Dad's life. So, Nana walks away from the morgue where Dad's body was, convinced in one breath that Dad's deep faith had helped him deal with death. Yet with the very next intake of air, Nana concludes that "there's nothing like eternal life." "We must all die! Accept it!" he screams.

We also meet Mum, to whom he wrote long letters, and each of which she still keeps. It was Mum who told him the story in the essay "Do It Well" about the builder who had built several houses for a rich man. But having been hired and paid to build another house with the best material he could find, he chose, being actuated by malice, bitterness and ill-will, to use the cheapest of materials, to lay a feeble foundation with weak walls, and to install a roof that shook and windows that clattered when the wind blew. "It was his worst work." To his shock, the rich man decided to reward him with that building. "I should have built this well!" The stories that only mums can construct!

We also meet his son who is totally into Afro-Caribbean music, and his daughter who enjoys rock classics, indie, grunge and Motown. Nana's life appears to be a classic story of contrasts.

In "The Unmarked Trail", easily my most favourite chapter, Nana challenges us to be curious and adventurous. Curiosity might have killed the cat, but Nana says if you seek to find and understand who you are, your place in the universe and your mission in life, then you must take that unmarked trail. Don't expect well-beaten and conspicuous paths.

In "The Journey" Nana says there is great peace and harmony if each traveler treats the other as they want to be treated. I find myself asking, what happens if I treat myself like crap? Would that justify my treating others like crap? And would there be great peace and harmony then? As if he senses my confusion, he provides an answer: the journey involves clearing the path, keeping the lonely company, feeding the hungry, healing the sick, redirecting the lost, protecting the weak and helping people find their destinations. But, Nana, did you say "clearing the path?" I thought the best trails were unmarked? Or do you mean that once we take the unmarked trails, we should clear them as a path for those following?

Throughout the book you will be blown away by his sheer mastery of history and literature. He recounts several historical tales and events, and backs them with his sources. He also shows his medical side in the several essays that refer to his chosen profession and the lessons he learns by simply being a doctor.

It is impossible to read these essays without asking

questions. And that's what's irritatingly narcotic about Nana's writings. He sucks you into his questions and search for answers, and then tells you that there are really no answers. And so he leaves you there, with more questions that beg or yearn for answers that he does not provide. Although he sometimes preaches a sermon that's almost existential and experiential, he laces it with theories that leave you hanging on a string or two that may soon break, and yet wanting more. Then he doesn't deliver the "more."

And so whether we meet him admiring nature in the village of Besease, or being a doctor in Lexington, in his trusted 1989 VW Golf or in the arms of a girlfriend in Leipzig whose ability to sleep soundly without a care in the world Nana was jealous of, you finish reading this compilation of essays thinking, "the more I know of Nana, the less I know of him." And I know he does that deliberately.

Enjoy the read. For this work, I give him two thumbs up, way up. Scratch that! TOUCHDOWN!!

Ace Anan Ankomah,
Lawyer and Author, Is There Not A Cause...To Rant?

Acknowledgements

This book would not have become a reality without the help and support of family, friends, colleagues and even strangers.

For all the hours spent in my office writing, hours I could have spent with them, I have to really thank my wife, Angela, and kids, Alexis and Drew. You let me chase a dream. Thanks, guys!

My brother Kojo Ghansah, thanks for always finding time to listen and help me organize those thoughts...just like dad did. You were more helpful that you will ever know. To my cousin Adadzewa Kottoh (née Otoo), thanks for challenging me all those years ago.
I am still trying to rise up to it.

To my sister, Abi, my brothers, Kweku and Paakow, my cousin Annette, my uncle Hans Kammermann, my father-in-law and Kofi Selby thanks for the encouragement.

Kweku Bedu-Addo, thanks for being such a good friend for so long and for a great foreword. Our conversations always forced me to think beyond my comfort zone.

Ace Kojo Anan Ankomah, a friend whose love for Ghana inspires me so much. Your words some three years ago lit a fire. It has been burning ever since. Thanks for reading through my ramblings and for a review that totally captures it all.

Emmanuel Dadson aka Aezor, my brother from Abaasa, what would I do without you? Your support has been indispensable.

Rev. Albert Ocran, thanks for always encouraging me to write, write and write again. Even when I had doubts, you had none. I will never forget those messages.

David Osae-Akoto, thanks for the deep conversations and encouragement. You are a good man. That blurb rocks!

Leslie Bannerman, my friend whose father knew my grandfather. Thanks for your wit and that review.

Cecil Nii Lante Sunkwa-Mills, I will always appreciate your wisdom. Tony El-Adas, you have encouraged me at every step of the way. Thank you.

Dr. Eugene Sangmuah, thanks for finding time to read through it. You are a good friend.

Egya "Bendilee" Crentsil , what would I do without you?

Dr. Esi Ansah, thanks for the "Table of Contents" and tips and suggestions.

Dr. Jud Chalkley, you have always listened and I have always appreciated your humanity, experience, and wisdom. Thank you for taking the time to read through it.

Suzanne Shewcraft, you did not only review the manuscript, you also helped me pick the title for this book! Thank you so much!

A big thank you to Chloe Howard for a good description of my journey.

Many thanks to Stephanie Mojica for editing the manuscript.

Nana Awere Damoah and Kofi Akpabli, you are taking a chance! Thanks!

Very special thanks go to my brothers of MOBA-84 (Mfantsipim School, Class of 1984). Ever since I got it into my head that I wanted to write, I have terrorized them with my views, ramblings, and poetry. They have had to tolerate me and my pieces for years now, even when they did not want to. Unwittingly, they have been my biggest fans and supporters. They have helped me organize my thoughts and given form to my ideas. Guys, thanks for all the encouragement.

Lastly, I am grateful for all those who read my pieces on social media, critiqued and encouraged me. Some of you are total strangers, only bound by the threads of a virtual world but your words have been extremely helpful.

www.ingramcontent.com/pod-product-compliance
Lightning Source LLC
Chambersburg PA
CBHW060304030426
42336CB00011B/937